A MATTER OF COMPULSION

The Story of Flory and Armand

JULIETTE PILON

Edited by Charmaine Bradley

© Copyright 2005 Charmaine Bradley.
All rights reserved. No part of this publication may be reproduced, stored in a retrieval system, or transmitted, in any form or by any means, electronic, mechanical, photocopying, recording, or otherwise, without the written prior permission of the author or editor.

Note for Librarians: a cataloguing record for this book that includes Dewey Decimal Classification and US Library of Congress numbers is available from the Library and Archives of Canada. The complete cataloguing record can be obtained from their online database at: www.collectionscanada.ca/amicus/index-e.html
ISBN 1-4120-4469-3
Editorial Assistance by Jessica Bouchard. Book Layout by Shawn Bouchard.
Printed in Victoria, BC, Canada

Printed in Victoria, BC, Canada. Printed on paper with minimum 30% recycled fibre. Trafford's print shop runs on "green energy" from solar, wind and other environmentally-friendly power sources.

TRAFFORD PUBLISHING

Offices in Canada, USA, Ireland and UK

This book was published *on-demand* in cooperation with Trafford Publishing. On-demand publishing is a unique process and service of making a book available for retail sale to the public taking advantage of on-demand manufacturing and Internet marketing. On-demand publishing includes promotions, retail sales, manufacturing, order fulfilment, accounting and collecting royalties on behalf of the author.

Book sales for North America and international:
Trafford Publishing, 6E–2333 Government St.,
Victoria, BC V8T 4P4 CANADA
phone 250 383 6864 (toll-free 1 888 232 4444)
fax 250 383 6804; email to orders@trafford.com

Book sales in Europe:
Trafford Publishing (UK) Limited, 9 Park End Street, 2nd Floor
Oxford, UK OX1 1HH UNITED KINGDOM
phone 44 (0)1865 722 113 (local rate 0845 230 9601)
facsimile 44 (0)1865 722 868; info.uk@trafford.com

Order online at:
trafford.com/04-2277

10 9 8 7 6 5

Poorly written
Horse behind cart
No fancy words
Straight from the heart
No apologies
Soul won't allow
Needs a transfusion
Don't know how

J.P.

ACKNOWLEDGEMENTS

Juliette was deeply grateful for the love Flory gave to all her children. She also was truly thankful for the many artistic gifts she inherited from her papa Armand.

FOREWORD

How do I describe growing up with my mother? With something delicious roasting in the oven, a painting-in-progress perched on the back of the washing machine, and the sewing machine whirring away like crazy, times were never dull.

In later years mom gave up the sewing machine to write her story. Whenever I visited her one-bedroom apartment there was still a painting on the go. Now, as well, her manuscript would be spread over her dining room table.

During those times life was a joy for mom. She couldn't wait to rise each morning to begin another busy and fruitful day. The evening was her time to relax, watching her favourite television programmes, a scotch and water by her side.

Editing mom's book has been years in the doing. It was, at first, a daunting task: the handwritten pages had been lovingly worked and reworked, her pencil longhand erased over and over again. Working on the manuscript reintroduced me to the vibrant characters I had heard about from mom and her sisters all my life. As I worked on the book these characters came alive for me again, as I hope they will for you.

I have to thank my daughter Jessica for her many hours of editorial help, as well as her husband Shawn for designing the layout of this book. Especially with new baby Jack in our lives, taking the time to help me is so very much appreciated.

Juliette turned ninety on January 20, 2005. Because her memory has failed her, it saddens me to know she is no longer aware her labour of love has been published. I believe that in another time and place she will become aware again.

My contribution to this book was a labour of love for my family - Jamie, Jessica, Shawn, and Jack. But mostly, Mom, it was a labour of love for you.

Charmaine Bradley

CONTENTS

The Goat With The Crooked Horn	1
Mama's Life	3
Québec	7
Going West	15
Beatrice	19
Reminiscences	27
Jane's Visit, Beatrice's Departure	33
Beautiful Hair	39
Visit to Brownsburg	41
Trapping	47
Willie and the Gun	55
Edmonton	59
Whisky Blanc	67
Moving to Town	71
Boarders	79
Yvonette	83
Napoleon Demarne	89
The Snowmobile	99
Armand's Inventions	107
M. Lecroix	117
M. Chalot	123
Juliette's Headache	127
The Boys	131

The Blind Pig, Rose's Visit	139
St. Jean Baptiste Day	145
Rose's Marriage, Cecile's Absence	151
Picnic and Playhouse	155
Rose's Arrival	163
Flory's Store, Lenny's Hand	169
The Goodbyes	177
Cold Lake	183
The Dance Hall	191
A New Way of Life	197
Living Quarters	205
The Trial	215
Old Man Renard	223
Corsets and Shoes	229
More Troubles	247
Berry Picking	253
The Hospital	263
New Baby, New Scheme	269

THE GOAT WITH THE CROOKED HORN

"Flory, I am calling you. Do you hear?"

"Yes, Armand. I'm coming."

Flory pronounced his name *Ahma*, with the accent on the first syllable. That was as close as she could come to the French pronunciation with its silent *d*.

"De mean cow wit de big horn puncture de *bébé* sheep in de belly. His gut are on de groun'. It will not live. I am t'inking I should put it out of misery."

"Maybe we can save it."

"I believe you cannot. It is not ver' pretty to look at."

The lamb's bleating and baaing were a heartbreak. Blades of loose grass, weeds, and hay clung to the intestines.

Flory insisted. "Go to the well for water while I get the boiling kettle and disinfectant. I have heavy linen thread and clean bleached flour bags."

Armand held the lamb while Flory washed the intestines, gently pouring water to remove loose hay and dirt.

"You are not a *docteur*, unless you keep it from me. How you put de gut back? How you know where dey go?"

"We can only do the best we can. If it dies at least we have tried."

Flory didn't know how or where to place the intestines, but she said a little prayer. The needle was threaded, she took a long breath and held it deep inside of her.

"Flory, take bigger stitch. You are not making one of your quilt. You are *nerveuse*?"

"No, Armand. Well, just a bit. I am glad it isn't one of my children."

"You do a good job. Now I will get a gunny sack. It will keep your flour sack clean. Also, it will serve as a corset."

The lamb was taken to the sheep shed where it was put in a sheltered corner on a clean bed of hay.

It was a long, restless night waiting for the first stream of light to peek from the edges of the green blind. Not a sound was made as Flory dressed herself. She hurried to the shed, and with a gentle hand stroked the lamb's head. It opened its eyes and gave a trebbled "baa" of thanks.

"It's alive, Armand. It's alive! It opened its eyes and baaed."

"Do not have high hope. Maybe tomorrow he will not baa. Den you will be baaing."

A MATTER OF COMPULSION

"I have a feeling that it will live. I'm going to put milk in one of my bread tins. I'll set it close. You never know. It may be thirsty."

* * *

"You will be happy today, I know for sure. Your sheep is standing on his feet. I say you are a good *docteur*."

"Oh, I hope it's strong enough. If it falls over it could die."

* * *

"Come, Flory! Come and see! Your little sheep is walking wit de udder sheep. Gee cripe dat is a miracle, eh?"

"Oh, Armand, it is a miracle! I feel . . . well, I feel it's the greatest thing I ever did."

"You do many t'ing dat is great Flory." He pinched her bottom and said, "Tonight, Flo: watch out below."

"Not tonight, Armand. We'll have to keep on having it during the day when Rosie's in school. I've asked you time and again to put a partition in that one long bedroom. Is it too much to ask? Rose is ten years old. Do you think that's right? And Leonard will soon be ten."

"I am sure dey sleep wit bot' eye shut. You worry for not'ing, but if it make you happy, I do it."

FLORY'S LIFE

They had a three-room shack, which consisted of two bedrooms and a kitchen with a lean-to. They referred to the lean-to as the back kitchen. It held dry wood and two extra sleeping cots for company. The table was built long to accommodate the threshers. Flory had begged Armand to cut it down to a neater size. His answer was always "tomorrow".

Tomorrow never came, so she decided to do it herself. She sawed off each long end as far back as the legs. It looked terribly naked and had lost its character, but she covered it with an oil cloth. Now she was sure no one would notice that eighteen inches had been taken off. The paint had been waiting for all of two months. *If I can use a saw, I can surely use a brush,* she thought. The window sills, the corner cupboard, and the table legs were painted a fresh blue.

There's so much to do around the place, but no, he has to go to the village. I know he goes to the village only for his little drinks of beer. He smells like father did when he came home after having his social pint. If it weren't for Rosie coming home from school I'd be lonesome. She's a happy girl. I am fortunate to have my sister with me.

She thought of the comfortable home her family had left behind in London. The fireplace with the wide mantle, and how pretty mother kept it with the two vaseline glass vases, one on each side. One broke when they moved to Canterbury Road. The other was given to her when she married Armand. It was still in her trunk along with all the other things she brought to Canada.

The children only ever saw the top half of the trunk, where Flory kept her best clothing. She had two skirts, one light grey, the other black with a panel of pleats on each side. There were three blouses, a grey silk, a black velvet, and an ivory. The two long nightgowns were made of the finest cotton ever made. The children found the most wondrous thing to be her ivory wedding dress, which had an oval yolk of frilled lace. There were two pairs of long gloves with lace inserts. Inside one glove, for safe-keeping, she kept a sterling silver chain of faith, hope and charity charms. The delicate gold-trimmed cup and saucer from the Crystal Palace was wrapped over and over in gauze to keep it safe. There were rare coins from the shop they had owned, which were kept in a little black bag with a drawstring.

Uncle Bill would sail to India where he stayed for months before returning to England. It was a special day when he came back, especially for Flory. Never once

A MATTER OF COMPULSION

did he return without a splendid gift for her.

She had a matching broach and earrings bordered in lacy scrolls, made of monies from India and dated 1881. There was a small pearl necklace which she had lost and then found on the way to Mission Church on Old Kent Road. She could never count the many times the story was told.

And there were other treasures from India. Also in her trunk were an ivory fan that she cherished and an ivory letter opener with a little gold handle. Although she loved her Grandfather's silver fob chain with a tiny black watch hanging from it, what she had loved most was the heavy gold-braided ring that Uncle Bill had bought her on a never-to-be-forgotten outing to the Strand on her sixteenth birthday. It had been stolen from Armand when they were courting.

Flory had collected little handkerchiefs. Now they were tied around rich auburn and spun gold locks from her brothers and sisters. There were parish magazines, quaint Christmas cards and photographs, each tied in a square of gauze. There was a book titled *Jessica's First Prayer*, which through the years was read to each child in turn. In a small cushioned box was an ebony crucifix bordered in silver. The figure of Jesus was silver and stood out on the black cross.

These were all Flory had, the treasures she held dear to her heart. She never took any of her precious belongings out of the trunk except for the grey silk blouse and dark skirt for special occasions, such as going to church or the christening of a child. Her gold looped earrings were a part of her. They had hardly been out of her ears since they were pierced at the age of sixteen.

* * *

Flory was ten years old when she went to Queen Victoria's Diamond Jubilee. All the girls were wearing Jubilee bonnets covered with flowers and coloured ribbons. Her mother Jane bought Didee and Flory the prettiest ones she could find. They were dressed alike in green velvet frocks with their golden hair tied back in large silk bows. On weekends they would go to Epson Downs or Hastings, always bringing home a large bouquet of flowers for mother and sea shells for the younger ones. Didee and Flory attended school on Queens Road, always one with the other.

The Hollowell family left England on April 18th, 1906. They arrived at Staynerville, Ontario on May 1st and heard that there was work in Brownsburg, Québec. They settled in Brownsburg at the Pilon Boarding

FLORY'S LIFE

House. It was there that Flory met the son of the house, Armand.

QUEBEC

"Mother, here comes Armand. Don't you think he's a smart-looking young man?"

"Yes dear, and I'm going to ask him to do me a favour. I shouldn't be going to the kitchen at this time of day when they are preparing food." She called the boy over. "How do you do, young man? Would you be so good as to see if there is milk for my baby?"

"Yes, Mrs. Hollowell. I will give you de whole cow if you give me your daughter."

"Not so fast, young man."

Armand had quickly turned to smile, then briskly walked toward the kitchen. He thought, *I had to say it. I could not control my feeling, but it is a warning. It is de best I can do for now.*

Jane Hollowell quickly got the message. "Do you remember when we went to the corner shop to bid farewell to Mrs. Reynolds and she said you would marry the first young man you met in Canada? Now, don't you think that's strange?"

Flory lowered her eyes and smiled. Little did her mother know that her Flory and Armand were already meeting at the park.

* * *

Brownsburg was a pretty village with a river that ran through the park. Armand called it the pique-nique groun'. "Flory, never forget. When Armand is not aroun' he is at de pique-nique groun'." Just to hear him say it drove her ga ga.

It was a busy household with as many as sixty or seventy boarders. The family's success was due to the fact that the Dominion Cartridge Company hired many people just off the ships. Room and board cost men $8.00 and women $6.00 per month.

None of the family was likely to notice the burning glances they had for each other. *Mère* Rose de Lima and *Père* Hormidas had four daughters, Berta, Dorena, Azelma, Marie-Anna, and two sons, Napoleon and Armand. They needed no hired help. Each one had his or her chores.

It was a balmy evening in August when Flory and Armand walked hand in hand along the river bank, Flory telling stories of England, then Armand telling stories

A MATTER OF COMPULSION

of Québec.

"I like you for my woman always, Flory, and one day we get marry. You like de idea?"

"Maybe, Armand, but I have my mother to think of. Maybe she wouldn't want me to marry a Frenchman. You see, not one of us can speak a word of French."

"I speak English. Is not dat enough for you? Dere is no maybe. I say it and I mean it." He changed the subject. "Where did you get dat ring? I never see one like dat. Flory, could you lend it to me for one day?"

"Armand, it has never been off this finger since Uncle Bill bought it for my sixteenth birthday." He looked at her. She melted, slipped the ring off, and handed it to him. He put it on his little finger. "Ah, it is so beautiful. Tomorrow it will be return."

"Why do you want to wear it, Armand?"

"I want to wear it because me and my friends gadder tomorrow to practise our violins. Do you mind?"

"Of course I don't mind."

* * *

Armand and his friends decided to go for a swim at the dam. After the swim they would go to Jean Luc's for their practise of singing and playing their instruments. After the swim Armand walked to where he had left his clothes. The first thing he did was reach for the ring he had left in his trousers' pocket. It was gone. He looked in the grass, shook his clothes. There was no ring. He panicked. He called his friends. "Help me! I have a ring on my finger, I take it off, I put it in my pant pocket. When you go for a swim de water make your finger small. I do not want to lose it. It does not belong to me. It is a ring made wit braid of gold. Mon Dieu! What will I do? I borrow it from Flory. I am a broken man."

"Ah, so you are friend wit dat new girl wit de gold hair. We hear about dat. Angebelle, what happen to her?"

"Never mind dat. I have to find de ring."

Armand didn't play the violin that night. There was nothing to sing about either. He kept his distance from Flory. He was sick inside and sleep didn't come for the pounding of his heart.

He was up at the break of dawn and hurrying back to the dam. Every move he had made was relived step by step. Going to the bushes, undressing, putting the ring in his pocket, rolling his trousers tight, then hurrying to his friends. Then suddenly he remembered the two men who were not sitting far from him. They had come out of the water when he was getting ready to go in. He remembered asking Jean Luc if they were his friends. Jean Luc said no, that they were from Ottawa.

Gee cripe! Dey must have see me put somet'ing in my pocket. Yes, it is dose sonofabitch dat take de ring. What can I do? What about her mudder Jane? Oh, I should never have borrow it! It happen because I want to show my friend.

When he drew his violin bow back and forth with his little finger slightly raised, his friends naturally would notice the heavy braided ring. Wouldn't they be curious? After all, it was an unusual ring from a very beautiful English girl. It was all in vain. Now the ring was gone. He knew he had to tell her, even if it meant losing her.

"Tonight Flory, you come for a walk wit me?"

"Yes, I'd like that Armand." She could feel that he was bothered. It wasn't like him to be so quiet. During the months of long walks, he had told her about his girlfriend Angebelle. He wasn't seeing her anymore. Not since Flory. She had naturally told him of Tommy in England, and how he walked beside her on the way to church.

"We didn't hear much of the sermon, what with stealing glances at one another. It did make my heart flip. Well, not because I liked him, but — oh Tommy was fond of me. When he saw me coming along, he was so ga ga over me he fell over a barrel of cockles and mussels."

Her heart was pounding. The mere thought of Angebelle winning Armand was unbearable. "Let us sit here Armand. There is something wrong and I can't stand it any longer." She looked at his black wavy hair and soft olive skin. It made her shiver.

He turned to face her with misty blue eyes. After a moment he placed his head in the palms of his hands in remorse. "I have bad news, Flory, and I don't know how to tell you. You must understand dat when I was swimming at de dam, I put your braid ring in my pocket to keep it safe. When you swim your finger get small. I have de ring on my small finger and I don't want to lose it, eh? When I come back to put my clothes on de ring is gone. I search. It is nowhere. Dere is a man. I see him. Jean Luc say he is from Ottawa."

"Is there no way to get it back? Don't you know how I loved it? No, you wouldn't know."

"Non, non. Do not cry. I promise you I get anudder ring for you. It will be from

A MATTER OF COMPULSION

me, not a uncle. I feel bad like a Judas. You will not like me anymore? I love you Flory, like nobody in dis world. I love you so strong I could eat you. Let me wipe de tear from your eye. Let me taste dem. Ah, it taste good and have just enough salt for me. Are you feel cross wit me?"

"No, Armand. I'm not cross, I'm heartbroken. Dear Uncle Bill. He brought me the ring and sailed away. We never, ever heard from him again."

"Come close to me, Flory. Let me hold you. Let me smell your hair. It is long, and de colour of a little horse my uncle use to have when I was a young boy. It was gold Flory, and it shine like real gold. Come close to me, real close. I will not hurt you. I cannot sleep at night. Your face is always before my eye. Let me caress you for a while."

He kissed her gently again and again. There was regret, sorrow, and deep, endless love.

"You are crying again. Do not feel sad. Tell me de truth. You know dat one day dis would happen. Do you not realize dat de ring was meant to be loss an' because you cry over de ring I feel sad and I taste your tear, an' because I taste your tear I love you. Yes, an' because I love you, we grow weak. An' because we grow weak we make love. It is as simple as dat. Now you are not happy. Ah, Flory, dry your eye wit dis *mouchoir*. And Flory, do not tell one person. Not yet. We will wait an' see."

That night Flory lay in her bed with a thousand questions rushing through her mind and not one sensible answer to any of them.

What will mother do when she finds out? Will she disown me? Oh, dear mother. Hasn't she had enough sorrow and grief? Didn't she lose Horace, Harry, Didee, and baby Esther? The last thing baby had done was walk to the corner store for a stick of candy by herself. Then she got pneumonia and died.

Two months later my sister and dearest friend Didee was sent to St. Thomas Hospital. Her limbs were swollen. The nurses were sure she could walk. She was left on the cold marble floor until she cried out, "Nurse, I'll lie here and die if you don't bring me a cover." They carried Didee to her room. When mother and I went, she said, "I'm going to die and I want to come home. Please let me come home, mother." We took her home. Mother immediately sent for Dr. Cook. Didee, he told us, had spinal paralysis. She was home for twenty-four hours. She was sixteen years old when she died. Mother lost her youngest and oldest within three months.

After Didee was laid to rest mother was never home. Every day she went to the cemetery, crying and talking to Didee. She lost sixty pounds. Father knew mother

QUEBEC

had to get away from the shop, so he sold it and we moved to Canterbury Road. She had to get strong. She was pregnant with her tenth child, Lillian. They made plans to sail to Canada. Lillian was seven months old when we came across on the S.S. Dominion. Now mother was pregnant again for her eleventh child. Neither Lillian nor Lenny ever knew their father. Exactly ten months after arriving in Canada we lost father at Smith's Falls, Ontario. The last words I heard father speak were, "Lord, into thine hands I commit my spirit."

I can't hurt mother. I wonder if Didee had been here with us would things be different? Would she have been with us walking along the bank? Oh, Didee. I miss you so. I need you now more than I ever did. I speak with you every day. You're still my dearest sister. If you were here I would tell you my biggest, deepest secret. I'm in love with a Frenchman. His name is Armand Pilon. Nobody knows yet, but I think I'm going to have a baby.

* * *

Two months had passed, and Armand told Flory that he was going to Montreal on business and would be back the following day. "Why are you going to Montreal, Armand?"

"I go on business. Do not tell me you will miss me for one day only. You make me happy for dat. Tomorrow night me and you will go for a walk."

* * *

"Ah, Flory, I can see you are happy to be wit me again."

He's got another thought coming if he thinks I'm going to ask him anything about his trip. She lowered her head, her hands parting cold blades of grass as though searching for something, pretending she didn't much care.

"You do not fool me, Flory. I know you ver' well." He took her hand, held it, then slipped the ring on her finger. She rested her hand in his.

"Armand, you will never be sorry."

Each side of the ring was shaped like a horseshoe facing the other. Each side was clustered with small pearls. In the centre were deep red stones. It was delicate and beautiful.

"You must not tell about de ring Flory. Take it off your finger before we go home.

A MATTER OF COMPULSION

You unnerstan', I have to tell Maman before anyone else knows."

* * *

The snow came down heavily until high banks lay along the roadside. Flory went to work as usual, but because she wanted to slip the ring on when she was alone, she put it in her pocket, placing a handkerchief over it to keep it safe. She walked down the snow-covered path that led from the house to the main road. When she got to the road, she felt for her ring. It was gone. She ran to the house. She had to tell Armand's sister Berta her secret.

"Oh, Berta, what will I do?" Armand gave me an engagement ring. We weren't going to tell anyone for a while. It was a secret. I put it in my pocket. I even covered it with a handkerchief. I didn't know there was a hole in my pocket."

"Come. I will find it for you. What pocket has the hole, and on what side were you walking?"

"The right side pocket has the hole and I was walking on the right."

"Stay where you are, Flory. Do not walk. Do not touch the snowbank, and do not cry."

Berta walked very slowly, side-stepping along the bank with utmost concentration, until she found the one small hole she had been looking for. She very gently lowered her hand into the deep snow and lifted the ring, crying out, "Look what I found!"

"Now Flory, this is how you keep things safe." She placed the ring in the corner of the handkerchief, then tied it in a knot. "You see? You can tie anything in your handkerchief. It will always be safe unless you lose your handkerchief, eh? And Flory, do not worry. I will keep your secret."

* * *

When Rose de Lima and Hormidas noticed how seriously in love Armand and Flory were, it wasn't long before Hormidas bought Armand a fancy carriage and a prancing black horse. Two young people in love, with their own horse and buggy, driving far into the countryside with nothing but happiness. Telling tales, all alone, where no one could see or hear.

"I used to go to the countryside in England. Oh, the green fields and flowers,

QUEBEC

Armand. I'll never forget it."

"One day Flory, I take you to old Québec Cité. You see some history dere."

"Armand, do you think your parents know that I am going to have a baby? Do you know that if anyone came to our shop in England, my mother knew which ones were pregnant. She did, and she was always right. Do I look as if I'm going to have a baby?"

"How can somebody know? Your face look de same an' your hair look de same to me. But maybe it is time to tell Maman." He wondered if maybe women did have a way of knowing. He feared that his Maman would think him deceitful.

Three weeks had slipped by before he mustered enough courage to face her. He stood bravely, looking straight into her eyes. "Maman, I love Flory. I would like her to be my wife, and Maman, we have to get marry."

"I understand. I was very sure it was that way. She will make a good wife for you. First I must speak with your father. Do not worry. You will marry Flory. We will pick a time and place."

They were married in the stone church at St. Phillipe on July 15, 1908. They were both twenty years old. Six months later a baby girl was born. Flory named her Elizabeth after her sister Didee. At four months old the baby died.

Maman Pilon put a white lace cloth on a high table. Flory dressed Elizabeth in her long christening gown. Maman Pilon lay her on the lace cloth, fixing her gown so it hung in folds. In her tiny hands Flory placed a large ebony crucifix that was bordered in silver. Jesus was silver and stood out on the cross. Not a word was spoken until Flory fell to her knees sobbing. Maman Pilon knelt. She put her arms around Flory. "You will have more bébés. You will love each one just as strong. You are young. You have a whole life ahead of you. Never forget Flory, that life is not always a bed of roses."

GOING WEST

Armand had a dream. He wanted to go West. At one time his aunt and uncle had bought a homestead at Legal, Alberta, just north of Edmonton. They had written colourful letters and sent them east. The crops were good and there were cattle to raise. It was, they said, the land of opportunity. Now that Armand had married, surely his mother would understand that he needed a place of his own. He idolized his mother, yet he was the only one of her children to leave Brownsburg.

Flory remained for the time being, continuing her work at the Dominion Cartridge Company. Armand wrote home saying how rocky and far the homesteads were from the village, church, and school. His father, Hormidas, joined Armand. It was unbelieveable. It didn't take long before he bought Armand the first farm next to the village. It was already cleared, and had a long sheep shed and one hundred sheep. It had a barn and a small granary. Best of all, the church and school were within walking distance for the children they would have.

Chère Flory:

You know, my dear wife, that we now own a farm. When you come, bring soap and towel for on the train. Do not put your head out of the window. You have long hair and the train go fast. It is dangereux. Also, I would like you to bring our rosier with you. Come soon to me. I see your face always before my eye. Do not forget to say your prayer. Goodbye, my wife. I am your husband with one million kiss for you.

Armand

"Mother, Armand said in his letter to be sure to bring Rosie to the west with me. Can she come, please?"

"If I let her go to the west, will you promise me you'll send her to school? You'll be living on a farm. Heaven only knows if there is a school."

"Mother, Armand's farm is the closest farm to the school, so you don't have to worry. I promise you she'll go to school. Oh, I am so happy, and I'll take good care of her."

* * *

A MATTER OF COMPULSION

The trip was long. When they reached Strathcona, the High Level Bridge was being built. They had to be lifted by a huge derrick to get to the other side. Rosie was crying, and Flory had lost the colour in her cheeks. It was no wonder, as she was expecting another baby. They arrived hot, tired, and hungry.

"Flory, you are here, my dear wife have come. Why you bring Rosie wit you?"

"Armand, you said in your letter to be sure and bring Rosie with me."

"Ah Flory, non, non. I say be sure to bring your rosier wit you - de rosier bush I buy for you. But it is good she come. She will be company for you."

* * *

Mr. Massey had built a hotel in Legal, but the village wasn't large enough for two hotels, his and Mr. Fortesque's, so he had a store and rented the upstairs rooms. It was an ideal place to stay while the farm shack was being built. Mr. Massey was a widower with one daughter named Edna. Rosie and Edna were the same age. Every day they went to and from school together.

When Flory walked into the kitchen it was a joy to see Mr. Massey in a white butcher apron, his sleeves rolled high, kneading the flour into a large mound of dough. She wanted desperately to learn how it was all put together. She decided that now, while he was in the midst of it all, would be a perfect time to ask. "Mr. Massey, could you teach me how to make bread, or is it your secret?"

"It is no secret. I'll be happy to teach you. When you make good bread you never go hungry. I will also teach you how to make your own yeast starter. Flory, your first lesson will be on Wednesday morning. Next Wednesday you'll do it on your own. It's easy."

"Won't Armand be surprised, and mother too. Why in England the bread cart came to the door each morning. I do think now that we have a farm, it will be a lovely thing to do."

* * *

It was 1910, and Flory gave birth to Leonard, a beautiful golden-haired boy with bright blue eyes. It was unusual, she thought. All eleven brothers and sisters had

GOING WEST

brown eyes. Not one had blue eyes, only her father. Her mother Jane never thought a baby was a baby unless it had brown eyes. She used to say it was the gypsy blood in them.

Flory loved the farm. She didn't know anyone yet, but then she didn't need a lot of friends. The wheat was so tall that Armand took a picture of Flory standing in it. You could only see her lovely face and a little of her white blouse. Armand named it "Un épi dans le blé." Flory's translation was "A needle in a haystack."

BEATRICE

"We should have a good life here. When de wheat is harvest, den de snow will come. It is perfect for me to get my own trap line. Also, I have some good idea." When Armand had ideas, he stayed home. He sat always in the same position, with his left thumb on his forehead, a deep frown on his brow, lots of brown paper and a pencil in front of him. "Flory, listen to dis idea dat I have."

"Armand, you need a button on your shirt. Take it off and I'll . . ."

"Gee cripe! Every time I have a good idea, you never listen. De goddam button have already been invented!"

"Yes, Armand, and I can't even write to my dear mother. There isn't one drop of ink in the home!"

"You want ink? I make ink. Get a small pot. I get de carotte. I show you how to make ink. I cut dem and put ver' little water. Dey must cook slow until dey burn shiny black. You may as well relax, Flory. It will take a while."

"I can't understand your thinking. You're like a child playing games."

"Ah yes, Flory. You have to add dat. You can never be happy."

When the carrots had burned dry and black, Armand poured a little water into the pot and pushed it to the side of the stove. When the burned sediment had loosened, he asked for a piece of cotton to strain it.

"Now, Flory, you have your ink. And Flory, do not forget to tell your mother Jane how well we live."

* * *

"I dream for you, Flory. You should see de sleigh I have draw. It will go on snow and on de lake. I can trap and hunt wit it. Also, I have a name for it. Dey already have de automobile, now Pilon will give dem de snowmobile. You say dat: 'snow-mo-bile.' It come easy, eh?"

"Armand, you are a dreamer. I don't think your father would ever have bought you this farm if he had known you preferred drawing so-called inventions to farming. When you are at Fortesque's hotel nothing gets done. You're always looking for a man to hire, so you say. You're either sitting with your thumb on your forehead, or walking in the fields. What in heaven's name did we come here for?"

"Bullshit! Complain, complain. You should have stay in England an' marry

A MATTER OF COMPULSION

Tommy. I show you dere is more in life. Yes, much more."

"Yes there is, Armand. I'm pregnant again."

"So, you are a woman an' I am a man. We cannot change dat."

* * *

Mme. Morin, the midwife who would deliver her baby, spoke very little English and Flory spoke very little French. They used their hands to express themselves like the French people do. It wasn't long until they understood one another very well.

Mme. Billet had eighteen children. They lived in a brick house on the corner of the road going to Diligence. She couldn't speak one word of English, yet she was a good neighbour who could be called on whenever Flory needed help.

* * *

Armand bought a garden of cabbages. Flory said there were all of a thousand of them and never had the sheep had it so good. Mrs. Prevost spoke English, so Armand made her an offer. "Beatrice, if you come to my place to show my wife Flory how to make sauerkraut, you can make enough for you and Maurice for de whole winter. What you say?"

"It's a deal, Pilon. I'll be there in the morning."

* * *

"Flory Pilon, how in hell do you get to the pump with that mean ram out there?"

"All you do is hold the wash tub on your stomach with the bottom facing out. When he sees that tub he won't bother you. Besides, he's too busy eating cabbage leaves. Armand told me to keep this stick handy. If it attacks I'm to hit it on the nose."

Beatrice walked slowly toward the pump. The only problem was that she had turned the tub the wrong way. The ram headed for her, knocking the tub and Beatrice to the ground. She screamed. Flory grabbed the stick and hit the ram on the nose, which started the blood rushing out. He walked away, rubbing his nose on the grass.

"You and your damned tub. What you should have is a suit of armour. Coming

BEATRICE

from England you should know that."

It was a happy day, with good talk and laughter. They became fast friends, and never did a week go by without them seeing one another.

* * *

"Tell me Beatrice, how did you come to live here in Legal?"

"It's a long story. I lived in Detroit and Maurice is from Windsor. He speaks French and English, but I do believe his French blood is stronger, because he so wanted to move to a French settlement and be a farmer. It was all the same to me. When you're in love, it doesn't matter where you live. He's very quiet. Never says a hell of a lot, but he's damned dependable."

"Does he drink, Beatrice? I mean, does he enjoy a drink?"

"He enjoys a drink, yes, but very seldom."

"Do you enjoy a drink, Beatrice?"

"I enjoy a little wine, don't you? It's like a special warm holiday when Maurice drinks. Maybe because he's more talkative, and he tells me things that otherwise I'd never know. Men are strange, Flory. Sometimes they won't open their mouths if they are full of it."

* * *

There was an early snow that year, but it didn't last long. The rain came down, packing the snow tightly until heavy slush lay all around the shack. Armand wondered if water could have seeped through the banking and into the cellar, especially the back part where the vegetables were stored. When he checked, he noticed that vegetables had been dug out of the sand and washed clean in a puddle of water. A few bites had been taken from a carrot. He knew muskrats had come in to feast on the vegetables.

"Flory, you never believe dat. We have visitor dat come where de vegetable are bury and I see dey eat some. Can you guess what it is?"

"Of course I can't."

"It is muskrat."

"Good gracious! What will we do?'

"Not'ing. Dey are more afraid of us. Dey come from de crique. Dey make dere home under de porch. Ah yes, I have one good idea. Dey are ver' clean. Dey do not eat witout washing dere food."

"Yes, Armand. Stack the fire and get Mme. Morin. It's time."

* * *

Flory had a girl. She was named Cecile Muriel. The year was 1911.

"Are you going to give your children French or English names?" Beatrice wanted to know.

"No, Beatrice. I'm going to give them one of each. I have Leonard Albert and this one is Cecile Muriel. When they grow up they can choose the one they prefer."

"Now isn't that a practical way of doing it. Do you think you are strong enough to come for dinner this coming Sunday? I'd like it if you could, because I'm having four and twenty blackbirds baked in a pie. You need a change, and bring Rosie and your babies."

"Oh, Beatrice, I would like that, and so would Armand. It would do me good to go somewhere away from the four walls of this shack."

* * *

"We are here, Beatrice. Gee cripe, it smell good. Flory tell me you make four and twenty blackbirds bake in a pie. She say when de pie is open de bird start to sing song. Dat is a good trick Beatrice. I wait to see dat. Where is Maurice?"

"He's out at the barn. Take your son and go for a walk. Put the baby on the bed Flory, and come and relax."

Flory looked at the pictures on the wall. She decided that when she got home she would take down the gaudy calendar hanging by the blue cupboard.

Beatrice peeked at the pie. "It's almost done. Not quite. A little more golden will do it."

"Flory, let's go to church next Sunday. Wouldn't it be nice to go together?"

"I'd like that. In England we went to the Anglican Church. Come to my place and we'll walk together. Between Armand and Rosie, surely they can mind the baby. Leonard's a big boy now."

The table was set. The men walked in and Beatrice took the pie from the oven. All eyes were on the puffy golden crust. Rosie was the most curious of them all.

BEATRICE

They must be birds, she thought. *You can see the shapes of them under the bulging crust.*

"Dat is ver' beautiful, eh Flory? I never see one dat big. Dat is made wit grouse, eh?"

"No, Pilon, they're smaller than grouse."

"Ah yes, partridge? Prairie chicken?"

"I won't tell. You'll have to taste it first." Beatrice never did tell what was in the pie.

* * *

"If Beatrice and you are going to church, why not she stay an' have dinner wit us, eh?"

"Yes, Armand, why not? I'm sure she'd like that."

Armand was in his glory. He liked to cook, but this day was very special. He took out the roaster, prepared the meat, peeled onions and garlic. Then he scrubbed the potatoes and took out a jar of sauerkraut.

* * *

It was a lively walk down the hill and over the bridge.

"Flory, when you go to church, do you get hungry?"

"I get so hungry I can't wait to get home. Why I can have a bowl of porridge, toast and tea for breakfast, yet the minute I set foot in church my insides start to gurgle. I was the same when I was in England."

"Well, I get so hungry I can't concentrate on the sermon. All I do is stare at the priest and wonder what his housekeeper cooked up for him."

"Do you think it could be the incense that makes us hungry?"

"I never thought of that, Flory. They do rock it back and forth and well, doesn't it smell spicy to you?"

"You know, that could be the reason. There must be something to it. I'll bet the whole congregation is starved."

They tried not to look at one another. They couldn't resist the temptation. Then the laughter started. They held their noses until it felt as if their temples would burst. Finally Beatrice stood, made a genuflection, and walked down the aisle to the door. Flory made a genuflection and followed closely behind and out the door. Flory needed that. It was the heartiest laugh she had had since coming west.

"Aren't we terrible, Beatrice? I wonder if the priest noticed. I truly feel I've sinned."

"Of course you haven't sinned. Jesus had a good sense of humour. Now take Adam and Eve. They had the greatest sense of humour of all. You should know that."

"Oh Beatrice, you do make me laugh. I feel I've known you all my life."

"When I lived in Detroit, my best friend Mary told me that she played with herself."

"Played with herself, or by herself?"

"Both, Flory. She played with herself, by herself. I told her it was a sin. Well that's what I was told. And do you know what she said? Oh, you'd never guess. She said, 'It's mine. It belongs to me and I can boil cabbage in it if I like.'"

"Stop, Beatrice. I'm going to wet my drawers. Listen to this. A young lady told the police officer that a man kept following her. The officer asked him, 'Why are you following this young lady?' The man said, 'Click, click. You know.' The officer told him, 'If you do it again, to the judge you will go.' Well he said it again so the officer took him to the judge. The judge said, 'Why are you following this young lady?' The man said, 'Click, click. You know.' The judge gave him one year behind bars. The man asked what for. The judge said, 'Click, click. You know.'"

"Am I supposed to laugh, Flory?"

* * *

The hot roaster and baked potatoes were put on a large breadboard. In a bowl Armand had hot sauerkraut. A plate of Flory's homemade bread and butter completed the menu. Armand set breadboard and all on the table.

"Now eat and enjoy. It is not fancy, but I make it especially for you."

"Armand, we're starving, and it smells so good."

"Yes, Pilon. We're so hungry we're sorry the good Father didn't serve us communion." Armand and Beatrice burst out laughing.

"Don't take dat so sérieuse, Flory. You know Beatrice by now. Dat is a joke. Loosen your mout' a little. You have to learn when a joke is a joke and when it is not."

BEATRICE

"Pilon, you should open an eating place."

"Yes, many times I t'ink about dat, but I have too much on my mind right now."

"Well tell me, what did you put on that meat? I don't think I've ever tasted anything like it."

"No, I am sure you have not. You see, you do not tell me what bird you have in dat pie, and I am sure dat I guess de right one. But I will be a sport and tell you. First I take de roaster. I put in a layer of pork and a layer of onion. Den I put a layer of muskrat and a layer of onion. You see I build it up, so I do it again, a layer of onion, and a layer of muskrat. You top de whole t'ing wit a layer of good fat pork to keep it from drying. Oh yes, de garlic, salt and pepper also. And den I roast it. Ver' easy to do."

They sat speechless. They didn't know if they should laugh or cry.

"Flory, tell me the truth. Would he do that?"

"I wouldn't be surprised. He's been telling me for weeks how clean they are. No, I wouldn't put it past him, and I'm damned sorry I ate it."

"You're nothing but a devil, trying to get back at me because of my bird pie. That's a hell of a dirty trick, Pilon. One hell of a dirty trick."

"Dat is a clean trick, Beatrice. When you learn about muskrat and how clean dey are, you will eat dem. Yes, and one day when de worl' get hungry, everybody will eat muskrat. Dis is not a rat dat go in de garbage. Dis is de muskrat dat wash everyt'ing dey eat."

"Well at least we enjoyed the sauerkraut and tea."

"Good. I am happy for dat Beatrice, because I have no milk, so I go out an' have to milk de mare."

"Damn you! Damn You! I wouldn't dare ask what you put in your sauerkraut!"

"Ah, dat is a secret like your bird pie. Everybody have to have dere secret recipe."

"You're not being fair, Pilon. We're going to think you put rabbit droppings in it."

"I never do a t'ing like dat. What you t'ink I am? I wash de salt away. I put pork crackling and I try a little dried sarsaparilla for a change. Oh yes, I t'row a handful of sunflower seed dat I gadder. I put more, but it take too long to crack de seed. Den I put it in de oven and keep turning it, so don't t'ink I am feeding you rabbit shit. If people hear dat, dey will say, 'Did you hear de latest news? Pilon make his wife eat shit.'"

25

A MATTER OF COMPULSION

Flory didn't quite like the sound of that one. Beatrice and Armand burst into laughter. It wasn't funny, but she wasn't going to let them think that she didn't know a joke when she heard one. She smiled broader and broader, without once raising her eyes.

REMINISCENCES

Armand had an idea. It was a much bigger idea than roasting muskrat, and all he could think about was how it could be done. He wanted to tell Flory, but he knew what she would say. "You and your ideas. Why don't you find work like other decent men." He had heard it so many times. But then, who knew. Maybe she would like this one best of all. Yes, he would tell her and watch the look on her face.

"Flory, listen to dis. You can have wheat farm. You can have pig farm and you can have cattle farm, eh?"

"Yes, Armand, didn't you know? Or is that why you want to rent out the farm?"

"Bullshit! You never wait until I am finish! I should tell you not'ing. Not one t'ing from one week in and one week out until it become month. Yes, and den year. I am sure you like dat."

"Armand, I do feel tired today. What is it now?"

"I was going to say why cannot I have a muskrat farm? A muskrat farm, Flory. Do you realize what dat mean? It is here, all here, right under our nose."

"Good God, Armand! What next? And what would people think? The village people will think you are another John Foster."

"Who in de hell is John Foster, and what have he got to do wit me?"

"Oh, nothing. It just reminded me of him. He studied the stars. This was when I was a little girl in England. His wife thought he was losing his mind and she told all the village people. Anyway, she had him put away."

"Where did she hide him? Dat poor man. If I be him I would put her away and trow away de key as well."

"No, Armand. She put him in an insane asylum. I don't want to talk about it, and I'm sorry I ever mentioned it."

"De problem wit you Flory, is dat you always worry about people. To hell wit people. Worry about me once in a while. People, cripe, dey t'ink if dey have butter on de table dat not'ing else matter in dis world."

"Armand, if you're not interested in growing your own wheat, or your own animals, how in heaven's name are you going to have a muskrat farm? You've got an invention on the go now. That's why you're eager to rent the farm out. You don't want to put the crop in. You don't want to work it. You want to work on your invention. Remember?"

A MATTER OF COMPULSION

"I did not say we would fill de house wit muskrat dis afternoon, Flory. I know it can be done. De bébés can have fur coat and for you a nice long one," he said, pinching her bottom.

"Don't think you can get around my good side. Your mother is sending you twelve dollars every month. I never see a penny of it. Where does it go?"

"Flory, you are being an English bulldog again. Yes, I see dat more every day. You should have marry Tommy. Maybe he make you happy wit his cockle and mussel."

"Maybe I should have, Armand. Who knows. You've done a lot of drawings, so why don't you start your sleigh now instead of again starting on something else? You are going to the hotel every day. Don't you care what happens to your family?"

She turned around to face him, but he was gone. She looked out the door. *Yes, there he goes, walking straight and cocky. What in heaven's name do you do with a man like that? Maybe I'm short-tempered because I'm going to have another baby.*

* * *

"Flory, what would you like this time, a girl or a boy?"

"It should be a boy, Beatrice. I first had a girl, which I lost. Then I had Leonard. Then Cecile. If I have a boy I'll name him Romeo George."

"You're a lucky woman, Flory, and never forget that."

Flory wondered why Beatrice would say such a thing, but she wouldn't dare ask. *When she's ready, she'll tell me.*

"Armand said that this coming year we would go to Brownsburg to visit Papa and Maman Pilon. I did have happy times with his sisters."

"How can he afford to go east? The farm is rented now and, well, I hear that he does go to the hotel a lot. Oh, I am sorry. Forgive me. I didn't mean to interfere."

"It's perfectly all right. If Armand wants to go, he only has to write to his mother and she will send the fare. He wants to see about his so-called invention, and I can't blame him for that. I mean, I have been blaming him for a lot of things for a long time. They've been so good to us, Beatrice. I really don't know what we would have done without their help."

Beatrice decided to be frank. "There's no use saying one thing and meaning something else, Flory. Armand is no farmer. He never will be. He has big ideas one minute. Then he's a dreamer, and a thinker. He should have been born rich."

REMINISCENCES

"He needs people, he says. That's why he goes to the village. Oh, I know he goes to the hotel to drink. That's what worries me."

"Oh, he goes to parties too. You told me so. He takes his violin to town and goes to Mrs. Martin's, and that is healthy for his nature. But I say Flory that it is time he took you to these parties. You're carding wool, knitting, making clothes out of flour sacks and soap out of fat, lye, and ashes. If you don't start going out with Armand, yes Flory, out to these parties or whatever, you will never meet people."

"Speaking of parties, when I was in England I often slept at Mrs. Brown's and helped her in her antique shop. I had to go up flights of stairs to get to my room. I always, every night, heard thumping noises and men and women laughing and carrying on. I was so frightened. One night I heard people coming up the stairs. I peeked out of my door. They couldn't see me, I was in the dark, but I saw them. The men looked quite dandy, but the girls were vulgar with all the bright colours and feathers they wore. Well, they looked like Guy Fawkes. I often wondered if Mrs. Brown knew about it because it was terrible for a young girl sleeping there."

"What do you mean, Guy Fox?"

"I mean garish, with red cheeks and red mouths, and well, not very nice women. Mr. Brown was blind, and do you know that if I reached for a cookie he would say, 'I see you, Flory Hollowell. You may have it, but I wish you would have asked.' As blind as he was, he could make beautiful fire irons and ever so many things for the shop. I liked him far more than I liked Mrs. Brown. His best friend was John Foster. He studied the stars. It was just something he loved to do. Like a hobby. His wife thought he was completely crazy because he would not stop. Do you know what she did? She put him in an insane asylum. Once in a while Mrs. Foster would visit him. He would plead and cry, with tears running down his grey beard. 'Liz,' he would say, 'you know I'm not crazy. Please take me home.' She never did. The last time mother and I went to see him without Mrs. Foster. Oh, it was so sad, Beatrice. His hair was long and white. He had changed. He looked so sad, as though he wanted to die. Mother said, 'Dear Mr. Foster, it won't be so long now until Liz takes you home. Keep your chin up. Flory and I will be back in a fortnight.' He died there in that awful place. And do you know that when he died, dear Mr. Brown died a few days later. I have no idea why, but it truly did affect me. I was so young and she was so cruel." Flory paused and then asked, "Why do I tell you these stories of England? Is it because I'm pregnant, or is it because I am terribly lonesome for something?"

A MATTER OF COMPULSION

"Flory, I love to hear your stories. When you tell them I can see you as a young girl. No, you forget how quiet Maurice is. He's a dear, wonderful man who can go all day without saying a word. I'm happy I came today. Can I pour us more tea?"

"One day I didn't have to go to Mrs. Brown's and mother thought we needed a change and that we would visit Aunt Flory, after whom I was named. We took the tram to Elephant and Castle and on the tram opposite me sat a woman wearing a beautiful hand-painted silk scarf. Every time I turned her way to look at it, she was looking at me. It made me feel uncomfortable. Then she got up and came to me. She asked if I had any time to spare. Oh, my heart gave a turn. I said that I was with my mother who sat two seats ahead of me. The woman waited a while, which made me wonder what she could possibly want. All I could think was that she wanted to hire me as a nanny. You know, minding the children. She went to mother and told her that she had been looking at me. Can you imagine? She said I had beautiful hair and colouring and that she wanted to do a portrait of me. I often think about that. A painting of Flory Hollowell as a madonna! Mother was speechless, she was! The woman told mother that she was Lady Lillian Perkins, and that she lived at number four, Deans Yard, Westminster Abbey. 'My husband,' she said, 'is the minister to the King of England.' She asked for mother's address, and it wasn't long before mother received a note from her asking if we could go to Westminster Abbey."

"Did you go, Flory?"

"Yes, we did. The door was opened and we were taken to the minister's rooms. He pinched my cheek Beatrice, and said that he could see why Lady Lillian was interested in painting me. Then Lady Lillian walked in. It was all so sad in a way. Mother standing there, so regretful at having to tell her that we were leaving England and sailing to Canada. She did a quick sketch of me. Then she told mother that she would be ever so happy if we could go back one more time before we left for Canada."

"Did you go back?"

"No, we didn't go back. Everything had to be sold. There was so much to do and of course mother wasn't strong. We were all so excited about going to Canada that nothing else seemed important any more."

"Do you have any regrets? I mean regrets over coming to Canada and then becoming a farm wife?"

"Sometimes I do. When I'm angry. Oh yes, Armand can make me angry. But you know, he has a way about him, and I can love him so strongly."

REMINISCENCES

"I like Pilon, but it seems as if he has been terribly spoiled."

"Yes he has. Spoiled by his Maman and spoiled by his Papa. When Armand wasn't happy with any of the homesteads he wrote home. It didn't take long for Papa Pilon to come west. He bought us this farm. By the time we got settled with animals and everything a farm needs, it cost Papa Pilon three thousand dollars. They also bought him a beautiful shiny horse and buggy to take me for drives in the country. I felt guilty because no one in the family had anything like it. Oh, we did enjoy visiting the aunts. They made us so welcome, and the uncles could all play the fiddle and dance. They always had homemade wine. Oh Beatrice, and their French *tortières!*"

"What is that, Flory?"

"It's French Canadian meat pie. It's made in a deep pie plate with chopped pork and spices. You slice it and the crust is thick and crumbly. Oh, I get excited talking about it. I truly don't know the recipe, but I'll get it, and when I do, Beatrice, you'll have it too."

JANE'S VISIT, BEATRICE'S DEPARTURE

There was a letter in the mail from Flory's mother, Jane. She was coming to visit and would bring along her Lillian and Leonard. Also a Mr. MacLeish, who she said would stay at the hotel. At the very bottom of the letter she asked Flory to have Rosie and clothing ready, as she would take her back to Smith Falls, Ontario. It was a terrible heartbreak for Flory. With a lump in her throat, Flory looked around, wondering what she could do to improve the house. The only thing to do, besides all the washing, was to scrub the floor with lye until the boards looked bleached. Then bake more bread.

It was a nice walk up the hill to Mme. Morin's. Bless Mme. Morin, the midwife. Flory would be lost without her. "I have come to have a cup of tea with you and to ask you a favour. My mother is coming to visit and she is bringing my brother Leonard and sister Lillian."

"Ah, your Maman come. You are happy?"

"Yes, but also very unhappy. My Rosie will go away with my mother. My Rosie works hard. She helps me with my baby. I love Rosie very much. Rosie *chante chansons*. She sings."

"*Ah, oui, oui. Chère Flory, la séparation!* She comes back, *non*?"

"I am sure Rosie will come back, but not now. Later, when she is older."

"Not to worry. Tell me the favour."

"I hate to ask you, but I am short of sheets."

"*Draps pour lits? Oui, oui.* I will bring them tomorrow."

Flory cuddled her grey head and kissed her cheek.

The next morning Mme. Morin came with fresh flannelette sheets. Then she handed Flory a ten-pound sugar sack filled with doughnuts.

* * *

Jane Hollowell arrived with Leonard and Lillian, who were dressed in starched white outfits with huge sailor collars. They were quite a contrast to her Leonard and Cecile, who were wearing long hand-knit stockings and clothes made of bleached flour sacks. Mother Jane's gentleman friend, Mr. MacLeish, sat in one position and stared at goodness knows what. Flory knew that it certainly wasn't the paintings on the wall.

A MATTER OF COMPULSION

There was great excitement that day. The children played in the field and got not one speck on them. It was a far cry from the times they played alone, walking in with dirty knees and straw in their hair. Flory had told them to stay clean, and they did obey.

The children were tucked in wherever they could fit. Now everyone sat round the kitchen table to reminisce about the days in England, the arrival at the Pilon home in Canada, and their special memories of Québec. Jane listened well when Armand told of his new invention, the snowmobile, and what a great help it would be to get to his trap lines.

"Mudder Jane, I tell you a story. One time when I go hunting for moose you never see track like dat. De biggest I ever see. You know what I call dat moose, Madame? I call him Big Ben. Flory tell me about de clock Big Ben in England. Dat name fit dis moose. You see, every day I go early in de morning at de same time, and every morning dere are fresh track. I say tomorrow I go much earlier to take a look at him. Ah, but I also have a spike dat have no head. I see dat moose. He was close. I fire, and den I run like hell. De next morning I go back and I find him. We haul more meat dan we can use, and also give some away. Yes, gee cripe, I work to get Big Ben. You see, I wanted to tickle dat by myself and I did it."

"You wanted to tackle it Armand, not tickle."

"Whatever. I do it."

Flory never corrected Armand, but she knew darned well that her mother would be happy to tell other members of the family that Armand Pilon derived a certain pleasure from tickling moose.

"You know Flory, Armand sounds smart enough, but all those soppy inventions don't clothe the children. He should get on with what needs doing around here and do an honest day's work. Never mind, I'll not say one word. It isn't for me to say one thing or the other, is it now?" Jane thought of Mrs. Reynolds in England saying that Flory would marry the first young man she met in Canada. *Why, she's like a rose among thorns, pregnant and expecting any time now.*

* * *

As sad as Flory was to see her family leave, it was Rosie who tore at her heart, standing there with one big bag that held all she had in the world, waiting for everyone to hug before she would take her turn. Flory walked toward Rosie and

JANE'S VISIT, BEATRICE'S DEPARTURE

with open arms enveloped her closely. The crying could be felt from deep within. "Oh Rosie, you have been a love. I'll miss you and still wait for you to come home after school. I'll miss you singing to the babies."

"Don't cry, Flory. It won't be long. I'm coming back to you the first chance I get."

Armand's eyes were misty. His nostrils flared and with a big smile he said, "Rose, do not forget, you have a home here wit us always, and Rose, I am happy dat Flory leave de rose bush in Québec and instead she bring de real rose to Alberta."

* * *

Mme. Morin came again. Flory was right. It was a boy. He was christened Romeo George. The year was 1913.

"You look sad, Flory. Do you miss your family?"

"Beatrice, I do love them all, but in my condition it was all too tiring having them here. Lilly and Lenny always dressed in white. Truly, the tub and washboard were forever on the go, and that Mr. MacLeish! You should have seen Armand trying to entertain him, his arms flying in all directions about one invention or another."

"Armand's one hell of a good man Flory, but I don't think anyone could ever tame him."

"Oh, he's peculiar, all right. The other day a friend of his came over. He had a sore on his arm that wouldn't heal, and do you know what Armand said? He told him to go down to the creek, move some stones to find bloodsuckers, then put the bloodsuckers on his sore and bandage his arm. The bloodsuckers, he said, would draw all the poison out. The man actually went white. He couldn't get out fast enough. I asked Armand why he had said such a wicked thing to the dear man. He just walked away and said, '*Merde*! Nobody listen!' Do you know what *merde* is?"

"Yes, it's bullshit. Maurice says it at least four times a day. Oh Flory, your husband is an odd one. He dropped in to see us the other night. I could tell he had had a few drinks. He said each life was like a chain, being only as strong as the weakest link. Do you know what the missing link in my chain is?"

"No, of course I don't."

"Maurice and I have never been blessed with a child. Never mind that now. We're leaving next week. I will try to see you again, but I doubt that I'll be able to with all I have to do. In case I don't Flory, we'll say our goodbyes now."

A MATTER OF COMPULSION

Flory walked toward Beatrice with open arms. "Beatrice, I don't think I'll ever have another friend like you. Not as long as I live."

"Don't say that Flory. You'll have more friends than you'll know what to do with. With a man like Pilon, you may starve once in a while, and yes he may come home running his hand up his fly, but for sure he will never be dull. He's so witty, I believe he could charm that steer out there."

They laughed, each knowing how the other felt. Beatrice wanted their goodbye to be short and sweet, with no tears. With one last lingering hug she stood back to face Flory. With a wide smile, and exactly one tear in each eye, she was out the door. When she reached the gate she turned back and waved.

The door closed. Flory walked into her room where she fell on the bed, sobbing. *Mother took Rosie away, and now Beatrice has gone. I'm sure Armand is at the hotel. Maybe he would have been happier with French Angebelle. I'm not going to lie here and brood over it any longer. I'm going to have a bath and wash my hair. I always feel so much better after. It's like wiping the slate clean.*

* * *

"Oh, Armand, you did give me a start. I thought you went to the village."

"No, I take a walk at de end of de farm."

"Beatrice came. She came to say goodbye. Now she's gone."

"Flory, it look nice when you feed de bébé wit your hair take down."

"I took it down because I want to bathe and wash my hair. Dear Beatrice has gone. I won't see her again."

"You have a cry. I can see dat. Flory, I walk as far as Defrene. Remember, I tell you I see oil on de pig? Well today I see black oil at de end where de wheat grow. Gee cripe, I am happy dat we have de mineral and de oil right on dis farm. You do not look happy for dat. Why?"

"I feel sad that Beatrice has moved away, but I was daydreaming, just thinking of what a good lovely man you are when you . . ."

"Flory, I do not trust you. You will start to tell me how bad I am. Goddam, I am me. Pilon today, Pilon tomorrow, Pilon forever, and nobody can change dat."

She lay Romeo in the big blue cradle and thought of what a bad time she had chosen to tell Armand how good he was when he didn't drink. She had tried on many occasions, each time on a different note. No matter how angry or how sweet

JANE'S VISIT, BEATRICE'S DEPARTURE

her temperament, she failed. There never was a reasonable answer. He would never commit himself to stop drinking. And yet he did try, drinking pots of black tea while he worked on his inventions.

BEAUTIFUL HAIR

"Flory, I jus' read de Bulletin. It say dere is a contest for de woman wit de most beautiful hair. It say de longest, de tickest, and de colour. We should go. Bechamp, he can take us. You are game for dat?"

"Well, it wouldn't make much difference if we went or stayed home. There must be umpteen women in Edmonton with hair as nice as mine."

"Do not be bull headed! Take de gamble. Dere is a prize to be give for de best."

"Oh all right. I'll ask Mme. Morin to mind the children, if it's only for the day."

"Yes, we be back early. Now I go to ask Bechamp."

* * *

The car kept on knocking, jerking, and sputtering. It would only go a short distance before one man or the other had to get out to crank it. Armand must have been angry at the whole thing. Flory sat with no conversation, except for the tip of her tongue hitting just behind her front teeth making "tsk tsk" noises as she shook her head from side to side. She could hear Armand saying his *sacré bleu* as he cranked on and on, until he suddenly screamed. The crank had kicked back. His wrist was either broken or badly sprained. When they finally did arrive in Edmonton, Armand was in so much pain he had to go to a doctor who told him that he was quite sure it wasn't broken. Armand's wrist was so well bandaged that he could not move one of his fingers.

"It hurt like hell, Flory, but it is better to have it sprain den broke."

"Oh, I am sorry, Armand. Shall we forget about the hair contest? You know it is getting on. It must be all over with by now, and I'm getting tired."

"It is getting late, but not too late. We will go."

* * *

"I am Armand Pilon and dis is my wife Flory. Is dis de place where de contest go on for de most beautiful hair?"

"Yes sir. The contest was on from ten o'clock this morning. I am sorry, but you are seven hours late."

"We come from Legal. We are late because dere was car trouble. No matter, but

A MATTER OF COMPULSION

I very much would like you to see my wife's hair. Do you mind? Come on, Flory. Dey have not got much time. Take down your braid. I have de comb."

"Armand, it's a lot of bother for nothing, don't you think?"

"It's no bodder for nobody."

As Flory undid her braid, not once did she look up.

"Stand up, Flory. Now you will see somet'ing," he told the men. "You want me to comb your hair, Flory?"

"No, I'll comb it, if I remember how."

"My wife is tired. She had a very long day."

Asking me to stand up. He knows darned well I sit to comb my hair. I must try to smile or they'll think I'm a miserable woman. Maybe I'm pregnant again. Who knows. We don't have time to rest until he's at me again. I guess I'm as bad. I can't complain.

Armand took three steps forward, then facing Flory, he drew each side of her hair like a drape, surrounding her body and hiding her face.

"What do you t'ink of dat, eh?"

"Ah, Mr. Pilon, it is sad you could not be here in time, eh Margot?"

"Yes, no one had hair like you have. The gorgeous colour, the thickness, and the length. Yes, I am sorry, Mrs. Pilon. You would have come in first."

Flory responded by giving her most understanding smile.

"T'ank you very much. We come, we are late, also I am satisfy. If I go home after de pain I have to get here, witout showing Flory, I do not sleep tonight."

VISIT TO BROWNSBURG

"Flory, would you like to visit Maman and Papa and see my sister and brudder dis fall?"

"I do need a coat. Mine is so shabby I'd be ashamed."

"You are too pretty. Nobody notice your coat."

"But Armand, I know I'm pregnant again."

"Good. You need a change. You visit my family and I see about my invention. Who knows what is ahead. Maybe one day you will have a muskrat coat."

* * *

Everything looked the same to Flory. The kitchen stove that never burned low, the big blue kettle that never stopped steaming. The bedroom they shared hadn't changed. There was the same wooden bed with all its character, dressed in the same patchwork quilt, the dresser still on the opposite wall, and there in the small cove where Maman had put it, the high table, still covered with the lace cloth.

She remembered how gently Maman had placed Elizabeth, and how she handed her the large ebony crucifix to place in her tiny hands. The memories brought tears of sadness. She remembered Maman saying, "You will have more babies and love each one as strong." *She was right. I now have three and am expecting another.*

Armand was in his glory, visiting with his old friends. They'd gather to drink beer and listen to his stories of the West. "Yes, I have some good idea. One I am still working on, but de most important one now is de Pilon snowmobile."

"How did you think of that, Armand?"

"Well, I tell you. I go hunting on Egg Lake. Dat is not very far from my farm. I see a prairie wolf on de lake. It was far away. So far away, it look like a field mouse. I have a good carabine, a Winchester, but I can not shoot. It is too far. If I miss, I lose de wolf. You know what I have to do? Well I tell you. I hide behind some stump. I get a long piece of binder twine dat I always carry wit me. I remove my muskrat hat and tie it wit de binder twine. I t'row dat as far as I can, den I hide myself. I pull a little on de string. It jerk a little, den anudder jerk and anudder. I have all day. I am in no hurry. De wolf see dat. He t'ink is alive, eh? I could see dat wolf coming. Den he stop to look de situation over. He come closer and closer. When he come close enough to shoot, pow! I get him, den I retrieve my muskrat hat. When I go

A MATTER OF COMPULSION

home dat night, I t'ink, if I have somet'ing dat travel t'rough de snow, I could trap and hunt witout a sorry horse dat stand in de cold. Also, I could set more trap. You understand dat you can go early and be home early. What you t'ink about dat, eh?"

"Ah, Pilon. You never will change. What would you have done if you hadn't worn your muskrat hat?"

"*Pas de problème, mes mitaines,* anyt'ing. Yes, my moccasin, scarf, or even my stocking, eh?"

"We miss your stories. Do you remember when your father had the cheese factory? You told him that he didn't need those big round boxes. That he should put the cheese in one-pound packages. You told him that he could have it in the stores and it could also be peddled from house to house. Remember your father saying you were a great dreamer?"

"You have to dream, Louis. It keep you healt'y. Everybody should dream. If you do not dream, you are only half a man. My fadder dream also, but he is a worker. I say dat if you dream and use your head, maybe you do not have to work so hard."

"Remember the fisherman who sang like a bird? How you practised your violin every night until you figured you were good. You asked your mother for a sheet to make signs. We had a good crowd that night. Do you still sing and play your violin?"

"Yes, Flory enjoy when I play. I also sing when I go to church, but I don't let de priest see me. I leave. I do not confess. I am Pilon today, Pilon tomorrow, and Pilon forever."

The girls clustered together, reminiscing about the years gone by. How Berta and Flory used to make hats that were extravagantly over-decorated with ribbons and bows, then modelled them, turning them back to front and side to front, giggling until they wet their drawers. They had great plans for having their own hat shop one day. The collection of hat forms, silk, ribbons, odd feathers and decorations still filled the old humped trunk.

Grandmaman, as Armand's mother came to be known, was plain, unadorned, with straight hair parted in the centre, a twirled neat bun resting just above her collar. She wore simple black dresses, always with a long white apron. Her face was pure goodness. She reminded Flory of a nun, and much like *Whistler's Mother* in her rocking chair.

Armand's sisters many times told of their Maman suddenly waking in the middle

VISIT TO BROWNSBURG

of the night to hear the rocking chair going back and forth. She knew then that there would be a death in the family. She was never wrong, they said. Early every morning she was the first one up with coffee brewing and breakfast cooking, a crate of eggs setting on the drain.

Grandpapa Pilon's hair was so curly that he swore it gave him his headaches. He would say, "It is time to have my hair cut. My head is aching again." They never really believed his hair caused the ache, but agreed it was indeed time for a hair cut.

Flory was happy to be part of their family. She had never heard a cross word or complaint. However, she had heard that every family had one black sheep. Could it be their beloved son, Armand?

Grandmaman enjoyed having her family together again, with each one having a turn at telling a happy story.

"Do you remember Armand, when you climbed the maple tree right to the top?"

"I remember dat tree, Berta. Gee cripe dat was a beautiful tree, eh?"

"Do you remember you only climbed the tree when you could not have your own way with Maman? She would coax you to come down. You would not, so Maman would give you some special gift that you liked. She would stand at the bottom of the tree and coax you. '*Viens, mon fils. Maman a fait un beaurer de crème avec sucre d'érable.*' Only then would you come down. He knows I speak the truth. He is laughing. Look, Flory. If he did not get his own way I believe he would climb that maple tree to worry you, eh Maman? I tell you, she suffered until you were safe on the ground."

"Well Berta, it is one way to get what you want. It is too bad we have not dose maple tree in Legal. We have poplar and spruce, but dey are very hard to climb."

Flory gave him one of her looks that made his laughter slow down and turn into an innocent cough.

The time came when they had to leave. There were many hugs, tears, and much coaxing for a return visit the following year.

They arrived first in Ottawa, then took the streetcar to the station. Flory was pregnant and tired. It was all very wonderful visiting everyone, the old aunts, cousins, Armand's sisters and brother and new babies, but she couldn't wait to board the train where she could completely relax every sinew in her body.

"Flory, it will not be long now, so we will be organize. I will take Cecile and Leonard. You take Romeo in your arm until we get off. We have to be careful.

A MATTER OF COMPULSION

Dere are so many people, if he fall he can be step on. When de people in dere seat ahead stand, we do de same and follow. It is not easy wit young one."

People were shoving ahead, holding their bags or valises up and away from the slow-marching feet. Armand was going down the steps with Cecile and Leonard, Flory following with Romeo in her arms. She looked down and saw the heavy braided ring on the conductor's finger. Her heart pounded. She wanted to scream out, "You stole my ring. Give it back to me." There was no time. She couldn't cause a commotion. She tried to hold back the tears. The more she tried, the heavier they fell. *So he was the one at the dam who took the ring from Armand's pocket. We could never prove it. He may have bought it in a pawnshop. Oh, I am sorry that I saw it. I was just beginning to forget.*

"What seem to be wrong, Flory? You look like you are sick. Why you cry? It is not de *bébé*? You are not ready for it, eh?"

"No, Armand. I'm all right. I saw my braided ring on the conductor's finger."

"You are sure of dat? It is not de only one in de world."

"It was, and I'll say it again a thousand times. It is the ring that Uncle Bill gave me for my sixteenth birthday."

"We have no time to look into dat now. It is almost time for us to take de train."

"The last gift Uncle Bill bought me was the gold braided ring. Oh God, my braided ring." She sat on a bench with Romeo on her knee. Leonard and Cecile were playing close by. Armand met someone and was chatting. There was no room in her mind for anything but the ring. Over and over again it was there on that big fat finger. He must have had it made larger. If only she could get that man's hand out of her mind. *Dear Lord, help me.*

Suddenly Leonard was hurled across the floor. He lay motionless. Flory's scream echoed through the station. Everyone gathered to look. Men in uniforms carried Leonard to another room. Then another man told Armand and Flory to stay where they were. "Do not worry. He will be all right."

Armand and Flory never knew what was given to Leonard. When they carried him back, he looked dead. Had he been given medicine or drugs? He lay limp in Flory's arms. The panel door of the electrical circuit had been left unlocked. Leonard had climbed onto the bench, opened the door, and touched the electrical circuit.

They boarded the train, Armand carrying Leonard, Flory carrying Romeo, with Cecille hanging on to Flory's coat. Leonard cried a lot. Then he would lay limp and fall into a deep sleep. When he cried Flory wished he would sleep, and when he slept, she prayed he would wake up.

"Armand, I'm so worried, I feel ill. Do you think he will be healthy and strong again?"

"Yes he will. Dere is no udder way to t'ink."

TRAPPING

The shack, no matter how humble, was a haven. To Flory it held all the comforts, and safety for her children. Dear Mme. Morin just up the hill, so close and handy. *I don't know what I'd do if she weren't there when I needed her*, Flory thought.

"Flory, I have to get ready to go trapping. I need some heavy sock. You knit a pair, maybe two pair, for me?"

Flory had so much carded wool for comforters that there were bags of it left over and Mme. Morin had a spinning wheel. Flory carried two full bags up the hill.

"Hello, Mme. Morin. I need your help. Armand's going trapping and he needs two pairs of stockings. Can you spin the wool for me? I've brought enough for you as well."

"Ah, I am happy. How your trip to Québec? You see your *maman et papa, soeurs et frère?*"

"Oui, Mme. Morin. I feel happy to visit, but I am tired, *fatigué*. Too much go on. *Excité. Trop de joie.*"

"*Ah oui, Flory. Je comprend.*"

"You are a very good woman, *bonne, bonne*. And soon, Mme. Morin, I will need you."

"*Oui, oui*, I can see. *Ah, oui, pas de problème*. Armand already come and tell me dat. I come when you need me."

She had tiny feet and tiny ankles that shot out quickly, growing larger and larger at the thighs. The top of one stocking measured twenty four inches around, while the foot measured six to seven inches long. Her legs were shaped like funnels and could have been mistaken for jelly bags. Everything in her house smelled like carbolic – her clothing, her knitting, even the tea she made.

Flory was grateful for Mme. Morin in many ways, but most of all that she had told Flory to nurse her babies as long as she could. That way, she said, you cannot get pregnant. Flory nursed each child for over a year, and there were times when she felt ashamed.

* * *

Armand ordered more traps, shells, rope, a small axe, and a pair of moccasins. *While I am here at the post office it is a good time to see my friend. Yes, I will go for*

A MATTER OF COMPULSION

a while. He crossed the road and went to the hotel.

"You are back, Pilon. How did you enjoy your trip? Did they like to hear about your snowmobile?"

"Not so fast. I am going to build my snowmobile, but first I am going on my trap line. I hear de price for fur is good and I can use some money. It take money to build my sleigh. Plenty of money. Yes, we have a good time in Québec. I see all my friend, and believe me, we have a lot to talk about."

"More *bière*, here!"

"Ah, we drink, salute. Good luck with your snowmobile, Pilon."

It was late when Armand walked in. Flory could see that he had been drinking.

"Armand, you have such a good family. I was hoping you would change after seeing how they live. You always say you are *t'inking*. Well, when are you going to *t'ink* of staying away from that cursed hotel?"

"Don't worry about it. I go trapping. Den you have not'ing to complain about. It do no harm for me to see my friend. Dey like to know about my trip back home."

"Yes, Armand. I feel as though tomorrow we will have another child."

Flory was never wrong. Mme. Morin was there in time to deliver a baby girl, the smallest so far. She was born on January 20th, 1915. She was named Juliette Florence.

* * *

Old Nellie was hitched to the sleigh, the gear was stacked and included thick sandwiches with Ontario cheese, black tea, a special pail to boil the snow, and the matches, which were put in a tight-fitting tobacco can. It was early morning, with a whole day to set traps. It was the most exciting time of the year for Armand. Now he only had to wait a few days before he made his next trip. Tomorrow maybe they would have a snowfall. If lucky, it would cover any sign of scent or tracks.

On the first day he got one coyote, on the second he got two coyotes, and on the third he got three. "If dat keep up Flory, gee cripe, I feel happy." On the fourth day he got one silver fox. "Did you ever see a fox wit a coat like dat? No, I am sure you have not, Flory. I set dis one on de side. I feel I get good money for him."

On his next trip he got a very large coyote. It was held in the trap by the very tip of its foot. Armand approached, and then suddenly stopped in his tracks. The coyote lunged, tearing the bottom of Armand's pants. It lunged at him again and

TRAPPING

bit the end of his rifle. He fired one shot and the coyote lay still. But it was not to be trusted, so Armand, grabbing his axe, hit the coyote over the head with all the strength he could muster. Hurrying, he pushed the coyote into a large burlap bag, then into another, tying it well, over and over again.

"Gee cripe, I have a close call wit dat one, Flory. You see he lay like he is not alive, so I go closer to see. He come on to me and tear my pant. I have only one bullet. I load it and he come again to bite de gun. I fire. If he get loose, I be gone, so I grab my axe and give him a bang on de head. Den I tie him up."

"This is the second or third time you've run out of shells. Last year you came back with a dangerous story. You're asking for it, Armand. You must spend two or three boxes of shells every time you go to the hotel."

"Do not be a bulldog. It do you no good. I have order bullet. Also, I order a small axe dat can fit in my pack. It have not arrive. Now I have wit dis one seven coyote and one fox. Dat is a good beginning for us."

"Did you look at all your traps, or is it too much for one day?"

"No, I have them in different direction. One time I go to one trap line, and de next time I go to de udder one. Flory, I tell you de trut'. When I skin dat big coyote, he wink at me. I do not know de joke. He wink as plain as daylight. He have some nerve, eh? Yes, he was a fighter. He tear my pant, he bite my gun, and after I get de pelt I tell him. 'You can go if you please.'"

* * *

Armand came home with a live black fisher. He put it in a wire cage and placed the cage in a barrel in the grain shed. "He will be safe dere. I want to take it in to Edmonton to show the fur buyer. It should bring good money, but I feel it is too beautiful. I cannot kill it. I will take it alive."

* * *

"Come wit me to see de fisher. Maybe he did not have a good sleep last night, but he be warm in de shed."

"Where is it, Armand?"

"It is gone. Dat sucker get away. I be go to hell."

The wire was neatly undone. The fisher must have leaped out of the barrel, yet

A MATTER OF COMPULSION

there was no sign of how it got out of the shed. Fishers were very scarce. He had lost good money, but apart from that, he would have been ever-so-proud to take a live fisher to the fur buyer.

"Flory, if de fisher had not escape, I would go to Edmonton. Yes, it would be wort' it."

By this time Armand had seven coyote, three weasels, one lynx, two fox, and one of the widest fat badgers you ever did see. What Flory didn't know was that Armand was saving some of the weasels to have an ermine scarf made for her.

"I hear de price of fox is high, so I hang on to de fox for a little longer. I take all de udder to sell."

"You should take the two fox, Armand. If the price is good, why not?"

"Because it could go higher, and maybe, yes maybe, dere could be one more in my trap, eh? It make it worthwhile to wait. You never know what I catch in my trap dis week."

That night he put the furs in a large bag, and was down at the train station early the next morning.

* * *

"Ah, Mr. Pilon, what have you got today?"

Armand shook the pelts and lay them out. Mr. Shubert bought everything he had.

"How is the price for fox now?"

"Do you have fox, Mr. Pilon?"

"Oh, I have only two now. I never take dem off de mold."

"You should have brought them. Fox prices are high."

"I bring them next time I come."

Armand did go to the Cecile Hotel, but he didn't stay long. Trapping was his joy, and he would be out bright and early the next morning.

"I do pretty good, eh Flory? I was t'inking it is time I set some snare for jack rabbit. We make some stew in a pie. You like dat?"

"Yes, Armand." She knew that when it was trapping time he was always a better man. *I know why,* she thought. *It's the gambling, the excitement. That's what keeps him happy.*

In the next two weeks, Armand had two more fox. One was smaller, but it was

TRAPPING

another good pelt.

"Dis time you come wit me to Edmonton. If we leave early, we be home early. You like dat?"

"I would like it, but what about the children?"

"It is simple. Mme. Morin take de two young one, and Mme. Defrene take de two older one. Mme. Morin feed de bébé *blanc mange* wit milk just like you. So we will arrange dat today." He continued, "Dat first silver fox, my first one, Flory. Dat is de best. Dere is anudder dat come close. De udder two are smaller, but it is a dandy catch I make. You will see de look on Shubert's face when he see dat."

* * *

"Good day, Mr. Pilon. What have you brought today?"

"Ah, you will be happy to see my catch." He took each pelt out of the bag, and shaking them one by one, he lay them on the floor with an all-in-one motion.

"Did you ever see fox like dat, eh?"

Well, Mr. Pilon, we have quite a few fox right now, and my partner isn't here yet. If you would like to go for something to eat or do some shopping, that would kill time."

"Dat is fine wit me. We go Flory, and come back later."

They looked at the store windows, and saw all the pretty things.

"See that braided black hat, Armand? Look at the size of the brim. Wasn't that a smart way to decorate it with two rose-braided buttons in the front? Oh, I do like that. What time is it, Armand?"

"It is time to go for somet'ing to eat. We are hungry."

They found a little spot further along and both decided to eat slowly to kill time. "Two hour is long, Flory, when your hope is high, eh? We will take our time, and walk back slowly. He should know by now."

"You're back, Mr. Pilon. Did you have a nice dinner? My partner didn't come in. I'm afraid he's gone for the day. You see, we have too many fox right now. I would not buy more without his approval. I'm sorry, Mr. Pilon. Maybe next time."

Armand didn't seem worried. He only said, "Fine, fine. I can sell dem some place else." He picked up the bag and left.

"Do not feel bad, Flory. I know fox, and doze were de best. I'm not worry."

Armand went to another fur buyer. He went through the same shake and lay

A MATTER OF COMPULSION

motion, which made him feel just a little bit more knowing than the city folk.

"Look at dat. Have you ever see more beautiful fox. I will sit down and let you see what you t'ink."

The fur buyer looked at them while feeling them the whole time.

"These are not good furs, Mr. Pilon."

"What do you mean, dey are not good? Dey are de best." He walked toward the pelts to have a better look.

"You have patched these fox, Mr. Pilon."

"I have patch dese fox? No I have not, but I know de son of a bitch dat did. I have been fooled. Nobody fool Pilon! No wonder dey are all ready and in de bag for me. Dey take my good fox, and replace dem wit patched fox."

"Armand, why didn't you look at them? Whatever will we do now?"

"Don't worry, Flory. Don't worry. Just watch me."

"I am sorry, Mr. Pilon, and I wish you luck."

On the way back to Legal, Flory could see that the wheels of Armand's brain were working as he sat silent and eager to get at whatever it was that he was going to do.

"Flory, I don't care if it take me t'ree year. I get dat man."

Every night for weeks Armand worked on the fox pelts, patching and matching. "You're not going to gain anything, Armand, if you cut a good fox to patch a poor one."

"I do not care if it cost me good furs. One or two is worth what dat sonofabitch do to me. Don't worry. I am using his own fox. Whoever patch dat do a bad job. You watch me. I learn to sew leather and buckskin when I be a boy."

When the fox were finally ready, he shook them and lay them for Flory to see.

"Armand, they look lovely, just lovely. I don't know too much about mended fox, but I must say they look perfect to me."

"How I approach dis sonofabitch is anudder matter. Maybe I spy, and when he go to eat, I get his partner."

* * *

"Well Mr. Pilon, we haven't seen you for a long time." It was the partner who greeted him this time.

"No. Some fur buyer come to Legal, and I sell him every bloody pelt I have. It save a trip for me. Is your partner in?"

52

TRAPPING

"No, he has a full day away, and won't be in until late. What have you got to sell today?"

"I have one good month. Gee cripe, de fox was good trapping. I hear de price is good, so I bring dem."

One shake, then another, lowering each pelt to the floor with his all-in-one motion. He got top price. When he had the money in his hand he said, "Tank you very much." Then he headed for the door. He looked back.

"I am happy dat was a good deal we make, you and me. You have your patch fox back, and I have my money. And by de way, my friend, you know de whole story. You are in dis togedder, bot' of you. Whoever patch your fox do a very sloppy job. I was ashamed to see it. Take a look at mine. Yes, if you want to be a crook in dis life, hire me to do your job."

* * *

Gee cripe, luck was wit me today. It is wort' all de hour I spend. Yes, I t'ink I deserve a drink. Wait until my friend at de Cecile Hotel hear dat. I have to tell somebody. It is too good to keep. I cannot laugh alone. It hurt inside. Flory be happy for dat. She will not mind if I do not go home tonight.

* * *

Flory knew that if he sold the furs he would go to the Cecile Hotel. "Armand, can you please tell me why you didn't go back when you first found out that man fooled you?"

"By de time I go back de fur would not be dere. Dey are not crazy. If I go back dey would not say dey were only fooling and want to play a joke on me. No, if I say I phone de police, or I am going to sue dem, dey would only laugh. I did not mark dem, my name was not on dem. I have no proof, eh? I learn a lot dis year. I put it under my cap."

Armand couldn't wait to tell his friends. They would get a kick out of that, he knew. He would pick up the mail, then go to Monsieur Chalier.

"M. Chalier, could you sell me one bottle of your wine? I would like Flory to taste it. Also, could you lend me a wine glass? I believe Flory miss de wine we use to have back home in Québec. Maybe she don't mind if I make some. I make some *biere* one time but when I open one bottle it go pow! It land on de ceiling and it fall like rain. It have too much pow an' Flory say she do not want *biere* in de home no more."

That evening Armand brought out the wine in the long-stemmed glass. "Take it, Flory. I want you to taste Chalier's wine. To please you I borrow dis. It always taste better in a wine glass."

"It does taste a lot like Tante Matid's, doesn't it? And the same colour too. Wonder what his recipe is?"

"I believe it is parsnip, dis one for sure. He make different one, sometime *pissenlit*. I get de recipe for old time sake."

"What is *pissenlit*, Armand?"

"It is dandelion. Yes, we enjoy some good time when we go for ride in de country. You smile more in dose days. Remember when you smile?"

"I didn't smile more. If I did, I must have been happier then."

He walked across the room, took his violin from its case, tuned it high, then low, ever-so-gently until it sounded just right. He got a table fork and inserted it in the bridge of the violin, swooping the bow back and forth, changing the position of the fork numerous times until he finally got the sound that suited his mood. He stood with legs apart, a deep frown on his brow, and started to play *Plus d'amour, plus de roses*. Flory sat knitting, not raising her eyes. She thought of that first day she met him. He wore a cocky straw hat that was ripped along the brim. A few black curls poked from the tear. How they all went out for the sugaring time. How they pulled taffy when the sap was boiled. The dipper was filled and poured over the snow. It hardened into ropes of candy. She remembered boiling the snow to make tea, and how good it tasted in a big enamel cup. She looked up at Armand and smiled. He stopped playing.

"You look pretty when you smile. What are you t'inking dat take you so far away?"

"I was thinking of after the sugaring when we all gathered for a *soirée* at Tante Matid's, eating slices of *tourtière* and drinking the home-made wine. We did have fun. I needed that after leaving England, and your family were all so good to me."

He felt the softness of her cheek. "Let us have one more of Chalier's wine, den Flory, take down your braid and we be close."

WILLIE AND THE GUN

"I have hire a man to work on de farm, Flory. He will have supper wit us."

"Armand, there are only three partridges for dinner, and they are small. I am angry. Why would you do such a thing? Are you that lazy that you can't do the little that needs doing around here? The farm is rented. There's nothing to do, but for a few chickens and animals to feed."

"Do de best you can. He is a hungry young man. Slice more bread."

* * *

"Dis is de new man. He have arrive."

"How do you do? Sit yourself down. Supper won't be long. Where have you come from?"

"I came from the East from a place called Brownsburg."

"Did you say Brownsburg?"

"Flory, don't you know your own brother?"

"Oh, Willie! I thought I recognized those brown eyes. That's why I asked you where you were from. You've grown so much. I remember when mother was with the Bell Telephone. You had your pony and you would deliver all the messages that came in. You were such a little lad then."

* * *

Willie liked the farm. He would help with the hogs or do anything Uncle Armand asked. It wasn't long before he made friends with the Defrene family who lived at the back of the farm. Willie had one wish, and that was to be able to shoot birds, especially since Armand had told him he was not eating chicken, he was eating wild game. Armand and he walked past the garden and down to the grove.

"See dose bird in de tree, Willie? Dey are what we have for supper de udder night. Dey are call partridge. One day we will get some."

"I can shoot, Uncle Armand. I'm quite good at it really. My friend and I go out in the woods. We shoot at stumps and cans. That's why I came to the West. You see, mother said you were a dandy Frenchman who went trapping for furs, hunted moose, and shot wild chickens. I had to come, Uncle Armand."

A MATTER OF COMPULSION

"Willie, dere is a lot to be learn about de gun. You only use it if you are hungry. De animal you trap is to give your family what dey need. De Indian tan de hide for clothes and moccasin. You know about dat, I am sure. How long you be here? Maybe I get time to take you for bird."

"I sure like this wild country, but mother said I can't stay. I'm only staying for a week, you know."

* * *

Flory received a letter from Beatrice saying how happy she was to be back with her family.

If you can imagine, Flory dear, we are now the proud owners of a car. It's a hell of a lot faster than that old horse and buggy we had, but how I loved to drive over to your place where we shared so many happy hours together. Our car doesn't eat all the hay and oats that we worked so hard for, but we're still working to keep it filled with gas. You can't win. Tell me, are you pregnant again? I envy you. How are you, Pilon? I miss your bread that soaked up the brown bits of goodness from your big iron pan. We had some good times together. Most of all I miss both of you and your damned unpredictable lives that made my life happy. Hang on to it. It could be most precious and rewarding some day. My love to all of you. With love and kisses, Beatrice and Maurice.

* * *

"Two t'ousand feet of lumber should be enough to make de house bigger, don't you t'ink? Maybe enough to build a new one."

"That would be lovely, Armand. I often think of my mother's parlour, with the big fireplace and all. Ah, not that I expect that, but we do need some more room with the four children."

"Do not get fancy idea. You are not de Queen yet. Maybe one day. Do not rush me so soon."

Why did I do it? Why did I mention mother's parlour? I shouldn't have, but why should he say such a wicked thing like me not being the Queen yet? I do believe he is the black sheep of the family. If it weren't for his mother sending him twelve dollars every month, we wouldn't have flour in the house. How much further from

WILLIE AND THE GUN

the Queen can I possible get?
"Armand, do you really think we can afford to build?"
"As I say Flory, relax. We will plan. We will take our time."

* * *

Willie was up and out early. Flory was sure he had gone to the Defrene's. He was enjoying his freedom - soon he would have to leave and go back to work. Flory was surprised to hear that Rose was now working at a feed and livery store. She didn't say so to Willie, but she did think that Rose was much too young to be out on her own. After all, Willie was a boy. You never really knew mother, and she wasn't one to tell anything. She could give a lot of advice to her children, but for herself, she was a locked door that could not be entered.

Willie ran to the house with blood pouring from his hand. He screamed, "I am ruined, Flory! I am ruined! I shot my hand! What will mother do?"

Flory ran for the wash basin while Armand found the tea towel for a tourniquet. Then he ran to Dr. Jeunais.

Willie's hand had to be dressed every morning and every night. Flory dressed it the first time, but it made her stomach turn. Having to put gauze through the palm of his hand, then pull it out from the back was too much for her in her condition. Armand knew that it could cause Flory to be ill, so he took on the job of dressing it each morning and each night.

"Where is de gun, Willie?"
"It's down in the grove, Uncle Armand."
"Where did you get de gun, Willie?"
"I brought it with me, Uncle Armand."
"Why did you not tell me you have a gun, Willie?"
"Because. I don't know why. I was going to tell you, Uncle Armand, but I was scared, mostly."

The creek was flowing strongly from the melting snow. Armand took the gun, and holding it back, threw with all his strength, his muscles surging. Away flew the gun. He didn't know where the flow would take it.

"Where you suppose Willie get dat gun, Flory? For sure his mudder will t'ink it is from me."

"I don't know. I did think it strange when I saw he didn't have a valise. He had a

A MATTER OF COMPULSION

long canvas-like bag. He must have wrapped his clothes around that gun. I never paid much attention. Who in heaven's name would ever think of a gun?"

Willie's hand did heal with a deep palm, and fingers that slanted sideways in the same direction.

* * *

Armand was going to the village more often. Being with his friends, the sound of clinking glasses and the hum of the beer parlour, excited him. It excited him because he knew his friends enjoyed his company. It was humdrum talk – the price of wheat or Bossy not giving much milk. No wonder one or the other would holler, "Pilon, you are here!" He could bring joy and laughter by telling them what were ordinary things to him, like fooling Beatrice Prevost by feeding her a three-layered roast made of pork, onion, and muskrat, then topping it off by serving tea with mare's milk. Or telling Joe Bedeau to bandage blood suckers on his arm to suck the poison out. Or he could bring complete silence from a very sobering story about his Maman, who would be awakened in the night by the sound of the rocking chair rocking back and forth. She knew then that there would be a death in the family, and she was never wrong.

Each day Flory would look out the window to see if the lumber pile had gone down. She began to wonder if she was going strange. She felt in her heart that the new house would go the way of all things. She missed Rose and Beatrice. How they could make her laugh. She remembered laughing when they took the children down the lane to the grove, and a huge snake crawled out from under the rocks. How they all ran! She read Beatrice's letter again and again. Yes, Beatrice was right. The snowmobile could be rewarding if Armand finished it. And yes, she was pregnant again.

EDMONTON

There was a loud knocking at the door. Flory quickly removed her apron. Any knock that loud must be from someone who meant it. A strange man quickly pointed toward the steer.

"Mrs. would you sell me your steer?"

"Yes, I'll sell it if I get the right price, and that is forty dollars."

"Well he's not very big. I want him for breaking land."

All the while she was wondering how she came up with the price of forty dollars. Why, she wouldn't know the price of a chicken, let alone a steer to break land.

"He is small Mrs. Would you take a little less, like thirty dollars?"

After he had left, taking the steer down the driveway, she had second thoughts. *What if the darned thing is worth far more, like one hundred dollars? Maybe Armand will never miss it. I don't think he knows what he owns. I'll feel my way around.*

"Armand, if you sold the steer, how much would you ask for it?"

"Well, let me see. I don't know why you ask, but if I sell it I would ask eighteen dollar. Why you ask?"

"I ask because I want to buy your steer. I will pay your price of eighteen dollars. Sold?" She knew very well he had been drinking.

"Yes, but where you get de money?"

"Well Armand, today I sold the steer."

"Your steer? How much you get?"

"Let's say I got a little more than eighteen dollars."

"You may be an English bulldog, but I like you for dat trick you play. Now I have news for you. Today I rent de farm for t'ree year."

"Three years? Good God! What are we going to do for three years? Oh, I am getting tired of it all."

"You are tired? Just take care of your *bébés* and I do de rest."

"Armand, are you trying to send me dotty? I don't think I can stand any more of your games."

"I have one more game, Flory. I decide to go to Edmonton to work. I cannot get work here, you know dat."

"I can't believe it! I can't believe it! I can't. You would work in Edmonton, but you won't work on your own farm. Oh I wish your dear mother and father knew

A MATTER OF COMPULSION

what was going on. Who or what are you running from, Armand. Why, you must be the laughing stock of the village."

"Do not make a sneer at me, Flory. I see dat look on a fox one time, when he get away from me."

* * *

Two days later the same man who had bought the steer came back. He must have noticed that the loft was packed with sheep's wool. He had driven his wagon to the barn. Flory didn't like going to the barn with a stranger. She was very frightened that he would throw her in the wagon and sell her to the white slave traffic. She did go halfway, then told him to fill his wagon and to be sure to take most of it from the back of the loft.

That day she sold her wool and made eighteen dollars.

* * *

"Flory, look at me. You have a home on de farm wit your *bébés*. I know I can get work in Edmonton. I will write you a letter. Edmonton's not dat far away. You see yourself how it is possible to go and come back in one day. I am not going to China, so wipe dose tear from your eye and smile for me."

* * *

She received a letter from Armand saying he was now working in a meat packing plant and had rented a room from a second cousin. It so puzzled her that she couldn't bear to think of it, yet it never left her mind. Not until she realized what a fool she was.

Here I am with my babies. I've got forty dollars in the palm of my hand, and I'm going to stay home and take care of my babies? You can bet your booty I won't! We'll go to Edmonton. I refuse to live like this. She did a huge washing, folding and packing most of it. The treadle sewing machine would be shipped as well.

They rented a small house in Edmonton. When they were settled Flory started to make shirts for the soldiers. She tried to make twelve shirts a day at eight cents a shirt. It was a good day when you made ninety six cents. Many a time it was less

EDMONTON

than twelve shirts.

With four children to take care of she never stopped. The three older children would go out to play. When they came in they were filthy from all the excavating and mounds of dirt. Even their shoes were filled with dirt. Flory wasn't happy. There were so many shirts to sew, besides the one box of fabric she had received that hadn't been opened. She longed to be back on the farm, but she would never complain to Armand.

It was a worry letting the children out to play. Flory was forever up and down, going to the window to see if they were all there together. She could see Leonard and Cecile, but not Romeo. She lifted Juliette into her arms, and ran outside. Both children thought Romeo was in the house. Flory kept on calling his name as loudly as she could. There was no answer. She didn't know in which direction to go. She asked every person she met if they had seen a little boy with white hair, a light blue shirt, and navy pants. No one had seen the child. She turned back, in case he had gone the other way. She phoned the police and gave her address. She continued asking people on her way back home. When she was almost home she saw a policeman on horseback with a white-haired boy holding the reins.

"Oh thank you, officer! Thank you so much. She put Juliette down and held out her arms to take Romeo, but Romeo was having none of that. He hung on to the reins with all his might.

"Romeo dear, you've got to let go of the reins." The policeman helped loosen his fingers. Romeo hung on to the policeman, sobbing his heart out. The policeman got down from his horse and had a few words for Romeo.

"When you grow up Romeo, maybe you will be a policeman and have a horse just like this one." Those words quieted Romeo for a second, then he said, "Why don't you give him to me now?"

Flory no sooner got through the door and fell into a chair, when Armand walked in with his hand bandaged half way up his arm. "Good God! What happened?"

"I have cut my hand at de meat plant. I will have to stay away from work until it heal."

"Well I have something to say. I can't sew all day and mind the children properly. They're covered with black dust. They have to play somewhere. Have you noticed the building going on next door with mounds of dirt and lumber, and the banging all day long? I can't let Juliette out. She sits on the floor all day watching my feet go back and forth on the treadle machine. Today Romeo wandered away and I went

A MATTER OF COMPULSION

crazy. I had to phone the police. The officer just brought him home five minutes ago. He's still sulking. Now you walk in with your hand bandaged. No, Armand. I'm starting to pack. We're going back to the farm."

* * *

In three days they were back home, the sewing machine not far behind, along with one box of shirts that she hadn't had time to finish. It was long, tedious work, but thirty or more dollars was a lot of money, especially after having spent most of the money from the wool and steer. The shirts were sent from Edmonton all cut and ready to sew. You received your pay when you filled the box with the finished shirts. Then a new box was returned to be sewn.

Flory had returned a box of finished shirts and asked that her pay be sent to her Legal address. "Armand, I haven't received one penny for all the shirts I made in Edmonton. Not one penny. Could it be lost?"

"Non, non. It didn't get lost. Have a little patience."

"My leg is so sore and I haven't had time to finish this box."

"Take your time, Flory. You do not have to worry wit dat. Make one, make two, den get up and walk for a while."

Every day she waited for Armand to come home with the mail. Finally she said, "There is something wrong, Armand. Something very wrong. It either got lost or they have fooled me. I'm going to write and find out."

"It hurt my heart to tell you, but I need some cash an' one day. . ."

"How could you cash my cheque without my signature?"

"De man at the post office cash it for me. He know you never go to de village. Don't look at me wit dat look. I confess to you. Is dat not wort' somet'ing?"

Flory quietly put the shirts back in the box. Some were finished, some were not.

"You'll be going to the village tomorrow, as usual. Send these back to Edmonton. It has gone the way of all things, Armand. The steer money, the wool money, your job at the packing plant, and now the money I made sewing shirts. I don't care, Armand. I'll never care again. I'm going to have my baby and that will be it. No more! Nothing matters! We'll go along like strangers. Get on with what you have to do, and I'll get on with what I have to do. No, nothing matters! I don't care anymore!"

She opened the heavy cellar door with hatred in her heart. She took the first step

EDMONTON

down and the cellar door slammed down on her leg. She screamed, "My leg! My leg!"

"Mon Dieu, Flory! Flory, what happen? I help you. I put you to bed. I put your leg on a pillow. Do not cry. I will fix it."

He kept on wetting the towels in cold well water to keep the swelling down. He made soup for the children. He put them to bed. He sat beside her on the bed. He told her that she was the only woman for him. "Try to understand me. Is dat too much to ask, Flory?"

"Armand, I'm not enough for you. I bear your children year after year. I've tried to learn the ways of the French. I've tried my very best to be a good farm wife. It wasn't easy. Oh, I could be more interested in your ideas, but you never finish anything you start."

"We are not old. Give me time. You cannot invent something in your mind and be rich tomorrow. You have to work very hard from your brain. You have to buy all de material to make it. Did you t'ink you would come from England, marry a Frenchman, and be happy for de rest of your life? Dat's what you read in story book. I trap. Dat take hard work. Yes, an' I take you to de opera in Edmonton one time. We make a trip to Brownsburg and de last t'ing I have to say is, Flory I do not want to be a farmer. You see, I will not have time to do de important t'ings in my life. Dere are plenty of farmer. It is not my fault my hand get cut. We live, and for dat we should be happy."

"No, Armand. We exist. We were rich when your father bought us this farm, and richer still when we had horses, cows, chickens, geese, pigs, and over one hundred beautiful sheep. Where has it all gone, Armand? Did you ever get paid for the sheep? No!"

"Gone? It is not all gone. I have my farm still. I was innocent like a boy when we come. I want to build my snowmobile. I have to do something for my soul."

"Oh, Armand. I'm sore inside. My leg is pounding. I'm very tired."

*   *   *

Flory expected it would be a boy, since it had been that way from the beginning. It was a girl, and a surprise. Flory named her Venice Albertine. It was May, 1918.

The pain in Flory's leg was getting worse. She had to remain in bed. Grandmaman Pilon had given Armand a book. It was very important to have, she told him,

A MATTER OF COMPULSION

especially living on a farm where you could be miles away from a doctor. Armand called it "The Doctor Book." He started reading it, searching for answers. He walked to Dr. Jeunais and told him that he was very sure Flory had a milk leg. The doctor glanced at Armand with a look that clearly said, "What would you know about it?"

"It look very bad. My wife is sick and if you can come today I tank you for it."

* * *

"Mrs. Pilon, you have a sore leg? I'll take a look at it. Yes, it is quite swollen. You are wise to keep it raised. I would like you to take a teaspoon of this medicine every three hours. Keep your leg raised and stay in bed. I'll be back the day after tomorrow."

* * *

"Armand, the medicine isn't helping my leg. It only makes me feel drowsy. I can't go on like this."

"I believe you, Flory. I go to Diligence and get de docteur Ferguson to come. He was a good docteur when we take Willie for his hand."

Dr. Ferguson came. He took one look at Flory's leg. "Mr. Pilon, your wife has a milk leg, just as you said."

"When I read my book I believe dat myself but when I tell Jeunais he look at me like I am crazy. He laugh, after he sneer."

The doctor covered her leg with a black salve, then he bandaged it. Oh, didn't Flory's eyes fill with tears of joy. It felt rested, it felt cared for, it felt secure. Dr. Ferguson also gave her different medicine to take. The other was to be disposed of.

"Oh, he is a good doctor Armand. I wish he lived closer. It is a bit far to Diligence. I can't stand that Jeunais. Romeo getting that terrible infection in the foreskin around his whatsname and him saying that it might have to be cut off. Oh God. I dread to think of what could have happened."

* * *

EDMONTON

It worried her when Armand went for the mail. The hotel door was always open, which meant that he could wander home at any hour. This was her fifth baby since they moved to the farm. The eldest girl, Cecile, was six years old.

"Do you think you could help mother? The baby's napkins need washing. If you bring the tub and washboard here by my bed, then carry two or three pails of water, that won't be too hard, will it? They're not very dirty, dear. They never are when you nurse your own."

Cecile held each napkin up for Maman's approval.

"Are they clean enough, Maman?"

"Yes dear. You are a love. One day you'll make a good wife for some man. If you could peel potatoes without cutting yourself it would be a help."

WHISKY BLANC

"I pick up de mail an' de Gazette. How you feel?"

Flory knew he'd had a few drinks. She could tell by his eyes. *I don't half mind. He's been so good, and he is home.*

"Cecile was a love. She did the baby's napkins for me and she really scrubbed them with my good soap."

"I notice dere are clothe on de line."

"Armand, would you heat some water? I want the children bathed tonight. Oh, I would enjoy a wash. It would make me feel better. Bring the washtub here by my bed so I can see the children."

Cecile didn't want Papa to give her a bath so she ran behind the shed where he couldn't find her. She was barefooted. As she ran around the corner a three-inch rusty spike went through her instep and out the other side.

"I t'ink Flory, we have more problem. I hear Cecile screaming her lung."

He ran inside with her in his arms. "Yes, you can cry. I know it hurt. Papa fix it and you will lay down."

"What in heaven's name is the matter?"

"Cecile step on a spike. Where is dat *gomme d'épinette*?"

"It's in the bottom of the big blue cupboard. Bring her to me, Armand. Whyever did you run out the door with no shoes on?"

She sobbed the words out. "Because I didn't want Papa to bath me."

"Why didn't you just tell him that?"

"I didn't tell him because I'm afraid of him when he....when he's drunk."

"He's had a few drinks, but he isn't drunk, dear."

"Well I don't care what you call it. I can smell it on his breath."

Armand had set the spruce gum in hot water. He slathered it on with a spoon, then bandaged the whole foot. The next day he used salted pork rind, which he left on overnight to draw out the poisons.

"Armand, I can't stand anymore of it. I want to get up." Flory's milk leg was still healing.

"Not yet. Give it anudder day or two."

"I feel that if I stay in bed I may get that terrible flu that's all through the village. I'd rather get it standing up. The longer I lie here the weaker I get."

"Yes, I can understand what you mean. I will help you, den you can sit at de

A MATTER OF COMPULSION

table."

Armand would heat milk and wine. He insisted she have a glass of it each day. It was, he said, good for her circulation. She was getting stronger, but she did have to sit down to knead the bread.

Cecile's foot was healing slowly too. She still limped, and dressings were put on every other day.

There was a knock on the door. She took off her pinafore and answered it. She hollered, "Good gracious, it's you Nap! Napoleon Pilon, I am happy to see you!"

"*Bonjour*, Flory. I come to de *ouest* to visit."

"Won't Armand be surprised. He went down for the mail. How are Maman and Papa and all the girls? I have a thousand questions to ask."

"All very good, Flory. Dey send love to you. I cannot say it fast. I only start to learn English."

"You do very well. I understand every word you say. I feel very proud myself. I speak a little French, and I'm getting better every day. Oh Nap, I have been sick for a long time. I have a new baby and a very bad leg. For three months I have been in bed."

"Ah yes. I see your colour is not rosy."

"No it isn't. I'm not very strong yet. Listen! Can you hear the church bell? Another one has died from the flu."

"It ring a long time. It must be a man dat die."

Armand walked in. Napoleon quickly got up and walked toward him. "Gee cripe, my brudder!" They hugged, shook hands, and kissed cheeks.

"Napoleon, you have come at a bad time, but also, maybe at a good time. Twenty people have die wit de flu. So we lose no time. I am going to make hot drink for all of us. You too, Flory. We have to kill dat germ. Before you go to bed you will have anudder. When dis bottle is empty I will get one more, and one more."

Flory could see that Armand had had a few, but she was sure that Napoleon hadn't noticed. They all enjoyed laughter and good conversation. It was like a special welcome party for Nap. There were hundreds of questions asked, mostly in fast French. Flory understood many things. When she didn't, she'd ask. "What did Napoleon say about Papa Pilon?"

"He say Papa is not feeling well but he say he believe it is because he get dose headache still. Yes, and Papa still believe his curly hair cause de problem."

It wasn't very long before Napoleon had a nose bleed. Armand was very

WHISKY BLANC

disturbed.

"Yes, he must have it. Mon Dieu, I pray dat Maman does not hear de rocking chair go back and fort' in de night."

* * *

"Flory, I go to de village. I bring dis back."
"What did you get Armand?"
"I get t'ree bottle of whisky blanc. De kettle is always boiling and I am not fooling anymore. It is here wit us. We can all die. You realize dat? Well I say we are not going to die yet, if Armand Pilon have anyt'ing to do wit it."

He poured twice as much as he should have, adding a little sugar and hot water.

"Drink it, Napoleon. You can always go to bed. Your nose is still bleeding. What you want? Blood or whisky blanc? It is de only t'ing we can try. De *docteur*, he have not'ing. It's a matter of compulsion. You shit or get off de pot."

Flory was sure he had missed his calling, the way he mastered the whole thing, and with such pride. Surely he must have been a bartender in a previous lifetime. He even gave the older children a teaspoon or two in hot, sweet water.

"Armand! What are you doing? You'll be punished for it!"
"God is too busy. He have his hand full. Worry about your *bébés* and who will take care of dem. De bell is ringing. One more have die. Can you hear it?"
"Yes, Armand. Make another hot drink for me."
"Now you understand what I am trying to do?"
"Oh God, Armand. I would go crazy if I lost any of my children. When I think of placing the black crucifix in Elizabeth's tiny hand it haunts me. There isn't a day that goes by when I look at my children and don't think of her. You understand, Armand?"
"I understand. I understand many t'ing. Now de *bébés* are sleeping. Napoleon is sleeping. It is time for you and me. Take down your braid and pray we do not hear de bell."

* * *

Napoleon was up early, looking out the window, calm, quiet, unconcerned, just watching the chickens pecking at nothing and anything they could find.

A MATTER OF COMPULSION

"You're up, Napoleon. How do you feel?"

"I feel happy. My nose is not bleeding dis morning. Flory, see de rooster? Can we have it for soup? I feel for it."

After much running they finally cornered one.

"Dis one look like it fit de pot. We get it."

"Armand, what have you done? You've killed my best laying hen!"

"It was de only one dat was easy to catch."

"I doubt you knew the difference. I am hurt. I'm angry."

"Cook it. We need soup more den we need egg. Do not be cross over little t'ings like a chicken."

"Yes, Armand. We are all feeling better. I am getting stronger, Cecile's foot is healing nicely, and the children are all well. Thank goodness for that. And you, Napoleon, you look as good as the day you came."

Flory truly believed that it was the whisky blanc that saved them all. Napoleon was the only one in the family who had any signs of the flu. After Napoleon left, Armand never brought liquor into the house again. He did just as he had before, going for the mail every day.

Flory realized now more than ever that Armand enjoyed the company of his French friends more than he needed ordinary, everyday talk from her.

MOVING TO TOWN

"Today I get some good news. Monsieur Robert want me to work in his store. I feel sure dat it would be good for us to live in de village."

Flory just sat, not moving a muscle, until she felt that if she breathed in any deeper her corsets would split.

"I sell my lumber to Monsieur Dutel. He say his house is too big for two people wit'out any kid. He want to sell it and build a smaller place. You should see Madame Dutel. She is small like one of our kid. I believe the reason is dat she have a huge hump on her back. She make lady hat to sell. Well, are you not going to say somet'ing? You sit wit a blank face like de egg from your chicken. Say somet'ing or do somet'ing!"

"You sold the lumber?"

"Yes, I told you. I, Pilon, sell de lumber. I am excited over dat. We are close to de school. De kid can come home for dere dinner and Dutel's house is across from de store."

"Take a breath, Armand. What exactly will you be doing at Robert's store, and what about wages?"

"You t'ink I am going to calsomine? No, I will be waiting on de customer from behind de counter. Flory, I would like you to see dat house. Let us go togedder. You will not be sorry."

"I'll go. The farm is rented so it wouldn't hurt to look at it."

*   *   *

After the shack it was a sight to behold. The living room, where they had entered, ran the whole width of the front of the house. "As you can see, Madame Pilon, I have no furniture in my parlour. I use it for my hat shop. The rest of the house Monsieur Pilon can show you. He has seen it before. And now I will return to my work."

"We like it very much, Madame Dutel. Do you have anything to sell?"

"*Ah, mais oui.* I have the dining room furniture, also this velvet Morris chair, very good to relax in. Also the kitchen stove, table, and chairs. Also my brass bed and dresser. Ah yes, I have too many dishes. . ."

"We will take everything." Flory glanced at Armand. He had the look of a thoroughbred horse. The expansive space of the whole of the house had melted her heart.

That night she lay awake. There were so many heartaches that should be forgotten. She would cherish all that was sweet and good, and leave the shack behind. Wouldn't her mother be surprised to see this house with a parlour, an upstairs, and all that decent furniture!

All the hardships and heartbreaks when Armand was nowhere around came to her mind. Leonard and Romeo setting the grass on fire, and how the hen house had started to burn with all her setting hens inside. She had sent Cecile to the Billet house to have someone come with a plough, while she had pumped and hauled pail after pail of water, trying to save it. The hens had escaped, but the hen house and all of the eggs had burned to the ground. The Billet boy had worked quickly, ploughing to try to save the shack. Flory kept pumping and hauling. How sore her body was. The next day she had had a miscarriage.

There was the time that Romeo and Juliette were nowhere to be found. Flory ran from barn to shed to hay stack, hollering their names. She ran down the path to the grove, and saw two small figures walking through the stubble.

"Maman, we walked through the wheat. We couldn't get out. We walked and walked. We were afraid we would die. Romeo said we should kneel down to pray. We did, Maman."

"It's true! We could hear the binder coming closer and closer. I lifted Juliette on my shoulders. All she could see was wheat. Then we heard the binder coming closer again. Then it would go away. We did the breast stroke to clear the way, but the wheat kept hitting back at us. Juliette said she was scared we might die. We kneeled down again and prayed harder. I pointed to a cloud in the sky and we walked toward it. The binder sounded closer and closer, then farther and farther away. I told Juliette to keep walking toward the cloud. We finally reached the stubble. Then we saw the horses coming with Mr. Brunette and the binder. He asked us what we were doing in the wheat field. He told us we could have scared the horses and he would have had a runaway. Then the binder could have run over us. He told us we were lucky to be alive."

Memories. Oh, the memories. Flory remembered scrubbing the floor with lye. She reached far with the scrub brush, leaving the saucer of lye behind. When she turned around it was too late. Juliette had dipped her fingers in the lye and put them in her mouth. Oh God, didn't they hurry. She held her while Rose spooned milk into her mouth, trying to make her vomit. Juliette lay limp in Flory's arms. Then

MOVING TO TOWN

she turned blue. How Flory screamed. "Oh God! She's dead, Rose! What can I do?" Then suddenly Juliette vomited all the curdled milk. Rose kept on spooning milk while Flory held Juliette and prayed. Early morning Juliette looked at her Maman with the clearest eyes, and said, "Mama."

Flory kept the little black sock with the heel and toe the colour of a robin's egg. The lye had burned holes of all sizes on the black part of the sock, but not one hole was burned on the heel or the toe. Flory thought it very strange and years later she would tell the story and show the sock to prove it.

When Flory had walked into the shack for the very first time she loved the smell of the new wood. A whole new life lay before her and Armand, with young love and new babies. There was so much to live for, so much to learn, and no one to teach her. She had loved Rose, and she had been taken away. Then Beatrice, the dearest friend she had ever had.

Mme. Morin, bless her, had thought her water hadn't broken. She sterilized a hat pin to prick the water sack, and all the time was pricking the top of Juliette's head.

She remembered the time the haystack in the barn was on fire. Romeo had crawled under the barn to shoo the baby pigs out. Armand had tied a rope to both of Romeo's ankles and held the ends.

"You are de right size to crawl under de barn Romeo, and get dose pig out of dere, or we will have more roast pork den we can eat. And do it fast. Scream if de fire come close an' I will pull you out."

Leonard and Cecile hauled water. Didn't they work! Through all the years after, whenever it was brought up, it was always the same. "It was Leonard who lit that match," or "It wasn't me, it was Romeo."

* * *

The year was 1920. Flory started to pack. It wasn't a big job, because they had so few belongings. The stove, table, and chairs would stay. The blue corner cupboard was nailed to the wall, so it had to stay. Now the farm hands could sleep in the shack and not have to drive home each night. She folded her carded wool comforters, bedding, and pillows, filling the two tubs and copper boiler. Her trunk was filled to the top with clothing. The big bread pan held the dishes. Armand packed his tools, guns, and trapping gear. In a box he had all the drawings of his inventions. His violin and the long-armed banjo leaned against the cream separator.

A MATTER OF COMPULSION

"Why are you taking the cream separator?"

"You never know. I t'ink I will need it one day. Yes, I am sure I will need it one day."

Flory didn't say a word. With the lovely big barn at the end of their new yard, he might very well buy a cow.

"We are like a family of birds leaving the nest, aren't we Armand?"

"No, Flory. De farm belong to us. Dat is de main t'ing, not de shack."

Mme. Dutel had left the furniture just as she had placed it. On top of the buffet was a statue of Joan of Arc. It had layers of paint, the last coat being pale blue. Upstairs she had left a heavy oak showcase and the tallest, biggest pram Flory had ever seen. It had a large compartment for storing baby things, with a door that slid across the top to hide any evidence of soiled napkins.

A cash register, covered in scrolls of gold and in perfect condition, was left in the parlour. In the cupboard under the stairway were all the dishes that Mme. Dutel hadn't needed, along with a box that held six tiny lamp globes, each one wrapped in thin silky paper. Everything was so tiny. Little bowls, tiny cups and saucers, little plates.

Everything that had been left was used as toys by the children, even the cash register. They would push the key that made the drawer fly out and argue over whose turn came next, until Flory had to slap their hands once and for all. And while she was at it, she let them know that they were never to touch the oak showcase. She didn't mind, she told them, if they played with the pram, taking turns to ride in it.

*   *   *

"Flory, I was t'inking. While your parlour have no furniture, how about we have a party to celebrate our own new house? You like dat?"

"Armand, you must be dotty. Who do I know? Not a soul."

"Why you t'ink I want to have a party, if it is not for you to meet people? It is a good time to have a *soirée* in your parlour. A parlour like your mudder Jane have in England." He smiled. A pungent breeze of liquor wafted from his nostrils.

Flory didn't say a word. What if he did have a drink with M. Robert when the day's work was done? It was so much happier having him right close to home. It was thoughtful of him to think of a party.

"Whoever would you ask, Armand?"

MOVING TO TOWN

"I know who to ask. Do not worry about dat."
"Well, I wouldn't half mind. I wonder what I could wear?"
"No problem. Wear what you wore when you went to church wit Beatrice."

* * *

It was unbelieveable, the many friends he had, and for every man a woman. *All these people he knew while I was on the farm. Oh, I was a fool. Beatrice was right. How nice it would be if I could dance. Look at him now with his long-armed banjo. He is a smart man. He's different. No wonder he went to the village every day. People like him. He's witty. I'm not like that. I could never make anyone laugh unless I did something awkward. Yes, it certainly is a far cry from the farm.*

* * *

"How you enjoy de party last night?"

"I did, but after being on the farm for so long it made me feel a little out of place. Anna Saigner was telling me what a lovely time they have at the basket socials. She also told me of the big celebration coming up on St. Jean Baptiste Day. All the big cardinals, bishops, and priests come from as far as Edmonton and Montreal. The children will be learning their catachism, then comes the confirmation and their first communion."

"Did you notice de blue shiny eye dat Mademoiselle Morrow have? Too shiny to be natural, eh? She must put something in dose eye, dey look like de star in de sky. Next week on Saturday dere is a party at Saigner's. It is close to us here, so we will go."

"Are you going to play the violin?"

"Yes, I take my violin and de banjo. Why you ask?"

"I like it when you play, that's all."

Flory knew he was drinking, but where did he go? To the hotel? Hardly, because he was always at the store. It must be with M. Robert. Even if he didn't get close to her, she could tell by his eyes. Yes, like Miss Morrow's eyes, bright like stars in the sky. Miss Morrow had stepped out a few times, but then so did most of them, and as Armand said, "Everybody have to go to de privy."

A MATTER OF COMPULSION

* * *

"A man come to Robert today. We talk for a long time. His name is Chalon. Robert tell me he have so much money dat he can not spend what he have. He never spend five cents. He is a miser. Can you beat dat, eh? And he never have a smile on his face."

"Well Armand, I am glad you met someone wise for a change."

"Flory, I feel sorrow for Chalon. He have no dream. I have dream. I am happy for dat. I say yes, I worry over matter of de house. I borrow money to buy it. I was t'inking maybe after a while, you Flory, could do something to help me pay de loan."

"Armand, you do know that I'm pregnant again, but I will help as best I can. What is this all about? What do you want me to do?"

"Don't excite yourself. I will let you know when I find out."

How can I make money, she thought. *I wouldn't mind sewing. That could bring in some extra money, but why can he not get along on what he makes at Robert's? Then there's the rent from the farm, and the money his mother sends each month. Lord knows I make all the children's clothes, even Leonard and Romeo's knickers. It was all too good to last. He's drinking more than I thought. I can't fool myself. He's just home earlier because he's there under my nose. I won't say a word. I'll be pleasant. I will.* "Do you think we'll have tramps come to the door now that we're in the village?" she asked him.

"No, I do not believe so. It is de farmer where dey go sometime to chop wood or do chore and for de work dey do, de farmer give dem food. Time is hard for de Galatian who want to settle in dis country. We are very lucky wit all de comfort we have now. Why you call dem tramp?"

"They came to my door one day when Beatrice was there. There were two men. The best I could do was fry them eggs and potatoes. I called them beggars. I didn't know what else to call them after they asked for food. It was Beatrice who told me they were called tramps or bums."

"Dey are men Flory, just like everybody. Dey need food to survive. If you say chop some wood or haul some water while I make you some food, dey are happy to do it. When you are hungry you have no pride."

"Oh, I'll never forget the man in white who came to the door once when you weren't around. Was I ever frightened. He walked back and forth, holding a bible in the palm of his hands. It was pretty dark out there, well much too dark to be reading the bible. I remember there was a full moon. Now how in heaven's name could he read that fine print? I locked both doors with butcher knives. He didn't knock or ask for food. Even if he had knocked, never would I have opened that door. He truly looked like Jesus, Armand."

"Yes, you tell me all about dat before, and I say you have a dream."

"Don't tell me it was a dream! I should know. I was there peeking out the window, watching every move he made. He walked fast, then stopped as though there was a line that was forbidden to be crossed. Then he turned around quickly and headed in another direction, always coming back to the line that he never crossed. Don't tell me it was a dream. You weren't home that night."

"Maybe Flory, it was a nightmare. Besides, you should not be frighten of dat. It could be Jesus and you do a bad t'ing to lock de door. You should invite him in de house and give him some of your bread and a glass of my parsnip wine!"

"Don't give me that smile of yours. I don't think you ever believed me, not now or then."

He lowered his hand down the front of her blouse. As she ran from him, he quickly pinched her bottom.

* * *

Eaton's had a contest. Whoever sent in the best caption to advertise the catalogue would receive a special prize, and for one year the winning caption would grace the cover of their new catalogue. Anyone who received an Eaton's catalogue could enter the contest. What prestige, to have your own written words emblazoned on the cover for all Canadians to read. Both Flory and Armand were interested, jotting down every thought that came to mind. Nothing sounded right, so nothing was sent in.

When Armand walked in with the new catalogue everyone gathered around the table to see and hear. On the cover, in soft colours, was the picture of a beautiful lady dressed in high fashion. She was sitting with the folds of her skirt falling like a fan from her knees to the floor. The caption read, "Styles may come and styles may go, but beauty is eternal."

"Gee cripe, whoever t'ink of dat, eh? Dat is it. It is very apropos for a catalogue, but I will say one t'ing, she have not your hair. No, she have not, Flory."

A MATTER OF COMPULSION

"Maybe not Armand, but look at her figure and clothes. I put on pounds with every baby I have. Now I am pregnant again. It seems as if all the women are going for bobbed hair nowadays. I don't think bobbed hair looks good on a stout woman, do you?"

"I don't care if dey are tin or fat. I believe a woman should have long hair, period."

In a way he's keeping me in a happy mood. I wonder what he wants me to do to help with the loan? Does he expect me to go to work? Where? At Robert's store? No, I can't let my mind run away with me.

BOARDERS

    Armand walked in with two men who Flory had never set eyes on. "Flory, I would like you to meet my friend Monsieur Senachalle and Monsieur Champagne. Dis is my wife, Flory. Do you mind Flory, if dey will be our boarder for a while?" Flory stood like a statue, staring just over their heads. "Day after tomorrow it is Monday," he continued. "Dat is de day dat dey will be here, not tonight. I feel sure my wife t'ought you would be here for supper. I do not play a trick like dat." He gave a little laugh, then walked them to the door.
    After they had left, he turned to her, "Don't be cross, Flory. What are we going to do wit de big dining room? We have a big kitchen where we eat our meal. So what are you going to do wit it? Look at de table clot' every day? Don't look at me like dat. It's for you! De money will be for you only. It will help me pay for de loan."
    "Do you know what I think of your little scheme? I think you are a wicked man, treating me like a workhorse. Oh, I know what's going on. You're drinking as much as you ever did. You're three sheets to the wind now. You're not worried about your precious job, no, because your liquor is at the store. I'll bet my bottom dollar M. Robert doesn't drink half what you do."
    "Bullshit! You talk like an imperial bulldog. My mudder have six living children and she lose t'ree or four. She have boarder to help Papa."
    "Well it didn't do her much good, did it? They bought you the farm along with everything else for three thousand dollars and they've been sending you twelve dollars a month since the day we moved to the west. I would say your dear mother worked for nothing."
    "Bitch! Sonofabitch! You are hard Flory, and not worth two cent."
    He walked out and slammed the door. She didn't see him that night.
    Maybe I'm a fool. He said the money would be mine. It might be worth it for a few months. Yes, I've made up my mind. I'll take the boarders.

* * *

    M. Senachalle asked Flory if she could board two of his friends. Yes, she said. Why not? If you have two you may as well have four. She had a feeling Armand was behind the whole thing. The boarders paid weekly, except for M. Senachalle. He always had some excuse from one week to the other. Flory didn't half mind when he

A MATTER OF COMPULSION

told her he would pay in a lump sum. She could stretch things and manage without it and could end up with more than she expected. There were five children, seven with the two of them, and four boarders. She was heavy and tired. She realized what a fool she was. She was making it easier for Armand to spend more money on drink.

"Armand, are you there?"

"Yes, I am here."

"I'm going to have to tell the boarders to leave. The baby is due very soon now, and I can't do it anymore. You are drinking again and I was trying to help you because you said times were hard and you needed my help to pay the loan. No, I am getting rid of the boarders this very day. I am!"

He looked at her sheepishly and walked away. It wasn't like him to give in without handing back some of the fight he had in him.

* * *

On Monday morning Flory served breakfast. After they had eaten well, she walked to the table. "I am expecting my baby very soon now. I cannot board you gentlemen any longer. You will not be expected for dinner or for supper. M. Senachalle, you have only paid for three month's board. Now you owe me board for another three months."

"Mrs. Pilon, can I leave my trunk here? When I pick it up next Saturday I will pay my board for the time owing."

"All right. I'll keep your trunk for you, M. Senachalle, and expect you on Saturday."

* * *

On August 1st, 1920 Flory had a baby girl with a mop of curly hair like Grandpapa Pilon. Flory wanted her named Delima Rose after Grandmaman Pilon, but Armand registered her at the church as Lilianne Elizabeth. Flory didn't find out until years later. The oversight didn't matter - never was she called by her name. She was the baby, and would be called "Baby" or "Babe" throughout her life.

M. Senachalle never did call for his trunk. It bothered Flory to think that she could so easily be fooled. One day in a fit of temper she broke the lock. It was

BOARDERS

a good trunk. She hated to do it, but it was now hers. She had worked for it and she could do as she pleased. There were hundreds of worthless papers, one grey blanket, and a billy club. *A billy club? Whatever would he use it for, unless he was a policeman at one time? How could he do this to me, the cur!*

* * *

"Today I meet a family. A man, a woman, an' two young girl. Dey need a place to stay for a while."

"No, Armand! I got rid of the boarders. With six children to feed and clothe, wouldn't I be a fool? I'll never do it again. Senachalle left owing me three month's board. Oh yes, he left his trunk behind, but the rest is history."

"Non, non, Flory. It is not de same. You do not feed dem, dey feed demself. Listen to dis. We have de parlor. It is empty. All dey need is two room for six month. De big furnace is in de parlor, dey get water from our pump. Dey use de outside privy. *Pas de problème.* We lock de door, de dining room door, Flory. You never see dem. All I have to do is cut a door from de parlor through to one bedroom. *Voila*, it is all ready to live in. It will be your money an' you are private an' dey are private. You agree to dat, Flory? Don't forget, we have all dose room upstair for us."

"Do as you like, Armand. I really don't care."

"You do not care, or you do not mind?"

"I said, do as you like."

* * *

The Morencys, with their two daughters, moved in. They were very quiet. Each morning one of them walked down the porch to the kitchen door, knocked quietly, and filled two pails of water, enough for the day. It was a help to Flory. Now she could buy flannelette for the baby and it was time she bought herself a sturdy pair of corsets for firm support.

After each child it was a chore ordering anything for herself, since she always gained weight. Items usually had to be returned to the catalogue, not once, but twice. She came up with the idea of measuring her hips, waist, bust, and length with pieces of string. Then she tied a note on each string, telling what the measurement was. The corsets fit ever so much better, and she was relieved of the big chore of taking in a gusset or letting in a V, as she called it.

The children would stand on a piece of brown paper to have their feet traced, always having a little more length added. If the shoes were too long, Flory stuffed the toes with sheep's wool.

The children always took their new shoes to bed with them, not because of fear of theft, but because they were a beautiful gift that was long overdue, and given with tender love from Maman. If the shoes were short, the children never said a word.

When there was nothing to amuse the children, Flory took out either Eaton's or Simpson's catalogue, telling them that if they tore one page the shoes would be taken away.

Eventually the Morency family moved away. They never became close friends, but always remained kind and respectful.

YVONETTE

"Children, Mr. Massey, dear Mr. Massey who first taught your mother how to make bread, is having a Christmas dinner for all the children in the village. He's going to roast the biggest turkey he can find. Now it's not for grown-ups. None of the parents will be there. Another thing. It is only for children who can eat with a knife and fork, and if you can't use a knife and fork, you will have to stay home."

At the evening meals Flory never stopped glancing from the corner of her eye. When she saw them using their thumbs to push food onto their forks, she would say, "Tut, tut. Try again, dear. This time use your knife instead of your thumb. You are all doing very well. I see no reason why any one of you will have to stay home. Under the tree will be a small gift for each child. Do watch your manners, and thank Mr. Massey."

As Maman said, no one had to stay home except for baby Delima Rose, who could not know the difference, and was much too young to eat turkey.

A table the length of the room was draped in white with as many placings as there were children. It looked so beautiful, with little dishes of good things right down the centre. You could just cry as you sat in awe, breathing in all the wonders. It was a new smell - the smell of life - like when Maman walked in after being in Edmonton. It was the opening of your own box of life.

* * *

The Roberts had a large store two stories high stacked with everything you could ever want. Their home was next to the store. It was a red brick house with a wide porch that echoed. The upstairs had a balcony that faced the Pilon house. They had two children, Yvonette and Arthur.

M. Robert and Armand had a lot in common. Mme. Robert and Flory would only exchange a few words, mostly about the weather or unimportant trivial things. Emilie walked on her side of the street, Flory walked on hers. Emilie had no reason to cross to Flory's side, because strangely enough, all her friends lived on her side. The bank manager and his wife, M. and Mme. Benet, and the Roberts were as thick as thieves. That's what Flory said.

Yvonette and Juliette were the same age, but Yvonette was brought up with all the finer things in life. At times the girls had their differences, but they always made

A MATTER OF COMPULSION

up after cruel words. There was a rain barrel on each corner of the Pilon house. Juliette was familiar with Flory's English songs, and she discovered the beautiful echoing sounds they made while sung into a rain barrel.

"Yvonette, do you want to come to my house and holler down the rain barrel?" This was a very special treat for Yvonette, and after any argument these words would help them to again become best friends.

"Would you like to come to the store after school? I'll ask my father if we can play upstairs in the stock room."

"Oh, I'd like that! I've never seen a stock room."

The shelves reached the ceiling. They were stocked with boxes of candies and chocolate bars, licorice pipes and gumdrops. Juliette wouldn't have dreamed that a stock room was anything like this. They tasted candies of all colours, then finished with the biggest chocolate bar they could find. There was much giggling and looking. *If Maman and the kids could see this, wouldn't they be surprised. They'd have a fit, I'll bet.*

They had often played downstairs, always in a corner that was partly hidden by a big black safe. Those were the days when they would turn page after page of comics from the Chicago Herald, doing nothing but read and whisper.

One day Yvonette asked, "Would you like to come over after school and we'll read the funny papers?" Juliette couldn't refuse.

There was so much going on in the store. She could peek around the large safe and see Papa waiting on different customers. Yvonette hadn't come in yet. Probably she had to go to the privy. She saw Mme. Robert measuring yard goods for a customer. It so fascinated her that she walked a little closer. She wanted to see how quickly Mme. Robert could measure out yards of material with a long ruler on the edge of the counter. It was all so easy compared to Maman's method of standing tall, looking straight ahead, measuring yards from the tip of her nose, flinging her arm out straight to her side. Every piece of material ordered from the catalogue was re-measured, not once, but twice. Maman stood regimental like a soldier.

Mme. Robert couldn't have been happy with Juliette, who was daydreaming while she watched.

"*Voulez-vous quelque chose, Juliette?*"

"*Non, Madame, je ne veux rien.*"

"*Alors, prends-le et pousses-toi.*"

The two women laughed as though it was one of the best jokes they had ever

YVONETTE

heard. Juliette briskly walked out, happy that Papa was nowhere to be seen.

"Maman, I went to Robert's after school. Yvonette asked me to. I was watching Mme. Robert measure yards so fast from a ruler on the counter. She asked me if I wanted something. No, I told her, I didn't want anything, and she said, 'Well take it and go home.' Then both women laughed so hard."

"Were you bothering them, dear?"

"No, I was waiting for Yvonette. Mme. Robert is never nice to me. I don't know why she doesn't like me."

"Never mind, dear. She's a show-off. A la-de-dah."

That evening Yvonette came over with a bowl of fresh strawberries. "Maman sent them for you, Mrs. Pilon."

"How thoughtful of your mother. Now don't go away. I'll fill your bowl with pickled beets. Do thank your mother. When I bake bread next, I'll send her a fresh loaf."

The peace offering for being rude to my Juliette. She was probably showing off in front of her friend. Then again, maybe she realizes what she's done and she's being plain friendly.

The next day Yvonette told Juliette that her mother had given her a slap and sent her to her room.

"What for? What did you do, Yvonette?"

"The strawberries were not for your mother. I was supposed to take them to Mme. Benet. Maman said she slapped me for not listening."

"I'm sorry we ate them. It was such a small bowl, Yvonette. Why didn't you take them to the Benets?"

"I don't know."

It's unfair to Maman. She was so happy. I don't think I'll tell her. And then she promised she'd send Mme. Robert a loaf of fresh bread. I will tell Maman she shouldn't give her the loaf. The la-de-dah!

* * *

"You never before see de lovely dog dis man have. He breed dem, Flory. I am going to buy two. Yes, dis fall I will buy two of dem for hunting."

"Sometimes I wonder if you are all there. We are barely feeding and clothing the children, let alone two thoroughbred dogs."

A MATTER OF COMPULSION

"Dey do not eat pork chop. Dey eat horse meat, and you do not have to sew clothe for dem. Dey have dere own."

"Armand, use your head. What in heaven's name do we need two dogs for?"

"I, Flory, need two dog for hunting. Dey will ride wit me in de snowmobile."

Suddenly they heard hollering and screaming coming from somewhere outside. Flory hurried to the window.

"Good God, Armand! Robert's store is on fire!"

"Gee cripe! It is wood and it is old."

He rushed out. People were running in all directions. He felt helpless. Nothing could be done. It was an inferno, with flames shooting from the windows. The heat was unbearable. People were moving away, not knowing when the second story would collapse. Armand ran home.

"Get some heavy blanket, Flory. We will hang dem to de window and trow bucket of water on dem. We have to save our window. Gee cripe, we can lose our house if de spark blow here."

"I only have two grey blankets. Will they do?"

"I haul de water. You go to de shed. Get de Senachalle blanket dat you talk about all de time."

There was a big oval glass window in the front door. Flory cherished it. Armand nailed Senachall's blanket to the door and threw a bucket of water over it.

"Oh Lord, look at it go, Armand!"

"He do not worry. Robert have good insurance."

Juliette thought how sad it was that she was the only one who had seen all the candy and chocolate bars, and now in her mind she could see them melting, then burning into ashes.

"I tell you we can be happy de wind was not too strong, and Robert, he have a brick house so he is safe."

There was no sleep for the Roberts or the Pilons that night. They watched as the store burned to the ground.

"Can you tell me why my ear is aching so? I can hardly stand the pain, Armand."

"It's the cold water and de heat dat give you an ear ache. I fix it for you." He slowly rolled a cigarette and lit it.

"What are you thinking of, Armand?"

"I am not t'inking, I am doing. Now Flory, I am going to blow a little smoke into your ear."

YVONETTE

"What a wicked thing to do to me! Do you think I'm crazy?"

"Trust me. It is not hot. I promise you dat. Your ear will not ache. Come on, come on. Which ear, Flory?"

"The one I'm holding, of course." She knew he had a knack for curing, so she gave in to his ridiculous idea of cigarette smoke for an ear ache. He took a long drag, cupped her ear close to his mouth, and slowly blew the smoke into her ear.

"It will not be long. It will not ache no more. Wit your little cunning way you are trying not to smile."

She thought it was a silly idea that only he could think of, but to have it work was unbelievable.

"Look at me. How is your ear ache?"

"It's fine, Armand," she said while holding her head down.

"Look at me an' say it to me." She looked at him. They both laughed heartily. Then Flory suddenly stopped.

"What is de problem?"

"How can we be laughing when you're out of work? What will we do without the store and with eight mouths to feed?"

That night Flory decided she would ask Anna Seigner if she could let people know that she was a good seamstress and that she could do alterations. It was the perfect place to advertise, as the Seigners had a store on Flory's side of the street. They also sold yard goods and Anna was the one who measured them out.

NAPOLEON DEMARNE

Flory heard a knock and opened the door. A stranger, well dressed and with a smart black moustache, took one step forward.

"I am Napoleon Demarne. I heard you were a seamstress. My daughter Clara goes to the convent and she needs a navy blue dress. Do you think you could make it?"

"Yes, I'll make it. When will you bring the material? Also, I will need your Clara for a fitting. Would Saturday suit you?"

"Saturday is a good day, Mrs. Pilon. I'll bring Clara and the material."

Now did I do the right thing? She thought of the days, weeks, and months when she sewed dreary shirt after dreary shirt for the soldiers, and how she never received a cent, not even a smile from Armand.

* * *

"Today I t'ink a lot about our life so I decide to go east to see Maman an' Papa."

"You wrote to your mother, didn't you? She sent you money for your fare. I never could trust you!"

"It is my money, and I go if I please."

"Armand, why do you have to go now? You've lost your job and we have nothing. Be a good man and stay home."

"You tell me I am a bad man because I want to see my Maman and Papa? You tell me I am bad because I want to see about my invention and it is all for you and de *bébés*."

"Oh stop calling them *bébés*. We have six children. Four of them are in school, and it won't be long before Venice starts. There is only one *bébé* and that is Delima Rose. Besides, do what you want! I don't think you'd stay home if I were dying!"

"You do not look like you are dying," he said, pinching her bottom with a smile on his face. "Yes, you are getting round, so you are not starving, eh?"

"Go! Go! I don't care if you never come back."

"Dat is what I t'ink you t'ink. I leave tomorrow."

Oh God, isn't he ever going to change? What is it that keeps me bound to this man? Sometimes I hate him. Sometimes I wish I had the gumption to walk out. Wouldn't you think he'd appreciate me for trying? Trying to do the very best I can.

A MATTER OF COMPULSION

I won't think about it. I can't. I'll move the sewing machine into the kitchen, under the window. That way I can keep an eye on my bread and forget about my precious Armand and his high-falutin' ideas!

Saturday afternoon M. Demarne and Clara came. He unwrapped the parcel. Flory felt the quality of the serge.

"Your Clara is about the same size as my Juliette. I'll get her dress and you slip it on, Clara. Now isn't that just what I thought. I'll make it with a wide hem so it can be lengthened if need be. I'll start on it in the morning."

"When will I call for it, Mrs. Pilon?"

"Saturday will be fine, M. Demarne."

She watched as they got into the buggy. *What a nice man he is, buying material for his daughter and being interested in her frock. I wonder where he lives. I'll start on it first thing Monday morning. I wonder what his wife is like. She can't be able to sew. I'll make it with deep pleats falling from a yoke. I should have made a cup of tea for them.*

The jumper was made just the way she planned. After pressing it she had to admit that it was smart, but plain for a young girl. She decided to embroider a small red rose on the yoke. *I'll put it on the left. Yes, and three small green leaves. I wonder why he didn't bring his wife along?*

* * *

"Come and see, Juliette. I found something really funny in Maman's trunk."

"Venice! You went in Maman's trunk? We're not allowed. She'll give you 'what for.'"

"I just opened the lid and peeked. If you don't want to see . . ."

"What is it?"

"Well it looks like a red rubber duck with a long black neck. I squeezed it and air came out of the neck."

"A red rubber duck? Show me. Maman's at the machine so she won't hear us."

"It's under her black velvet blouse. See! I wasn't lying. Squeeze it yourself."

"I wonder what it is. Oh Venice, it isn't a duck." The sewing machine stopped. They quickly covered it with the black velvet blouse, then closing the lid they quietly tiptoed out of the room.

"We won't tell anyone. We'll keep it a secret."

"Funny, isn't it? If it belonged to Papa it wouldn't be in Maman's trunk."

"No. It's pretty though, the colours and all. Maybe she brought it from England. Maybe it's an antique bag to hold air to get the fire started. She did tell us she worked in an antique shop in England."

"Don't ask, Venice. Maybe it's none of our business."

"If I did ask, she'd know I was in her trunk."

"Venice, I know how we can find out. We'll look all through the catalogue until we come to it. Maman orders everything from the catalogue, doesn't she?"

"Here it is. Look! The same thing. It says *Red rubber balloon spray, black hard rubber pipe, tight-fitting shield, capacity one half pint.*"

"This one says water bottle and syringe. It pays to buy good rubber goods."

"This one's flat. This is all doctor stuff. Look here! It says bedpan and douche pan. It's for when Maman gets sick, like when Baby was born. Yes, that's what it's for."

"Well now we know. Don't ever go in Maman's trunk again. But why did you stop halfway down? I wonder what she keeps on the bottom."

* * *

Nap arrived with more blue serge and asked Flory if she would make Clara another dress.

"Yes, I thought she should have two. As you noticed, I made a wide hem so next year it can be let down."

The fragrance of homemade bread drifted through the house. When Flory saw him glance at the eight golden loaves on the table, she smiled and asked, "Would you like a cup of tea?"

"Thank you, yes, if I can have a slice of your bread."

Nap knew that Armand sometimes drank and had to be carried home. He thought how difficult it must be for Flory and her six children. In a small town, the less you say, the more they tell you. He decided he would never mention what he knew to Flory.

Flory thought Nap an attractive man. She wondered what he did for a living.

"Robert's store was well stocked. It must have been one big fire."

"Oh, it was terrible! We thought our own place would go up in flames. The heat was unbearable. Armand said if there had been a wind, we could very well be

A MATTER OF COMPULSION

without a home today. Do you know my husband Armand?"

"I have met him."

"You do know he worked for M. Robert? Now he is out of work, of course. He decided to go to Brownsburg, Québec to visit his family."

"How do you like living in the village?"

"I like it. The farmhouse was much too small with only two bedrooms, so we rented the farm out and bought this."

"You have a good farm there, so close to the church, the school, and the stores."

"Yes, and it wasn't too big. It was just right for us to make a good living, but you see Armand is no farmer. He was in his glory when M. Robert offered him a job. He wanted to buy this house and when I told him I liked it, oh he was happy. After he rented the farm out for three years, he thought he would enjoy working in Edmonton, but it didn't work out."

"I heard that he didn't like it."

"Oh, I despised it far more than he did. I couldn't wait to get back to the farm. I truly think he's aching to work on his invention."

Flory wondered just how much Nap knew about the snowmobile and Armand's drinking. How she had laughed when Beatrice told her that in a small town everyone knew the ins and outs of Mac's backside. It was no laughing matter. She knew that now.

* * *

"Can you tell me what your father's doing? Not one word from him."

"Well, if he has a big family Maman, he might be visiting them."

"Visiting? There are six mouths to feed and he hasn't sent one penny home. Visiting, you say? I can see him strutting around like he's lord of the manor, and his mother, dear Grandmaman, looking at him through adoring eyes."

"Why does Papa get drunk? If he likes it, why does he look so sad the next day?"

"God only knows, Juliette. Your mother will go crazy if he doesn't stop."

"Listen! Do you hear noises?"

They ran to the window and saw a horse-drawn caravan. It had stopped just past the house on the main street. Children were running in all directions, each one carrying a box.

NAPOLEON DEMARNE

"What in heaven's name are they running away from?"

Leonard ran in. "Look ma! A man gave it to me. He gave it to me for nothing. All the kids got one."

"Give it to your mother, Leonard. It says *Corn Flakes Breakfast Cereal*. Whoever would be giving food away? If you got one, why shouldn't Romeo have one? You go back dear."

She slapped water on Leonard's head and combed his hair straight. It looked three shades darker. She removed his shirt, telling him to put his sweater on.

Romeo came running in with a box of *Corn Flakes*. "Why does Leonard get two?"

"Just comb your hair, change your shirt, and put some shoes on. Then you'll each have two. Run dear. You'll catch up."

* * *

"It's you, Nap. I just this minute finished it." She held up Clara's dress with pride, and a craving for praise. "I embroidered a vine of forget-me-nots on this one just to make it look different. Do you like it?"

"I like it. I like it very much. I like your bread, and most of all I like you. There's a nice surprise for you in the buggy. I'll get it."

He walked in with a can filled to the brim with thick, rich cream.

"Oh, Nap. I will repay you with sewing or anything you need doing. I'll wrap two loaves of bread. I know it isn't a proper payment for all that cream. Nap, is your wife not well? Forgive me for asking."

"I lost my wife. I have five children, Earl, Marvin, Louis, Leo, and Clara. Earl and Marvin are on their own. Clara comes home on weekends and Leo and Louis go to school in Diligence, where my farm is. I've been wanting to ask if you could come on Saturdays to do a few small chores like baking bread. I would pick you up early and drive you home in the afternoon."

"I don't have to think about it. I'll come. Yes, you can pick me up early Saturday morning."

That night there was a lot on Flory's mind. *Did I do the right thing? What would Armand think, and heaven forbid that Emilie Robert should ever learn of it! I'll be going on Saturday. I'll take Venice and Baby with me. Cecile is old enough to take care of things until I get back. They all know their father hasn't sent one red cent*

A MATTER OF COMPULSION

home, not even a short letter.

* * *

Look at all that lovely cream! A whole can of pure goodness. First I'll make butter, then I'll make a big molasses cake and pour cream on each piece. Why should I worry? I do wish I had more sewing to do. I can't neglect the children. They're always needing something. There's no thanks knitting stockings for the boys. They only last for a while. I just turn around, it seems, when I have to knit new heels in them.

She heard a noise on the porch. When she opened the door Nap was there, holding a box.

"I brought you two fat chickens. Do you mind?"

"Come in, Nap. Set them on the table."

As natural as breathing, they walked toward one another. He leaned forward to kiss her. She did the same. Her face turned the colour of her rose blouse. Quickly she said, "I made jars of black currant jam. Do you know that in England you could only buy it at the chemist shop? Yes, it has so much iron and goodness that it was considered a medicine. Why are you looking at me like that?"

"I can't help it. I'm upset over this whole thing, and you know it."

"I want you to open the cellar door, Nap. Now please go down and bring up two of the large jars. See, you can tell by the dark colour of them. She quickly put two loaves of bread in a sugar bag.

"Flory, what are you doing? I can't take your food. Please!"

"No, right is right. You paid me for making Clara's dresses. You brought me all that cream and now chickens. Tell me Nap, did you have to come to the village today?"

"Yes I did, and I'm in a hurry."

He leaned forward quickly, brushed his lips against hers and said, "Until Saturday."

* * *

Oh Armand, you are a thoughtless man. Don't you remember the beautiful times we shared when you said I was the only woman for you? You couldn't live without me, you said. Didn't you love me? Didn't I love you? Didn't you keep whispering over and over not to make a sound, to be very still so as not to disturb the birds? We were so quiet and so close and I became pregnant. And when we lost dear Elizabeth didn't you hold me close and we were quiet again? I loved you Armand. I loved you enough to last a lifetime. I am a fool. They are two different men. So very different. Armand has to feed his soul, hit his forehead with the palm of his hand, pound his chest with his fist. And the most heartbreaking thing of all is his drinking. Really, the way he tries to walk cocky and straight, running his hand up his fly to see if everything's in order. What a dreamer!

* * *

"Maman, you should see Yvonette's brand new hat. It's black velvet and the brim is lined with pink shirred silk. I looked at it real good. Mme. Dutel made it for her. Oh Maman, it's the prettiest hat I ever saw. I'll bet it's the prettiest hat in the world! She said it was for going special places like church. Her mother said she could wear it today because it's windy. She must want us to have a good look at it, the way she keeps looking over here. So we have seen it. Oh Maman, I looked at it real good and I know exactly how it's made. I felt it, and she let me try it on."

"Well Juliette, I'll make both you and Venice one exactly the same. You bet I will."

"Where will you get the material?"

"Well dear, your mother happens to have a lovely black velvet blouse in her trunk. It's very good quality. I brought it from England. After it's steamed it will look like new, and it's not that expensive to buy a half yard of pink silk at Anna Seigner's."

"Will Mme. Robert be mad?"

"No madder than she was when Yvonette brought me the strawberries."

* * *

Father Giroux was very handsome in his long black robe. He hadn't been around to the house for some time. Flory knew he would start the conversation exactly as he had when they first moved in. First with the weather, then how the children were, and finally, M. Pilon. He did just that, and then got to the main subject: the church dues.

A MATTER OF COMPULSION

"Father Giroux, my husband isn't home. He went east to see his family. I am very sorry but I cannot afford to give you money."

"M. Pilon hasn't been to confession, has he? And you have not been for a very long time, Mme. Pilon."

"No, but all my children go Father."

He reached out and lay his hand on hers.

"Mrs. Pilon, a good Catholic family must all go to church. You must try to do better. How long will M. Pilon be gone?"

"Oh, I don't think he'll be home for another good month."

"That's a long time," he said, squeezing her hand. He stood pondering for a moment, then walked to the door. He turned back and again patted her hand.

"If you get lonesome while M. Pilon is away, you can always come to me."

She stood at the oval window to watch him cross the street. She pictured him in his fine silk robe embossed with gold, like a sunburst covering his back. He stood in the pulpit cursing all women who wore low-cut dresses. *Wasn't that strange? I can't picture myself going to the rectory for a visit. No, I know better than that. He's a man, just like the rest of them.*

* * *

Louis, Clara, and Leo were playing in the yard when they saw the horse and buggy coming through the gate. They stood wide-eyed while their father helped Flory out.

"This is Mrs. Pilon, and this is Venice and Baby. These are my sons, Louis and Leo. You have met Clara."

Flory smiled. She couldn't think of anything to say that would sound right. She walked toward the house with her two young ones, Napoleon leading the way with his three not far behind. Her heart was pounding. She felt like an intruder, and all for a batch of homemade bread? *I'm not fooling myself. I'm starved for attention, for someone to love me purely for who I am.*

"I could teach you how to make bread. Do you know who taught me? Mr. Massey. He showed me how to make my own starter. I keep it in a crock. I just have to beat in a little sugar and flour. It makes it bubbly and active. When I finish setting the bread, is there anything special you'd like done?"

Giving her chores was the last thing he'd ever do. He could tell by her fast talk

NAPOLEON DEMARNE

that she was nervous.

"You have a sewing machine, Nap. I'll see if anything needs repairing. Now I want the five of you to go out and play. Tonight you'll have nice fresh bread, and I'll make a cake for you. Would you like that, Nap?"

"Yes, and I will go and finish my chores."

Someone had done a washing. She started to fold the sheets and noticed how worn they were. She cut them down the centre and sewed the outer edges together, laying one over the other to make a double seam.

"What are you doing, Flory?"

"I'm doing what I have to do when my sheets get thin. I tear them down the centre. See? Then I sew the edges of the sheet together and hem the worn parts, which will only be tucked under the mattress. That way you get twice the wear out of a sheet." She looked up. "Isn't it a smart thing to do?"

There was a moment of soul searching. "Ah, you are a thrifty woman, Flory." He cupped her face. She willingly kissed him. "Flory, when you are through sewing I'll drive you home."

It was a glorious day. Never had she felt so proud, so praised, and so needed. *I can't believe it. It was all so easy. I made eight loaves of bread, a cake, patched three sheets, and cleaned two cupboards, and I'm not one bit tired!*

* * *

"I can see by your face Flory, dat you do not expect to see me."

"To tell you the truth Armand, I don't care one way or the other."

"I am here wit you. Ah Flory, give me dat smile you have save for me."

"You never sent me one penny for food, not even a note did you send."

"You sew. I know you are good at dat. You have brain. You know what to do."

"I know what to do? No, but I'm learning. There were days when I had no sewing. If it hadn't been for that one hundred-pound bag of flour and my own preserves, goodness knows what I'd have done. Not once have I charged anything at the store. I wouldn't have had the nerve to ask for credit. Now I go to Napoleon Demarne every Saturday. I make bread, patch things. Anything that needs doing, I do."

"You have a good brain to do dat. You see I did not have money myself. Ah my Flory, I knew dat you would find a way." He paused. "I see Robert is building a new store. He waste no time."

A MATTER OF COMPULSION

"Do you think he will hire you again?"

"I do not depend on dat. I was t'inking I will start my snowmobile. It is time. I want it ready for de winter. I go to Edmonton an' get what I need. An' Flory, I will use your parlour to do some of de work."

"Is your mother going to send you money? Oh, I don't know why I haven't the gumption to write to her. You are a rotter!"

"Since I go away you learn some fancy word. Very fancy. Do you want me to build my snowmobile, or not to build it? Do you want me to be a farmer? Yes, I feel you do. Well, I say no! I cannot work in pig shit no more. Maybe you like me to wear a tie on my neck dat choke me. No! If I put a tie on my neck put a bell on it. Den you can keep track of me. I have to breathe. I have to be free. Do you understand? Ah, what you know about it? You cannot answer dat. You know I miss you, Flory. Tonight I be wit you."

Wasn't I a fool to think he might not like it if I went to Nap's place. He doesn't care. Never is he interested in anything I do. Yet he expects me to make a big fuss over his invention. Yes, and keep my mouth shut when he comes home drunk. There are only three important things in his life. His inventions, his liquor, and me for his pleasure. Oh, it's my pleasure too. If only I could be strong. Maybe tonight I will be.

THE SNOWMOBILE

"Maman, look at all the apple peelings. Mme. Champs threw them out. I went back and filled my pinafore. Aren't they long and red? There wasn't one mark on any of them. They threw them out, Maman. I didn't steal them, did I? Aren't you happy? I'm going to pump some water on them. Why don't you answer me, Maman?"

"Do not ever do that again! I have some pride left."

"Nobody saw me. The Roberts are all at the store. Mme. Champs threw them out. I looked up. There was nobody in the window. They're like new. It would be sad to leave them there."

"Yes dear."

Mme. Champs is Mme. Robert's mother. She does the cooking. The hired girl is Annie Muse. She is the maid. She does the washing and ironing. She keeps the place spotless. M. Robert is rebuilding his store. They have everything they want to eat, and now Yvonette is having a real playhouse built. They're working on it now. But my Juliette has to pick up the apple peelings they throw out!

"Look! There goes Mme. Champs holding her skirts up, filled with more fresh fruit."

She could so easily have gone out the back door of the store and straight across to her kitchen door, but no, she has to come out the front door, the long way around, hoping we see her. The show off!

"Juliette, last month you and Cecile came home with mildewed oranges from the crates at the back of their store. I suppose they didn't see you then? If your father didn't spend money on bits and parts for his so-called inventions and the cursed drink, maybe you children could have an apple or an orange once in a while."

"But Maman, those oranges were good when we cut the little bit of mildew off. We put them on the oven door to warm, remember? Weren't they juicy and sweet? You said so yourself."

"Do not, either one of you, ever do it again!"

* * *

"Leonard, what are you scratching your head for?"
"I keep scratching, but the itch won't go away."

A MATTER OF COMPULSION

"Let mother have a look. Good God! You have bugs in your hair! Romeo, are you scratching?"

"Yeah, I sure am."

"Let me see. You're both loaded with lice. Get the Edmonton Journal."

"Why? Are you going to see if our names are in the paper?"

"Open it and put it on the floor. I'm going to soak your heads with coal oil and fine-comb the lice onto the paper. Kneel close to the paper. Then I'll wash your heads with Fels Naptha. And girls, you are next. The school must be infested with lice."

They hated the coal oil and worried that even the nuns at the front of the class could smell it.

"Leonard, go to Dr. Jeunais. Ask him if he has anything for lice."

Leonard came home with a bottle of larkspur.

"The doctor said most of the people use it and he said it doesn't smell bad."

Each day the moment the children stepped in from school the Edmonton Journal was put on the floor. It was a never-ending job, and after one week of it Flory decided she should have a talk with Sister Superior.

"I'm sorry to have to tell you, Sister Superior, but the school children must be infested with lice. I have been treating my children first with coal oil and now with larkspur, and truly, Sister Superior, it is a hopeless job. If you could tell the class that unless all of them are treated with coal oil or larkspur and their heads are fine-combed, it will be hopeless. My husband, M. Pilon, said that lice jump from one head to another. He said it was the only entertainment they had."

Sister Superior had a large grin on her face as she nodded in agreement.

* * *

"Today I buy two pure breed dog. Ah, dey are beautiful. One have gold hair like you have. I will call de bitch Queenie and de fadder is black so I will call him Blackie, like me. Animal can get to look like dere owner and sometime de owner get to look like de animal. So we take no chance, eh Flory?" he said as he pinched her bottom.

"I have nothing to say to you. I don't want to see them. Tomorrow is Saturday. I'll be going to M. Demarne. Enjoy their company, Armand!"

THE SNOWMOBILE

* * *

When Flory walked into Nap's house she could see that someone had washed the kitchen floor. She thought it could only be Leo. He was Nap's best boy and he was her favourite. It was one chore less to do, so while the bread was rising, she washed her hair. There was no time to do it on Friday, and Sunday after mass Mme. Maillot would be coming for a skirt fitting.

One thought after another rushed through Flory's mind, each ending with her first one, Armand and his two thoroughbred dogs.

One day I'll do something of my very own. I will! she thought as she steadily combed each strand of hair, laying it aside and moving on to the next strand. Soon it lay on her shoulders, looking like a sunburst of gold. It was a big chore, yet it always made her feel happy, calm, and serene. It was a special time for her innermost thoughts to be dreamed.

"Oh, you did give me a start!"

"What do you mean I gave you a start?"

"You frightened me!"

"Flory, I've never seen your hair combed down."

"Of course you haven't. It's down because I washed it."

"How long is it?"

"I don't know how long it is, but I can tell you I often feel like having it cut."

"Let me measure it. May I?"

Flory didn't half mind, in fact she almost felt young again. *Why am I doing this? Is it because Armand never sent a penny home or wrote a line, then when he came home he was able to buy thoroughbred dogs and go to Edmonton for the darned snowmobile parts? He doesn't worry about me or the children. If it wasn't for me taking in sewing and meeting Nap, well I don't know what would happen. Why Nap even set out a dozen fresh eggs for me.*

She stood tall while Napoleon measured her hair. "It won't be as long as it was last week. I always trim a little off the bottom."

"Your hair is so thick it covers your whole body and it's forty-eight inches long!" With both hands he gently parted her hair, then holding it firmly back he looked hard into her eyes. "You keep your marriage together on Armand's dreams and promises, don't you?"

A sudden calmness came over her. "No, Napoleon, I was let down too many

A MATTER OF COMPULSION

times with his dreams and promises. Yet I do believe he is worth saving. I just don't know how. I truly don't, Nap. You do know that Armand drinks? Everyone in the village knows. I've managed to live through all the heartbreak, but there are times when I could easily go, leave him forever, never to come back. Then in a day or two I mellow and wonder how I could have thought such a thing. I keep saying it time and time again: 'Next time. If he ever does it again I'll leave him next time.'"

"Here, Flory. Sit down. Braid your golden hair. It's starting to curl."

* * *

The parlour was Armand's workshop. Metal, wood, saw horses, bits and pieces, and his precious propeller were scattered about. The propeller had once belonged to Wop May, who became famous as one of the first bush pilots in northern Canada. It was a good propeller, all but for one very narrow strip which had been slashed off on one of the sides. Many times Armand had thought of putting a clock in the centre and hanging it on the wall, but Flory didn't much care for the idea. He was glad he hadn't done it. It deserved a rightful place once more, and no better place than on the Pilon Snowmobile. *Yes,* he thought. *I am excited about it, and I have not seen my friend for awhile. Dey have great interest in my snowmobile.*

* * *

"Pilon, *mon ami*, you are back. We hear you went to Québec."

"Yes I go to visit my family, also to do some business. Now Remi, I have decide it is time to finish my snowmobile."

"Ah Salut! Good luck to you. Tell me Armand, does Madame Pilon believe in your snowmobile?"

"She pretend she do not. She always try to change de way I am, but Pilon is Pilon an' you cannot change dat. Beauchamps, he will work wit me. De body of de snowmobile will be made of metal just like an automobile. I cannot cut dat in Flory's parlour."

"Hey Paul, Pilon is going to put his invention on the road this winter. What do you think about that?"

"We heard about your invention for a long time. Now we will see it. Have you got a date set?"

THE SNOWMOBILE

"Yes, you will see it. Dat is a promise. I never take back my promise, and also it go fast. When I have finish my udder invention you will also see dem, because all of you will have dem in your house."

"Bring more *bière* here!"

"What are you inventing now, Armand?"

"Not so fast. One at a time. Dis one is not so big, but it take bigger equipment to make it. I don't tell not'ing to nobody. It have to work before I talk."

Armand was the centre of attention. He needed that. He had been telling them for a long time that it wouldn't be long before he'd have the snowmobile finished.

"Yes *mes amis*, dere is much more in life den farming, or a *bière* parlour to drink in. And now I will tell you about my pure breed dogs dat I buy. De bitch I call Queenie. Ah, she is beautiful. She have gold hair and is streamline like my snowmobile. De udder one is a male. He is black like coal. I name him Blackie. Dey will ride wit me in my snowmobile."

* * *

"I have a feeling your father is at the hotel."

"He could be working at Joe Beauchamp's place."

"No, Romeo. He would have come home for some dinner. Be good boys. Go to Beauchamp's. If he isn't there, go to the hotel."

"We'll go to Joe Beauchamp's but we won't go to the hotel. We're sick of it. Everybody turns around to look at us. Did you have to go to the hotel when you were our age?"

"Leonard, that will be the last of it. How dare you talk to your mother like that!"

"Come on, Romeo. Let's go."

Romeo told his brother, "Len, if he isn't at Joe Beauchamp's we'll walk toward the hotel and wait a while. We won't go in."

Joe Beauchamp's workshop was on the Robert side of the street. Papa wasn't there. The hotel also was on the Robert side of the street. They walked slowly, cursing Papa to one another, calling him all the unsavory names and words they could think of, one trying to top the other. When one of them saw Papa crossing to the Pilon side of the street, they quickly turned, running home to warn Maman.

"Papa's on his way home. Please don't talk to him, Maman. Can't you hide?"

"I will not play hide and seek. That's just what your father would like. No. I live

A MATTER OF COMPULSION

here. This is my home! Is he drunk?"

"Well he's shifting from one side of the sidewalk to the other and there ain't no music. He was checking his fly last time we looked. Yeah, he's drunk."

Armand walked into the house. Flory started, "Armand, I'm going to leave you! I'm sick and tired of it all. I'm also going to write your mother. She should know what's going on here. Oh, how blind she is, sending you twelve dollars every month and giving you extra money for your so-called snowmobile. Aren't you ashamed of yourself?"

"English bull dog! Imperial sonofabitch. All you do is complain. You're no goddamn good!"

He hit her chest. She fell to the floor and didn't move.

All the children feared Papa when he was drunk. Even the boys weren't that brave. Baby and Venice would run upstairs and hide under the bed or in a closet. One of the older girls would run outside to peek in the window, and the other would run upstairs to peek over the banister. It was like looking down into an arena to watch the cock fight.

This time it was different. Papa had struck Maman and she had fallen to the floor. Juliette ran outside and saw M. Robert coming down the sidewalk.

"Please, please M. Robert! Come quick! Papa just killed Maman!"

His arms hung limply, his feet glued to the sidewalk.

"Please come, M. Robert!" She ran and he followed.

Maman was sitting, Cecile close beside her. They were pale, and not a sound was heard. Maman was wet, the floor was wet, and Papa wasn't there. He must have gone to bed. It was Cecile who revived Maman by throwing water over her. M. Robert put his arm around Juliette and told her that Maman had fainted. All Flory said was, "I'm all right, M. Robert. Thank you for coming."

* * *

"I've got to do something about your father."

"Well why don't you marry Napoleon Demarne?"

"Leonard, what are you talking about? I'll have you know that M. Demarne has been very kind to all you children."

"Oh it's nothing, Maman. I guess you kissed him because he was good, and Papa wasn't here."

THE SNOWMOBILE

"I probably did. I also kissed Mme. Morin every time she delivered one of you."

* * *

"You've known that I love you for a long time, haven't you Flory?"

"I felt that you did, and I meant it when I said I very often want to run away from it all. Not my children. God knows how I love them. Nap, do you realize I have six children and you have five. Have you thought about that? Have you thought of what it could be like if yours and mine fought like cats and dogs? My boys fight. I mean fight to prove who is the strongest. Of course the winner is always right and the loser is never wrong, and so they fight again."

"Yes, Flory. I have thought about it a thousand and one times until I came to one conclusion. The older ones could go to the convent. The younger ones would go to school here. Then when Baby becomes of age, only if you agree, she could go to the convent with her sister Venice."

Suddenly each child, each face, flashed before her. How wonderful Armand was when he didn't drink. How he could penetrate the very core of her soul when he played the violin. How she waited until the evening meal was over when she could finally sit. How Baby climbed up on her lap, then Venice and Juliette would sit at her feet, one on each side, hugging her thighs. She thought of Cecile, her eldest girl, who had done so many loving chores when she was only six years old. Only today she had washed the kitchen floor. Romeo, always watching, looking at people, sizing them up as though he alone was the tailor. He could tell you what Mme. Rochon wore at last year's midnight mass. Leonard, her eldest, a strapping boy, growing into manhood, with a mop of golden curls, and freckles on his nose. *He deserves store-bought knickers at his age. He's too big for the nuns to handle, or the priest. The last time the priest visited the school, he remarked on how quickly the boys were growing. "Some of you," he said, "are hard on our nuns, especially Leonard Pilon, le poulain." Now his friends call him Pilon le poulain. No, I enjoyed carrying my babies. I couldn't wait to see each tiny frowning face, to cuddle them close, to put my ripe, full breast to their searching mouths. Put them in a convent? God forbid, not while they have a mother.*

She wondered how Napoleon felt after suggesting it, how hurt he must be at her silence. She looked up and smiled.

"I don't expect a quick answer, Flory. Surely it will be the hardest decision you ever have to make."

"What a lovely, thoughtful man you are." She thought that if Napoleon and Armand, with all the good in both of them, were mingled together, she'd have one perfect man.

*   *   *

That night the pillow didn't fit Flory's head. *Yes, I will,* and *No, I can't,* rushed through her brain. There were no two days alike since the first day she had met Armand, so who was to say he couldn't change tomorrow?

I wonder what he would do if he suddenly found himself with no children, no house that was alive, and me gone. What would Maman and Papa Pilon think? What would his sisters and only brother think? Would I miss him and regret it for the rest of my life, feeling guilty at the same time because I had no cure for it all? I wonder if it's me. What if Napoleon Demarne was dull, so dull I had no tomorrows to dream of. So dull I dreaded the sunrise and never waited for the sunset.

ARMAND'S INVENTIONS

"It is a hot day for dis time of de year. I never see it dis hot. If it keep up, by de time winter come, summer will be here for a long time."

The children walked in, complaining of the heat. "It's just as hot in the shade, Maman."

"All sit down. Don't go outside. You'll be cooler in the house."

"Gee cripe, I do something to make dem feel a little cooler. I will go to Robert and get some vinegar. You, Flory, pump de water until it come cold."

* * *

"What are you doing now, Armand?"

"I make a drink. I pour vinegar in de glass, add cold water, now a little sugar an' soda. You stir it like hell until it fizz. Taste some, Flory."

"No, I don't care for any. Give it to the children."

"Come on kid, Papa have a cool drink for you. Now you taste dat. It will make you feel cool, Papa know."

They took tiny sips, unable to decide whether they liked it or not.

"Drink it an' when you have finish, sit down an' relax."

After a while they walked in, one after the other, complaining of stomach cramps and wanting to throw up.

"You all complain. It is not dat hot."

"Armand, how white they are. They're lying limp on the floor, pulling their knees up and moaning."

Armand could only think of one thing. He ran to Robert's store.

"Robert, where is your vinegar?"

"It's downstairs. Why?"

"My kid are poison." Armand ran downstairs as fast as he could go.

"Here, Pilon, in these pails."

"T'row it out right away. Right now, Robert! Did you sell some to udder people?"

"No, you're the first one who bought vinegar."

"Well get off your ass. My kid are dying. Get all de milk, cream, anyt'ing you can get!"

A MATTER OF COMPULSION

After the pails were dumped, Robert ran to Armand's. When he saw the sight of the Pilon kids frothing at the mouth, he went white.

"Robert, move! Get all de milk you can find. I have use what I have. I go too."

Flory was crying and praying out loud. "Dear God, don't let them die. They're all I've got, Lord. If I lose them, I have nothing. Dear Jesus, can you hear me?"

Armand ran in with more milk. "Raise dere head. When you give dem milk, give dem very little and do not stop. That way dey will not choke."

The children lay like the dead. Finally, one by one, they started to vomit.

"Do not worry about de vomit. If we can get dat out of dere system dey may live."

"The vomit is foam, white foam, Armand."

"Good! It is taking de poison out of dere belly."

* * *

"Now they are safe, tell me how it happened?"

"Yes I will tell you. Dat Robert, he sell his vinegar barrel yesterday. He put de vinegar in galvanize pail. It eat t'rough and remove de galvanize metal from de pail. I know it is not de soda, or de sugar, or de water. Non, I t'ink it have to be de vinegar."

"Thank heavens Venice and Baby were upstairs, and not once did they complain about the heat." Flory had suggested they play with the big pram, taking turns at playing mother.

"Yes, we have one hell of a day when we can lose four of our kid. Robert, he must have worry. Yes, he don't know too much about galvanize pail. He could have poison many people."

"The children have no go in them. They're pale and lifeless. Do you think they'll get strong? Why, they can barely keep their heads up."

"Let dem sleep. We will keep our eye on dem. What dey will need is a good tin soup. I make some."

"Can't you say 'thin soup'? You say 'tin glass,' 'tin bread,' 'tin woman.'"

"Ah Flory, you use to be tin, now you are not, but I like you de way you are. Yes, we are lucky. Robert, he sure haul milk, eh?"

"He tried so hard, didn't he Armand?"

"Come. We are tired. Take down your braid and we be close."

ARMAND'S INVENTIONS

* * *

The boys came home to tell Maman that they had been far back in the woods and under the tangled brush they had found a still.

"How do you know what a still is?"

"We know what a still is, but we don't know who it belongs to."

"Promise me boys, that you won't tell your father. It could give him ideas. That is, if it doesn't belong to him."

Flory's thinking was quick. *I'm beginning to see the light at the end of the tunnel. Maybe that's where he got the money for his dogs. Maybe he trades moonshine for horse meat. Maybe he makes all his deals sitting at Fortesque's Hotel. How blind I've been. I won't say a word, and I won't lose my temper.*

When Armand side-stepped throught the door, she lost control. Her heart beat like a drum.

"You're not only drinking beer, you're drinking alcohol! That's what moonshine is, isn't it Armand? From now on you will sleep upstairs. Oh, not once in a while, but from now on!"

"I do not give a goddamn where I sleep. Tell me one person who want to sleep wit de Queen of England! No, you and your fancy idea do not bodder me."

"Can't you stop drinking, Armand?"

"Drinking, Flory?" he said, while running his hand up his fly. "You take care of de kid and I take care of de problem, an' never forget," he said, as he pounded his chest three times, "I am Pilon today, Pilon tomorrow, and Pilon forever!"

"Armand, you always say you want to breathe, you want to be free, you want to invent. Then why are you always sitting on your backside at Fortesque's Hotel?"

"Forget about it. You tell me enough time."

* * *

"We are going to have some corn on de cob. I see you have some boullion and some cook potato. I will boil de corn in de boullion, den I will take de bouillion and make potato soup wit a lot of onion and a little *crème* dat you bring from Napoleon Demarne. It should be good wit a corn flavour. You like dat?"

There he goes with his magic remedy. He's being so good again, sending Venice for

A MATTER OF COMPULSION

fine-cut tobacco to pack in his pipe. Yes, and yesterday looking at me in his innocent way, asking me to have compassion. How can we be cross with one another all the time? There he is with his shirt sleeves rolled up and his shirt buttons undone to bare his chest. When he puts a fork in the bridge of his violin, he says it has a different tone every time, even when he inserts it in exactly the same place. He is one complicated man. I can't for the life of me understand what pleasure he gets at the hotel, when he could be home doing things with me. Not even a small garden was put in on all that beautiful land. He has got to be the laziest man in the village.

* * *

The coal oil lamps were lit early now. The snow almost covered the length of the veranda. Flory was annoyed that Armand and the boys hadn't dug a new hole for the privy. *It was the same last winter on the farm. A great mass of human dung protruding from the hole, frozen solid until we had to raise ourselves by standing on the seat. How the muscles in my legs shook. Oh, wasn't it cold!*

Armand ran in. "Gee cripe dere was a hell of a fire at de nun's home. De candle caught fire on de lace in de chapelle. Everybody holler, '*Feu! Feu!*'"

"How did you happen to see it?"

"I am talking to Robert outside when I hear it. I go. I run inside. Cripe, it is a fire. You should see all de fancy t'ing burning an' dey fall to de floor to start anudder fire, eh? I run in an' I say, 'Dis is no time to pray.' Yes, Flory, dey were kneeling to pray. I say, 'Get your bucket and go to de well.' Den I ask one nun where all de piss pot was. She look at me like I am crazy. She say dere is one in every bedroom. I say, 'You get one, I get two.' I trow de piss on de chapelle, de curtain, anywhere. De nun do not care now, and she bring in de last pot. Wit dat and de water it is not long when everyt'ing is under control. You see, it was de salt in de piss dat do de job."

"You mean to say they have ordinary pots like we have?"

"No, Flory, dey have commode wit a handle and a lid, but de quality of de pee pee is de same."

The next morning at school Sister Carreveau leaned close to Juliette and whispered, "*Ton père est vite comme un poisson.*" Juliette only smiled.

* * *

ARMAND'S INVENTIONS

"Maman, at school today Sister Carreveau said that Papa was as quick as a fish. Why would she say that?"

"There was a bad fire in the chapel at the nunnery last night. Your father was fast. He put it out. It could have destroyed the whole building. He does have a good head on his shoulders. Too bad he doesn't use it more often."

* * *

Flory was sure the dogs were warm enough in the barn and that the boys hadn't forgotten to feed them. Armand had gone to Edmonton to pick up what sounded like an important part for the snowmobile. He was excited about it and told Flory he would be home early. That night Flory and the children sat around the big kitchen stove with the oven door left open for comfort.

"Maman, can we sing your songs?"

"Yes, dear. Which one would you like first?"

"*The Old Man and the Photograph.*" They all sang:

An old man gazed at a photograph in a locket he'd worn for years.
His nephew then asked him the reason why the locket had caused him tears.
'Come listen my friend and I'll tell you a story both sad and true.
Your father and I were at school one day, met two little girls in blue.
Two little girls in blue land, two little girls in blue.
They were sisters, we were brothers. We learned to love the two.
But one little girl in blue land, she stole your father's heart.
She became your mother, I married the other, and now we have drifted apart.

"Can we sing *I Don't Want to Play in Your Yard?*"

"Now I want you all to be quiet and listen. Your father's coming home. He's close to Rochon's corner right now. He's coming. He's coming."

"Where is he now, Maman?"

"Shhh. He's coming down toward Hunter's Bake Shop. He's coming. He's at Bart's store. He's coming to the Dukette garage. M. Dukette lets him out of his car. Now he's walking fast, passing Saigner's store. He's pretty close. He's coming. He should be stepping on the porch just about . . . "

There was complete silence, each one staring at the doorknob. It turned and Papa walked in.

"Oh Papa, Maman said you were on your way. You're home, Papa! She did! She

A MATTER OF COMPULSION

said you were coming home."

"Gee cripe, what is all de commotion? I tell Maman I come home. Is dere somet'ing wrong?"

Flory sat quietly with a little smile on her face. "Everything is fine, Armand. I only told the children when you would be home."

"How do you do that Maman? Can you always do it?"

"Not always, but when I do I'm never wrong. It comes to me so strongly. I can feel it through my whole body."

* * *

Word spread throughout the village. Pilon was going to have his snowmobile ready and on the road Friday after supper. Flory couldn't understand why he had chosen that time. It would be dark. *Maybe*, she thought, *if he fails, they won't see the disappointment on his face.*

The snowmobile had been at Joe Beauchamp's for some time now. Wop May's propeller would be attached and it would be all shined up and ready to go.

"It's Friday today, Armand. Are you taking the snowmobile out tonight? Why isn't it here?"

"I have not change my mind. I am going to pull it here to my house. Dat is where I start to build it an' dat is where I start from."

When Armand returned with the snowmobile, Flory asked if he was hungry.

"Look at my snowmobile, Flory. It look good. It have a good line, eh? No, I am not hungry."

"There are people out there, Armand!"

"What you expect? Dis is a big occasion. It is not everybody dat t'ink to build a snowmobile. Dey t'ink de world end because we have de airplane an' de automobile? It do not end. It will keep going."

"Do you feel all right? Are you nervous?"

"I feel good. Don't worry about me. I have two stiff drink of whisky. Yes, pure wit no water. Dat make you fly an' dat is what I am going to do."

"Fly? Is that why you put the propeller on? Oh, Armand, you are a strange man. You seem to have a love for that darned propeller. You even wanted to put a clock in its centre, remember?"

Flory looked out. The sidewalks were lined with people now. *Why shouldn't I*

ARMAND'S INVENTIONS

go out on my own porch if I choose to. I'm not that shy, am I? I know darned well the Roberts and the Benets are watching.

She could see people with their arms flying in different directions, their heads thrown back in wild laughter. *Dear Lord, don't let him be the laughing stock of the village.*

Armand put on his heavy coat, pulled on his muskrat hat, and tied his long blue scarf around his neck. "I go now. If you can manage to, wish me good luck."

"Oh I do, Armand! I do!"

When Armand pushed the snowmobile to the road and revved the motor until the vibrant echo filled their ears, the crowd cheered and hollered, "Good luck, Pilon!"

Away he flew, his muskrat hat pulled low over his ears, his scarf blowing at a straight angle. Flory spoke out loud. "Let it be right, Lord, so we can hold our heads up high." She stepped out as far as the sidewalk. He was still going strong, then over the hump in the road until he was out of sight. Everyone was running to catch up, thinking he would stop at the hotel. No, Armand decided to drive past the hotel and on to Rochon's corner. He would make a good round turn there and head back to the hotel.

When Armand arrived they were all there waiting, cheering and shouting his name. Beauchamp thought perhaps Armand couldn't shut the motor off and was on his way to Edmonton. Romeo and Leonard were proud. Their friends, the Regimbal and Chavalier boys, had come far from the country to see how fast the snowmobile would go. When it flew past the hotel, Leonard said, "It's the first time the old man forgot to stop there."

Now, Armand thought, *dey will know dat when Pilon say somet'ing he mean it. I do a big happy t'ing tonight.*

*   *   *

"Sit down, sit down, Pilon. The beer is on us. Now we understand what you talk about. We used to say Pilon has crazy ideas all the time. We did, eh Zanon? But your invention works and it travels fast."

"Yes it works, an' now I know what to do. You have to try it to find out an' tonight I learn dat my snowmobile can be more simple still. Yes, no fancy frill. I am happy tonight and I know dat Flory is also happy. She don't say much about my invention but I know Flory very well."

A MATTER OF COMPULSION

It was a special night. Everyone was asleep except for Flory. She stayed awake, hoping that Armand would drive the snowmobile home. It was one special night when she hungered to have her man close to her. So many thoughts rushed through her mind. *He drinks, he's lazy, he's cruel, and he's cocky. I keep forgiving him over and over again. I'm putty in his hands. I hate myself for it.* All the hurts whirled round and round in her mind, only to be defeated by an overwhelming surge of love that she could not control. She lay still and sobbed quietly. She thought of his honesty when he told her he had had two stiff drinks without water. *I liked that. I didn't half mind. I'll bet the hotel is doing good business tonight.*

* * *

Napoleon Demarne had a black horse named Pet. He kept her well groomed. Her coat was soft and shiny as satin. He had a black buggy with red and gold scrolls bordering the edges. A scalloped red flannel throw was folded and placed over the back seat where Flory sat. This time she had left Venice at home and taken Juliette. Napoleon had placed a blanket on the floor of the buggy where Juliette and Baby would sit. The only thing of interest the children could see were Pet's huge flanks with her tail swishing up once in a while to pass gas. They giggled down their coat collars. Then Juliette leaned over and whispered loudly, "Baby, you'll think I'm crazy, but I really like that smell, don't you?" She laughed so hard it made both of them stare at Pet's tail, hoping to see it go up again.

Baby had a mop of curly hair like Grandpapa Pilon's. She was tiny, shy, and looked like a sad doll. When she was little, her legs were bowed. Flory wondered if the child had rickets. As she grew her legs grew straight. Baby was M. Demarne's favourite. He never came to the house without bringing her candy drops or gum. Being very shy, she would only peek around the door, but the minute he was out the door she would ask, "Maman, when is Mr. Gum coming back?" Venice had been in school since September. Now Baby was the only one at home.

"Nap, you have no idea how many people turned out to see Armand's first ride in the snowmobile. Why, they were cheering until I couldn't believe it. Oh, I was happy when the cheering started and kept on going, Nap. He had worked on it for so long, but he did have high hopes. He was brave. I wasn't half proud of him."

Nap looked at Flory steadily, with very little expression on his face. She suddenly realized what she had done.

ARMAND'S INVENTIONS

"Don't be hurt. I feel you are the only person who ever understood me. Far, far more than..."

"Don't, Flory. Don't feel sorry. Don't apologize. I first knew when you said he was worth saving, and that you were going to tame his wild ways. I hope you succeed."

"But Napoleon, I saw the snowmobile in the making. I've seen it grow. I saw the drawings of the whole thing inside and out, the metal and chips in my parlour, sawdust on my front porch. And yes, he is a smart man. When the darned thing took off with everyone running after him, I was proud. Yes, I love him. Yes, I hate him. Yes, there are times I could run, run, and never come back. Then there are the other times, the peaceful times that come after the war. The other times... Oh, I never wanted to hurt you."

She walked toward him smiling, then looked into his eyes. Gently she cradled his head to her breast and slowly she lowered her lips to his. He didn't move from his chair. He was in a cloud of wonderment. This kiss, given so willingly, so tender and meaningful. Was it goodbye, or a promise for the future?

M. LECROIX

The old shoemaker, M. Lecroix, lived on the back road. It wasn't a road yet, but all the trees and brush had been slashed in a long strip from Hansom's Bake Shop down to the creek. In the meantime, Armand had to walk down a long path between Mme. Peltier's house, the music teacher's house, and the village tennis court, to get to his place.

"M. Lecroix, de shoe maker, is good company. He have a lot of brain and much story to tell. I ask him to come to our place to see my drawing."

"Not the snowmobile, Armand?"

"Non, non. My clothes pin. I was telling him how strong it will be. He say he would like to see it."

"Do as you like. I can always make a cup of tea."

* * *

"Ah M. Lecroix, come in. Come in. Flory, I like you to meet our shoemaker, M. Lecroix, de man dat fix our kid shoe."

The man quickly offered Flory a bread tin. It was filled with a deep chocolate-coloured dessert.

"Oh, you are kind. Look children, the gentleman has brought something sweet for us."

"Madame, it is a *mousse au chocolat*. I learn to make it when I live in Belgium. I will serve it if you have small dish."

* * *

"Ah, it was delicate, eh Flory?"

"It was all of that. The girls didn't look up until the last spoonful was gone. Isn't he a dear man. Imagine him doing a thoughtful thing like that. Did you hear what he called it, Armand? I wonder if he made it himself."

"He call it a mousse made wit chocolat. It was very smoot, like velvet. He say wit my new clothes pin I cannot lose, dat I should get a patent on it. He only see my drawing an' de wire I will use."

"You already know about patents. You still haven't done anything about the

A MATTER OF COMPULSION

snowmobile."

"It take money. I have spend many dollar on my snowmobile. We will wait a while."

The following week M. Lecroix came with another chocolate mousse, and again they talked about patents and inventions.

* * *

The weekends were a joy for the kids. They would scatter from one end of the village to the other. Betty Hansom, Ella Morris, Cecile, and Juliette would get together to decide where to go or what to do that was exciting.

"Let's walk down the new road. It goes right past Old Man Lecroix's place. He always has candies and stuff. Have you ever been to his place?"

"No, neither one of us," Juliette answered. "We were scared of him. We did walk down the path to the tennis court. That's where he grows his garden. We crouched down and ate some of his peas. Now he has visited us, so we know him. Everyone calls him Old Man Lecroix. He isn't that old. Papa calls him M. Lecroix."

M. Lecroix had the most cluttered and interesting place they had ever seen. There were iron feet on long iron stands, shelves that held nails, tacks, heavy spools of thread, odd soles, and odd-shaped leather of every description. Everything that could be hung trailed from long hooks. Anything else was on the workbench. In the midst of it all, and just under a small window, was a bulky bed. It was higher than any bed they had ever seen. It looked as if it had been stuffed with straw. A grey blanket had been firmly tucked in at the foot of the bed.

"So you have come to visit me. Sit down on my sofa. There is no room for chairs in my workshop."

He brought out a bowl of mixed candies and said, "Help yourselves." They couldn't believe it. Maman was right. He was a dear man. They certainly weren't used to having a bowl of candy passed from one to the other. It was all so extravagant.

On weekends Maman would give one of the girls five cents. "Go to Perra's barbershop for an ice cream cone. Don't touch it, and ask him to cover it well or the sun will melt it." She would take out four saucers. After dividing the ice cream into four equal portions, the cone would be crumbled and sprinkled over each dab of ice cream. It was a weekend treat. It made the girls happy, and they never asked for more.

M. LECROIX

Being at the shoemakers was the most fun the girls had had in a long time. Sitting on a high sofa with a bowl of mixed candies being passed from one to the other was a treat indeed.

"Now if you all stand, I would like to show you something very interesting." He lay Ella on the bed, pulled down her drawers, and started to fondle and kiss her private parts. Cecile and Juliette stood like clay figurines, unable to speak or move.

He unbuttoned himself, took out his penis, and said, "This is where babies come from." Then he worked his penis back and forth until something like jelly appeared.

He held out his hand to show the girls. "See this? Well this is what makes a baby. Every girl should know that."

"I have another room I would like to show you." He opened the cellar door. Going down was a narrow, steep ladder that disappeared into the darkness. The floor was packed firm. Two gunnysacks served as mats. Another bed like the one upstairs held a quilt made of stitched gunnysacks. He opened a trap door and said, "I also have a well down here. I don't use this room very often. I usually sleep upstairs. I live alone, but I am very comfortable and happy, with many good things to eat."

There was complete silence when Juliette and Cecile were walking home. Each child had her own thoughts. Cecile finally said, "He did some very bad things."

"It wasn't our fault, Cecile. We would never have gone alone. Are we going to tell Maman?"

"No, we can't tell. She would go crazy."

"We'll never go back there again. If Papa invites him and he brings one of his chocolate mousse...well we'll just think of something before next weekend."

* * *

A few days had passed. Mr. Hansom walked down the long strip of road. He turned and walked to M. Lecroix's shop. He grabbed Betty, who was inside, by the hair and shoved her out the door. "I'll get you for this, old man!" he shouted.

Mr. Hansom and Mr. Morris were widowers. Mr. Hansom had two people to see. One was Mrs. Pilon, the other was Mr. Morris.

A MATTER OF COMPULSION

"Mrs. Pilon, do you know what's going on at Old Man Lecroix's place?"

"No, but I do know he's the boot maker and mends shoes and makes chocolate mousse."

"He does more than that! He entices young girls by giving them candy, and Mrs. Pilon, your girls are involved."

"My girls involved? Involved in what? My girls? Dear God, whatever for?"

"I phoned the police, Mrs. Pilon, and your girls will also be questioned."

That night Flory waited until Venice and Baby were in bed. "Now your father and the boys are not home. We are going to talk about a few things that both of you know about. I'm sure both of you will tell me the truth. Mr. Hansom came today. He told me all about M. Lecroix. Now I would like to hear it from you."

"Well Maman, Betty and Ella had been to his place before. They said he was fun and always had lots of candy, so we went."

"Yes, and then what?"

"He did some bad things, Maman."

"He showed us how to make babies."

"Did he touch you?"

"No Maman, he didn't touch either one of us. He only touched Ella and he touched himself too."

"How did he touch Ella?"

"He kissed her."

"Where?"

"Do we have to say it? We told you he kissed her, isn't that enough?"

"Did he kiss her cheek?"

"No, it was her dicky."

"Are you telling me the truth, in the sight of God?"

"Yes Maman, and he showed us a room with a ladder to go down. It had a bed and a well down there. He went down. We didn't. It was dark down there, so we just looked down."

* * *

A few days later Mr. Hansom came to tell Flory that the girls would have to go to court in Edmonton. Also that the girls would have to be accompanied by a parent.

"Mr. Perra, the barber, will drive you to Edmonton."

M. LECROIX

"Good heavens! It won't be long until everyone in the village knows."

Mr. Perra had the longest black shiny car they had ever seen. Flory sat in the middle with one girl on each side of her. She rocked back and forth, as though to help the car along. Except for her repeating over and over again, "Oh God, whatever will we do?" there really was nothing to say.

After Mr. Perra stopped at the courthouse to let them off, Flory said, "Look at me, both of you. Remember, no matter what the judge asks you, tell the truth and don't be afraid."

When they entered the room they saw Mr. Hansom and Betty. Further along the row of seats Mr. Morris sat close to Ella, and was holding her hand to comfort her. It was sad that neither girl had a mother, yet Flory could see how warm and attentive the fathers were toward their daughters. How Mr. Hansom had found out she'd never know, yet he had walked right through Lecroix's door and found Betty there.

The judge walked in wearing a black loose-sleeved robe. He sat behind a high bench. Betty was called first, then Cecile. Their quiet voices could not be heard. The younger girls were then called. He first questioned Ella.

"You went to Mr. Lecroix, the shoemaker, and he gave you candy?"

"Yes." She could barely be heard.

"After you ate your candy what did he do?"

"He sucked me and then he showed us how to make babies."

"Did he do anything else to you? How did he show you how to make babies?"

"He showed us in his hand."

"Did you see his hand?"

"Yes, he got it out of his tail, then he showed us his hand. He said that's what babies were made of."

"Juliette Pilon?"

"Yes."

"What happened after he gave you candy?"

"Nothing happened, except he showed us all how to make babies, then he opened a cellar door. There was a ladder that went down, and he had a bed down there and a well."

"Did you see what he did to Ella?"

"Yes, we were all standing around the bed."

A MATTER OF COMPULSION

* * *

Mr. Perra, the village barber, of all people to have to drive us to court. I can see the news travelling from the barbershop, across the street to the bank manager, from him to Mme. Benet, from there to Dr. Jeunais, then to lah-de-da Mme. Robert, then from the confession box to Father Giroux, and on to the nuns. Oh Lord, it's bad enough to have their father three sheets to the wind every other week!

* * *

Sister Carreveau lay her hand on Juliette's. "Do not look sad. We know it was not your fault."

"Sister Carreveau, we didn't know. The other girls said it would be fun because he always had candy."

"They should have told you what the candy was for."

* * *

"Maman, Sister Carreveau said the girls should have told us what the candies were for."

"Did you know what the candies were for? Well they didn't either, not until it was too late. You can thank your lucky stars Mr. Hansom got the whole thing stopped. I shudder to think of that cellar with a bed and a well. You were good girls not to go back. All I can say is ten years in prison may be a long time, but who's to know how far he would have gone with that well down there next to the bed. Oh, I am sorry I ate his chocolate mousse!"

"What did Papa say, Maman?"

"Your father couldn't believe his ears. Praising your father's invention and bringing that chocolate mousse! I do believe, in his cunning way, he was coaxing my daughters to visit him. One thing your father did say was that it was a very good lesson for both of you. He also said it was never ever to be mentioned again."

M. CHALOT

The snowmobile and all the leftover tools, wood, and metal were moved to the shed, and the front parlour was swept clean.

"Leonard! Romeo! Come to help Papa. De cream separator is in de shed. I want it move to de front parlour."

Flory heard Armand. "What in heaven's name are you moving the cream separator for? Isn't the shed big enough to hold it?"

"I want it in de parlour. I tell you when we buy dat, I will need it for my clothes pin."

"You never did! You said it might come in handy. I thought you might buy a cow, with that big barn out there."

"So now you want a cow!" Gee cripe do you realize dat we are in de village? Robert, he would be happy to have a big cow shit at his front door and how you t'ink Mme. Robert would like it stuck on her heel? Non, de barn was for de horse at one time. Now it is for de dog."

"It wouldn't hurt to have chores for the boys. All they do is hang around with the Fortesque boy. I'm worried they could grow up to be lazy. Not everyone can afford to become an inventor. Not without a mother's help, they can't. Why the boys can't even milk a cow, and while we're talking take your shirt off. It needs washing, and it wouldn't hurt to use a little boot blackening on your shoes."

"Yes, I am sorry I did not eat you when de time was ripe. I regret dat very much."

* * *

Taking the cream separator apart, then rebuilding the whole front of it to mould and model twenty inches of wire into perfect clothespins that would never break apart like the wooden ones, took a genius. The handle was to stay where it was, and turn as it did when separating the cream from the milk. It took sixteen or more turns, including a three-twisted spring, to turn out one clothespin.

"Gee cripe, I make my first clothespin, Flory. Come and look at it."

"Do you think it will work, Armand?"

"It is only de first. It will need to be improve. It have a good line, but de next one I make will have a hump on de nose dat will give it more character."

A MATTER OF COMPULSION

Isn't he a good man when he stays away from the drink. He's so involved with his clothes pin and the bundles of ready-cut wire. They weigh hundreds of pounds. I was a little brisk with him, but I can't help it. Besides, what woman would let a man haul a cream separator into her parlour, and I haven't said a word about it.

"Flory, did I tell you about M. Chalot, de rich man who never spend five cent? He die' yesterday. I hear he cannot be bury in de catholique cemetery because he have not gone to confession. Can you believe dose t'ings? Maybe he do much confessing in his life, but maybe it was not to de priest. Don't tell me Flory, dat de Almighty only hear de priest, eh?"

"If he does Armand, you'll be worse off than M. Chalot. At least he had enough money to give himself a decent burial somewhere."

"If I die, dig a hole and cover me wit a blanket, not too heavy. Also, you know how I hate to wear a tie. Yes, rich man die an poor man die. Money do not matter. We all go back to de soil."

"What would your mother think if she heard you talk like that?"

"Don't worry, Maman know me. I like priest if dey act like ordinary people, but I do not like priest who expect you to confess some sin dat dey cannot do anyt'ing about."

M. Chalot had a red barn with a ladder that went all the way up to the roof. His house was on the opposite side of the street, hidden by the trees. On windy days it had been a joy for Juliette to climb to the rooftop, where you could sit and watch the waves of golden wheat blow in. She had seen him only once at Robert's store. He was a tall, thin man with deep, dark, sunken eyes.

"Maman, at school today Sister Superior said M. Chalot will be buried in the Catholic cemetery. She said the priest found out he went to confession in Edmonton and Maman, she said a hearse with four black horses will come all the way from Edmonton to carry his coffin."

"Yes Juliette, I'm sure he'll be happy. I'm sorry, I meant I'm sure everyone will be happy that M. Chalot will rest in the Catholic cemetery."

* * *

Juliette had never been to a funeral, nor ever seen a casket. It was a very meaningful but sombre gathering, made possible only by his last confession in Edmonton. The mourners were slowly walking toward the casket. The dismal sound of the organ echoed death. Many of the mourners touched their foreheads, while others made the sign of the cross. There was a smell of holiness, different from the smouldering incense at Sunday mass.

No one cried. Did no one love him? Did he have a family? Suddenly it was her turn to file in line, to walk ever so slowly toward the candles that surrounded the casket.

She thought how she would like to do as Yvonette did. She would walk up to the Virgin Mary just as though they were friends, put her money in the slot, then kneel to pray.

Yvonette often asked her, "Do you ever pray to the Virgin?"

"Yes, but I forgot my money," or "Maman had no small change." There was always an excuse. The Virgin Mary was there every day of Juliette's life. She looked down at Juliette with open arms. *I know I can kneel and pray without having to light a candle*, Juliette thought.

She was nearing the coffin, and quickly made up her mind that never would she look inside. The coffin was bathed in pure white light. Suddenly a magnetic force that she could not control drew her eyes lower and lower. M. Chalot was dressed in black. It looked as if puffy white material surrounded his sunken eyes. Her heart stopped for a while. She felt it. She calmly walked to the church door, opened it, and breathed in the fresh air. It was the first time she had seen the horror of death. She vowed she would never, ever look again, and she would not tell Maman.

* * *

"I said, 'Go upstairs and get my wool bag.' Did you hear your mother?"

"Yes."

"Why are you crying? Is it such a big chore?"

"Oh please, Maman, it's dark up there. I'm afraid."

"You're afraid of what?"

"You'll be mad if I tell you."

"You're as white as a ghost. Whatever happened?"

"It's all my fault. I should have stayed home. I went to M. Chalot's funeral today and his eyes were sunken so deep. I can't get him out of my mind."

"Whatever would you go to an old man's funeral for? You didn't even know the man."

A MATTER OF COMPULSION

"I did, and Sister Superior said that anyone who knew him should pay their respects. At first I just went to see the black horses. Then when everybody walked in, I followed."

"Yes, and where did you meet M. Chalot?"

"I only saw him once at Robert's store but every time it was windy I'd climb his barn to see the wheat blow in. I never went into his house and he never saw me."

"Going to his funeral. You naughty girl. Anyone would think he was your grandfather."

JULIETTE'S HEADACHE

"Two men just brought Papa home. He's on the porch, flat out. You never listen, but this time please go to your room and lock the door, Maman! Leonard and I will carry him upstairs and put him to bed."

"Do whatever you want. I don't care. You can take him to Edmonton and have him put in jail if you like! It's the most disgraceful, low-down, heartbreaking thing your father could ever do to hurt us all."

I knew it was coming. He's been too good and happy working on the separator. He had to go to that cursed hotel to tell his so-called friends that his cream separator was now turning out clothes pins.

The next morning Juliette saw her Papa sitting on the edge of his bed. She hurried downstairs.

"Maman, Papa is going to die. His face is swollen and his lips are all puffed out! Aren't we going to get the doctor?"

Flory didn't answer. She took out the blue enamel jug and filled it with cold well water. Slowly she walked upstairs, quietly she tiptoed to his bed, and quickly she poured the whole jug over his head. Then she turned and ran downstairs as fast as her legs could take her.

Armand was up in a flash. He picked up Mme. Dutel's heavy oak showcase and threw it after her. It tumbled down the stairs, glass flying in all directions, and just missed, by the grace of God, Maman's legs.

The kids scattered.

It was the end of the show, the big finale where each one was left with one more deep wound that never completely healed.

* * *

The sidewalk didn't go down quite as far as the creek so it left a crawl space, a secret crawl space, where Juliette could hide for hours, where she felt safe from all the cruelty life handed her. It was a place to pray and a place to cry, until the short staccato sobs pounded at her heart.

You're mean! Both of you are mean! Don't you know how much we love you? Do we have to nail ourselves to a cross to prove it? Do you care? How long do we have to plead? Didn't we plead enough Maman, when you locked yourself in the

A MATTER OF COMPULSION

upstairs room? You said you would never come out because you wanted to die. I brought you food and water. I sat on the floor outside your room, begging you to open the door. "Go away," you said. "I'm not hungry."

"Maman, just take the food please. You can lock your door again." You didn't open the door, Maman. All I wanted was to see your face. You loved Papa more. You wanted him to go to your door and get you to open it.

Tears flooded Juliette's eyes. The green grass looked misty, like morning dew. Her hand went out to touch it. She parted the grass and there it lay. *Twenty-five cents! Someone dropped it and it's mine. I found it and this time I will keep it.* Her godfather, M. St. Martin, came every year with twenty-five cents put into a small aspirin box. She was never there. Maman would take it, promising to give it to Juliette the minute she came in.

"You are a naughty girl. He's such a good godfather. Why do you run and hide? Are you that shy? He's left you another twenty-five cents."

"I don't know why I hide, Maman. You can have it. I give it to you."

"Oh, you are a love!"

* * *

As Juliette sat at Maman's feet with her head resting against her thigh, she thought of the sidewalk and the grass that reached out of the cracks to peek at the world. She thought of the twenty-five cents she had hidden away.

"Maman, I have a headache. It comes and goes. It really hurts."

"How long have you had it?"

"Well, for about three or four days, on and off."

"Why don't you go upstairs and have a little rest?"

She walked upstairs and took the aspirin box from its hiding place. She looked at the twentyy-five cents, which showed the king wearing his silver crown. She rubbed it, feeling its smoothness. It would have been a lovely secret to have. Not to spend, but something of her very own. But it wasn't worth the pain. *And I'm not going to cry.*

"Look, Maman! I found twenty-five cents under the sidewalk. Here, take it. I give it to you."

"When did you find it, dear?"

"Oh, about three days ago. Yes, when you were in bed."

JULIETTE'S HEADACHE

"You are a love. How does your head feel?"
"It feels better. The pain has gone."

THE BOYS

The boys were becoming hard and short-tempered. Flory had cleats put on the toes of their boots to save them from wearing out. When there were cross words between sisters and brothers, the girls had to move fast or they got kicked on their shins. The pain was excruciating, zinging up your leg and coming out your backside. Then you had to sport a navy-marbled lump on your shin for weeks.

Every morning the boys had a bed fight. "You're pushing me! Get over on your side!"

"I haven't got any bloody blankets, that's why I'm pushing you!"

"You're a goddamn liar. You had all the covers. I froze all night!"

"Bullshit! I'm working all night trying to pull my legs out from under those dead horse legs of yours."

"Bugger!"

"*Crotte de cochon!*"

"Coward!"

"*Blatte!*"

"What did you call me?"

"You heard."

"Today you'll eat shit for that. Wait and see!"

That night Armand took the broom up and set it by his bed. When the boys acted up the next morning, he used the broom on them.

* * *

Baby was the only one who ever had a real doll. She treated it like a real baby, and every night they went to bed together. This particular night she was carried to her bed, so her doll was forgotten. She woke early and remembered playing with it on the boy's bed.

"Lenny, did you see my doll? I want it. Lenny, can you hear? I left it on your bed."

"Get the hell out of here! You woke me up!"

"I want my doll. Please Lenny, find my doll."

"You want your bloody doll? Well here it is." Holding the doll by its feet he plunged the head up and down in the pee pot. "Now take your pissy doll and go to

A MATTER OF COMPULSION

bed."

No child cried harder, and no heart was more broken. The paint ran down the face until the eyes became distorted. The painted hair disappeared and the head turned into a meaningless piece of clay.

"You killed my baby! You killed the only baby I ever had! Papa! Papa! Lenny broke my doll apart. She has no eyes. Her hair is gone. Oh Lenny, why did you do that?"

Armand grabbed the broom. "Why are you crying, Bébé? What happen?"

"Oh Papa, Lenny put my doll in the pee pot."

"Lenny put your doll in de pee pot? He held the broom high and brought it down hard, each stroke banging across the boys' bodies. When it hurt on their backs they turned onto their sides, ending in the fetal position and holding on to their heads.

"It wasn't me, Papa. It was Lenny!"

He held the broom high. "Dis one is extra for you, Leonard, for what you do to Bébé's *poupée*. Dis one is for you, Romeo, because you do not'ing about de problem."

After Armand left the boys talked about their father. "I hate him. One day we should beat him up for the rotten things he does to us."

"Yeah, one day maybe we will. We'll scare the shit out of him and see how he likes it."

Baby wrapped her doll and lay it in a shoe box. It stayed forever hidden in her heart, and many years later she would tell of peeking often into the box, hoping the doll had healed.

* * *

The boys had an old bicycle. They were trying to repair it with all the parts they had collected. They also had a tin of black paint to make it look like new. The girls sat in the loft with their legs dangling over the edge. Every time they asked a question, one of the boys would look up.

"Are you still there? Girls have to know everything and see everything. You'll never ride a bicycle, so why don't you go somewhere else?"

"Is that paint good, Romeo? Does it dry fast?" Juliette asked.

"Yeah, it dries pretty fast. Why do you ask?"

"Well I wondered how long you had to wait until you could ride the bicycle, that's

THE BOYS

all."

"It might take a few hours. Maybe by tomorrow we'll be riding it."

After the boys had gone Cecile and Juliette hurried down the ladder and into the barn.

"Do you think we should do it?"

"It sure would surprise Maman. Let's try it."

"Yeah, if we do them right now they'll be dry in no time."

"Remember that bicycle when it was old and rusty? Well look at it now."

"Yeah. Look at our shoes. Old and scuffed now, but patent leather in three hours."

The shoes soon looked just like new.

"We can't wear them until they dry. We'll go barefooted, and hide them in the loft."

After checking them all of a dozen times, they were still a bit tacky.

"Cil, I'm hungry. Aren't you? It must be close to supper time."

"So am I. They're not too wet. They're almost dry. If we put them on, and walk real slow, I bet they'll be dry by the time we get home. Just don't bend your feet or they'll crack."

They walked very slowly, but that didn't help. Every piece of loose grass, foxtail, and spear grass stuck to their shoes until they looked like porcupines. They tried to rub them clean with more grass, but the shoes became an unsightly mess.

"They were beautiful Maman, shinier than when they were new. You would have been so happy."

"They were Maman, and that's why we did it. We wanted to surprise you."

"Haven't I got enough problems? I'll try to clean them with coal oil. In the meantime you'll go barefoot. They may look better or they may look worse, but you'll wear them. They're all you've got."

"Please don't tell the boys. We put the paint back just the way it was."

"Well then, we won't upset the apple cart."

* * *

Mme. Benet lived next door, on the side of the house that faced the creek. There was only one window that faced her way. It belonged to Flory and Armand's bedroom. She was a good soul who Flory could depend on to keep a watchful eye

A MATTER OF COMPULSION

on the children whenever Flory and Armand went to Edmonton. This particular day she waited for the boys at her fence.

"I know it was you who shot holes in my pail. I'm going to phone the police. You'll pay for this." She walked to her back door and disappeared.

"Hell, a few little holes? She can still get water. She hasn't got a telephone and there's no police here. She's trying to scare us."

* * *

"Hey Romeo, I just saw Mme. Benet going up the hill. Let's make a bet. We each get one chance."

"One chance for what, Lenny?"

"The bet is, the one who hits the pail gets to ride the bicycle first."

"Yeah, but who gets the first turn?"

"I do. I'm the oldest. Besides, you always say you're a better shot."

"All right. You go first. Ha ha! You missed! I'll show you how. That's the way you do it. Now I ride the bicycle first."

"First let's get the gun back before Papa catches us or you know what he'll do."

* * *

The next day there was a knock on the door. "Mrs. Pilon?"

"Yes."

Oh Lord, she thought, *What has Armand done now?*

"Mme. Benet telephoned, complaining about your boys shooting holes in her water pails, not once but twice. I am here to warn them that if it happens again they won't get off this easily. Where are your boys?"

"I truly don't know officer, and I wouldn't know where to look."

"The pails must be replaced."

"I will talk to them. Believe me, I will. Thank you officer. You can rest assured it will never ever happen again."

* * *

"Yes boys, and where were you today?"

THE BOYS

"We took the bicycle over to Maurice Chaleur's place. He has a bike, and he said we did a darned good job on ours."

"Your mother had a visitor today."

"Yeah? Who was it?"

"It was a policeman with a gun in his holster. Yes, and he told me that two boys had shot holes in two of Mme. Benet's pails."

"Two pails, Maman?"

"Yes, two pails. Mme. Benet replaced the first one and hung a new one up. Again it was shot with holes. Naturally, she had to phone the police. She would have overlooked it the first time, but twice was too much."

"Did the policeman tell you that?"

"He told me some of it, but I got most of the story when I visited Mme. Benet." She looked at the boys, her eyes shifting from one to the other.

Then in a rage she held her head and screamed. "It's all right for your father to break my heart. It's all right for your mother to wash clothes late at night so you can have clean ones for school. It's all right for me to sew and knit your stockings. Yes, it's all right for mother to make thirty loaves of bread a week to feed you!" She took a long, deep breath, then let herself go limp. Tears flooded her eyes. She lifted her apron and held it tightly to her face.

"We'll never do it again, Maman. Please, we promise we won't. We'll pay for them."

"You'll pay for them with what? What did that dear lady ever do to you? Giggling at her because she eats hot porridge and breaks a raw egg over it, or because she likes green tea instead of black tea. You are both cruel. Both of you. If your lazy father had stopped inventing, and worked the farm, you'd have some chores to do, instead of getting into trouble. Now get out there and chop some wood. Do something constructive for a change!"

"Are you going to tell Papa?"

"I haven't decided yet. He did tell both of you never to touch that gun without his consent. You should know that he meant it. How could you disobey your father? If I told him, he would never, ever trust you again. Do you hear me?"

"Yes, Maman."

* * *

A MATTER OF COMPULSION

The boys always did exciting things. Juliette could hear them laughing in the barn. She slowly climbed the ladder to the loft and listened.

"Why don't they know that it's time to have pups?"

"How the hell do I know. Let's put him on her again. Dammit, this is the fourth time. This time we'll both hold them in position."

Blackie was big and strong. He was having none of this nonsense. He lowered his head from their hold, his heavy paws landing firmly on the packed clay.

"Lenny, they're no damned good. Papa bought the wrong dogs."

"Yeah, he never does anything right. He must have been drunk when he bought them. Queenie has a dumb look on her face every time we put Blackie on her."

"It's not Queenie's fault, Romeo. It's that big fuckless Blackie. He's no bloody good. Just like everything the old man does."

"What's that noise?"

"Juliette, are you up there? Get the hell out of here. Can't you find something else to do besides hanging around the barn?"

"I was just going to tell you what Maurice Chaleur told me. If you don't want to know . . ."

"What did he tell you?"

"Maurice Chaleur told me that the wind was blowing so hard and strong that it blew his uncle's mouth to the other side of his face and it's been like that ever since. I thought you'd like to know. I'm going now."

* * *

Fanny Ryder joyfully called out, "Hey Juliette, would you like to see something?" She was much older than Juliette, so naturally what that "something" was baffled and excited her. Maybe their cow had a calf! Maybe it had died! No, it couldn't be that. She sounded much too happy, stimulated, and eager."Follow me, but don't talk. If they look back, they'll see us. Stay in the low bushes and get down when I get down."

"Who is it, Fanny?"

"It's your brother Leonard and Marianne Gilbert."

After following for a while, Juliette couldn't resist asking, "Where are they now?"

"Sh! They're down in the grass. Watch, and you'll see them get up. Shshsh!

THE BOYS

They're up! Let's get out of here! Follow me. Walk in the bushes and be quiet. We'll get down to the barn, and they'll never know."

Juliette was stunned. She couldn't talk, and even if she had been able to, what would she have said? How long had it been going on, and how long had Fanny been following them?

There and then Juliette made up her mind. Never would this be revealed. Not to Papa. Not to Maman. Not to anyone. And especially not to Leonard.

A MATTER OF COMPULSION

Grandmaman and Grandpère

The Boarding House, Brownsburg, Québec

A MATTER OF COMPULSION

The Farm — Un épi dans le blé

The Farm

Flory

Grandmaman

A MATTER OF COMPULSION

Flory, with Leonard and Cecile

Flory circa 1930

Flory's house and store in Legal, Alberta

A MATTER OF COMPULSION

Juliette as a teenager

Family in front of Dance Hall

Leonard, Cecile, Romeo, Juliette, Venice and Baby circa 1922

Cold Lake with Dance Hall on lower left

A MATTER OF COMPULSION

Dance Hall and Hotel

Armand and Flory in front of Dance Hall

The family at Dance Hall entrance

A MATTER OF COMPULSION

Juliette and Venice

Auction Sale

Juliette and Hector

A MATTER OF COMPULSION

**DEPARTMENT OF
MINES AND NATURAL RESOURCES
DEPUTY MINISTER'S OFFICE
WINNIPEG**

June 6th, 1944.

Mr. Armand Pilon,
General Delivery,
Victoria, B. C.

Dear Sir:

    I have your letter of May 8th in which you inquire with respect to publications on muskrat raising in captivity.

    While we have no printed material on this subject available in this Department, I understand that there is a publication entitled "Muskrat Raising", which you might be able to obtain by writing to the Fur Trade Journal of Canada, Box 31, Toronto 2, Canada.

Yours very truly,

D. M. Stephens,
Deputy Minister.

DMS/MD

Official letter regarding the raising of muskrats

A MATTER OF COMPULSION

Another of Armand's inventions

A MATTER OF COMPULSION

Rocky Rapids, Alta.
March, 14/38.

Dear Juliet:-
        I am gratful for your answer; it is consoling to think some one bears patience with me. This I maintain after reasoning that I am part of the human composition in the great story of life.

And so you would like to read my story? Perhaps you may some day. I have set it aside---I am resting----working at other things. Later I shall go back to it when I shall be able to criticize it from an other angle, then I shall have it ready for publication.

    Does my Juliet ask much from LOVE--? She is like you, her demand in love is big; big with a thousand years of wonder, bigger with her growing soul.

    Not all people are that way, Juliet, and I am glad to find you expressing what I always felt you were. It is beautiful the way you write, the way you say those things. Often you humble me. In the commet of literature I am but the very tip of its tail, and with its slightest fading I should not be at all. Yet I carry on for each day's toil brings something new, and adds to my increasing store. It is by this increasing store that I first learned your value.

    Yes you wasted a little time(we all do that). But, now that you have started in earnest,how good it feels. Oh I know I have been mean, but I was anxious for you to express the sleeping wonders of your soul. You know I have always been proud of you, and it hurts when I can't have you being better than any other--you understand.

Letter from Ernie Marskell

A MATTER OF COMPULSION

Page 2.

About myself, what shall I say? Not so much. Juliet, concentricity has been one of my weaknessess which I should like to overcome. Don't make me worse than I am, asking me to talk about myself is only undoing all that which I have faught against these many years.

You know, what I thought I was is a person I have wanted to be, But gee you have no idea the usless thing I had to mould. When I realy studdy myself and see what has been my first moulding--I wonder----Did the Hand Batter of the Potter shake?

Homesteading, a quieter life with its comfortable margine of simple routeen, is what I thought more natural to me. This, and to forget the dizzy height of finer things, I thought would bring contentment. It didn't , Juliet, and now I know there is no other road than the field of writting; only then am I happy; only then do I live.

Now, I strike again the key of high serenities.
My soul set free sings, again,
Of love, of life, sweet purities.
Awakens that silent muse, my brain and fingers through.
And I see infused the wonders yet to do.
For man is barren without himself expressed.
With his values given, he, himself, has blessed.

As ever Ernie.
Will write again if you answer.

Letter continued

A MATTER OF COMPULSION

Armand's sisters in Québec

Flory

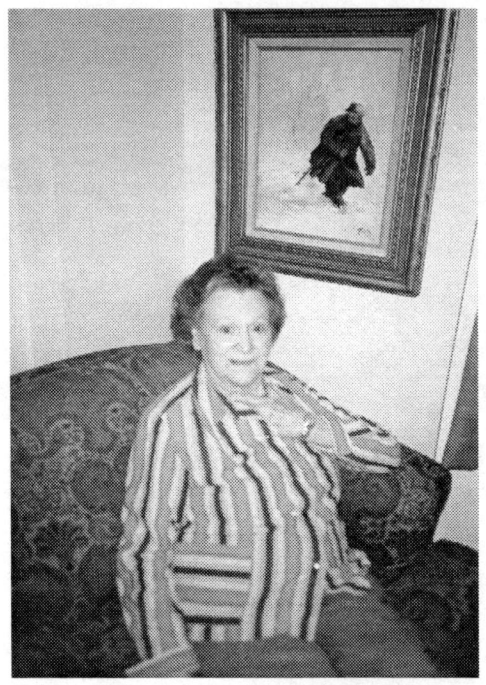

A MATTER OF COMPULSION

Juliette with her painting of Armand

Flory

JULIETTE'S PAINTINGS

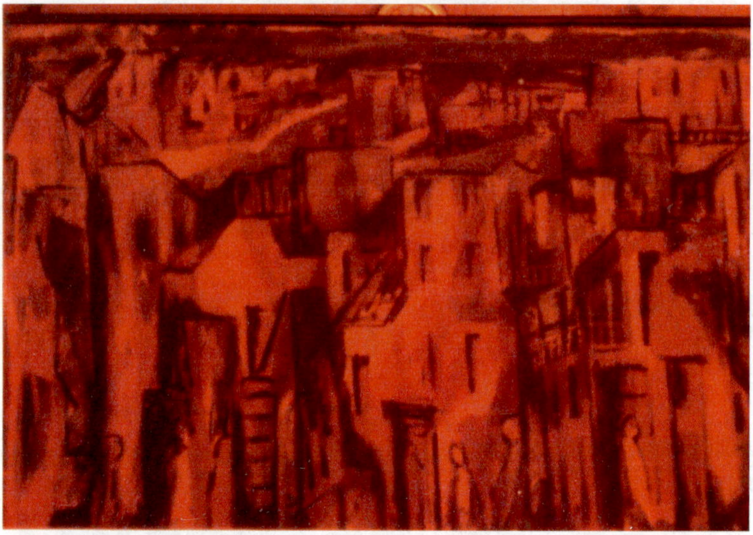
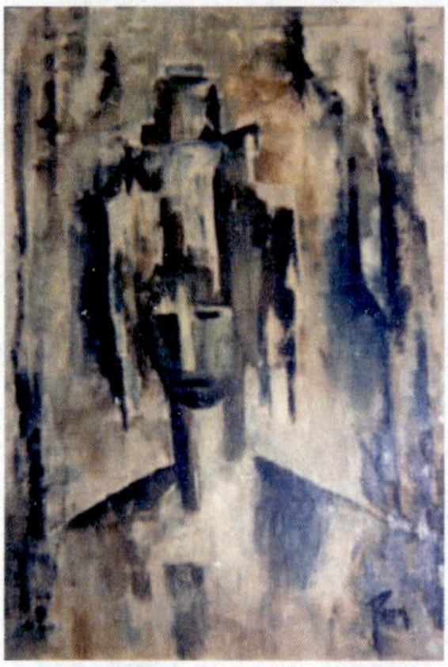
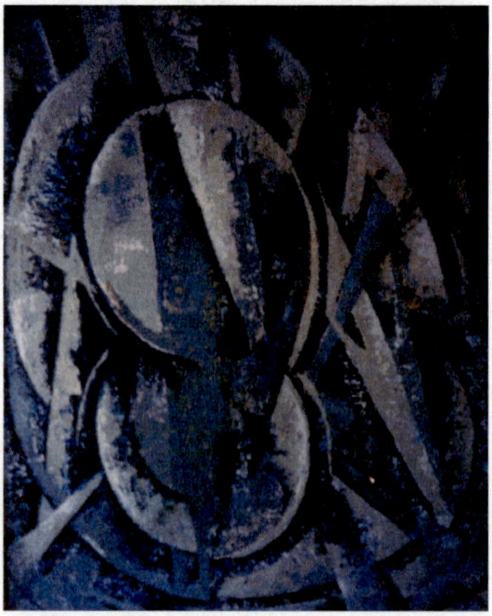

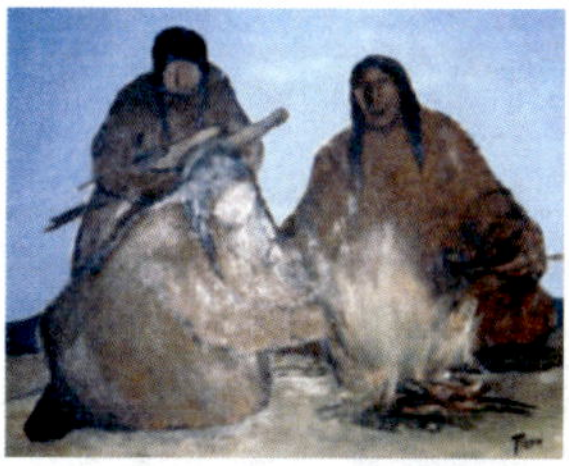

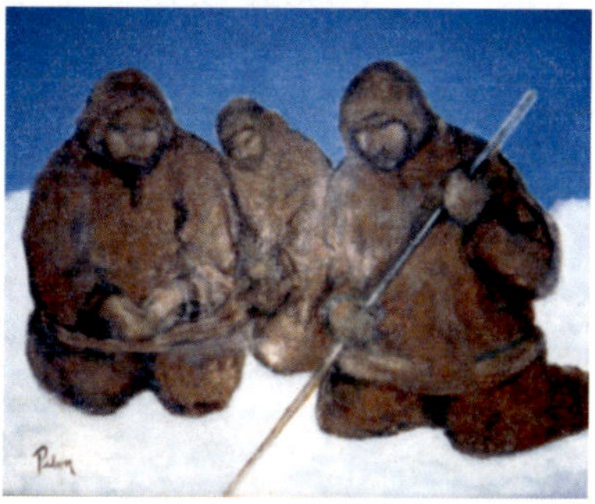

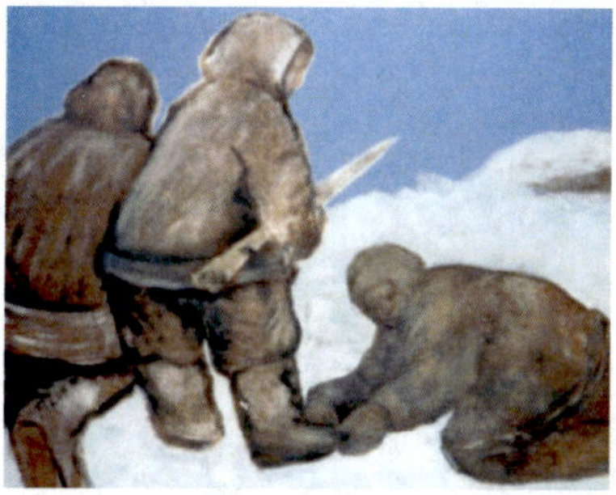

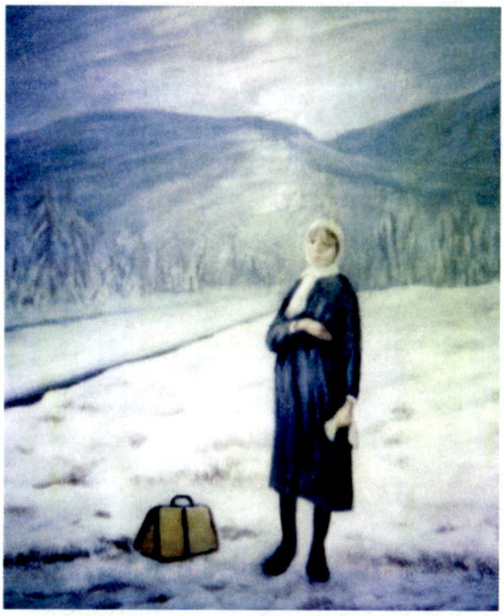

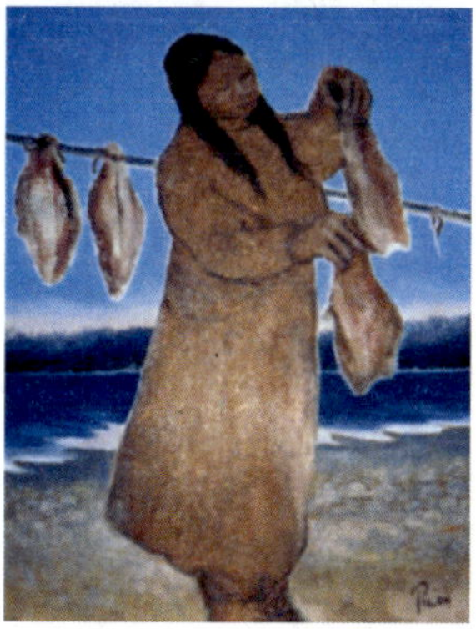

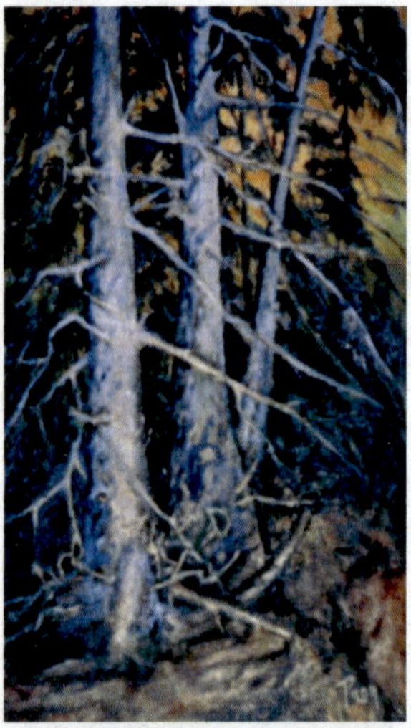

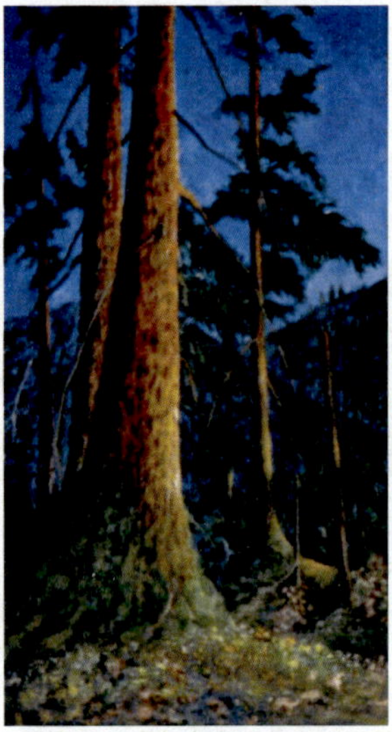

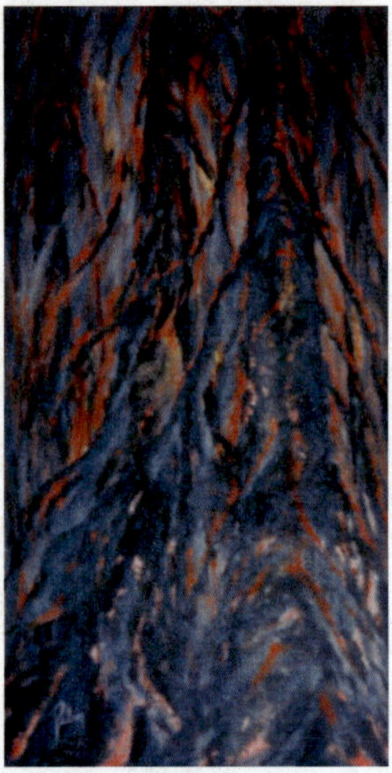

THE BLIND PIG, ROSE'S VISIT

"The housekeeper for Fadder Giroux have to go to Montréal. She have a big tumour in her belly an' have to have it remove. Can you figure dat, eh?"

Flory didn't look up. *Forgive me for what I am thinking, Lord.*

"Will she be back, Armand?"

"I do not know. Somebody say dat she was sick before. Fadder Giroux is very disturb. Robert say de priest tell him she take care of him very well."

"I'm not surprised."

"What you say, Flory?"

"I said I'm not surprised she had to go as far as Montreal to have it removed, but surely The Royal Alexandra Hospital in Edmonton could have operated?"

"Maybe it is a serious one."

"Yes, I'm sure it is."

* * *

"Flory, dat cream separator do a good job. I am happy I take it from de farm."

"Don't you think you should be looking for work?"

"Gee cripe. Dere is no work, but Joe Beauchamp was telling me somet'ing an' it sound like a good idea. Listen to dis. De men like to play card. Dey make bet and enjoy to play poker. Dere is a door from de parlour to your bedroom. If we put our bed in de dining room, we could . . . Don't look at me like dat, Flory. Dey will pay. You don't t'ink it is for free."

"Armand, why should the children suffer for your mistakes? They never have anything like other children do, and when they do ask, I forever have to tell them maybe next week. They don't believe in either one of us. God knows what they'll grow up to be."

"Flory, I feel I can make some good money from my clothes pin. If it sell it will go like hot cake. I only take de time to go in de room, take out de card an' . . . "

"Get on with it. You'll be sorry one day."

"It is very simple, it cost not'ing, and de kid can have what dey need. It would be for dis week and de week after. Dere is only one problem."

"What would that be?"

"You, Flory, will have to sleep wit me. Ah yes, I know you miss me. Look at me

A MATTER OF COMPULSION

straight in de eye and tell me de trut'."

"Go chase yourself, Armand. You are nothing but a dreamer."

The brass bed was moved into the dining room. The round dining table and chairs were moved into the bedroom, along with the buffet.

"Are you crazy, Armand? No, I mean it. Are you going crazy?"

"*Pas de problème*, Flory. Now it is a private room where de men can play card, amuse demself, and maybe have a little drink. Nobody can see inside wit a blind on de window. Mme. Benet can see not'ing."

* * *

Armand wasted no time. There were decks of cards in the top buffet drawer. Jiggers and glasses were in one section, along with the big blue enamel jug for water. The chairs were cosied around the table. It didn't take long for word to get around. "If you want to play cards, go to Pilon's," followed by a wink.

Flory knew nothing about his blind pig, a still he had started out in the woods. With that, and his invention, he had no reason to go anywhere. It was a perfect set-up behind his own front door. Anyone who entered, only came to see his invention. And how easy it was to step into the room with the round table. Until now he'd hid liquor in the black currant bushes, and even in the napkin compartment of the big baby pram. Now he kept it in the bottom part of the buffet. *Why not?* he thought. *Flory is happy dat I am always home working on my clothespin, and I have a little business on de side. Why I never t'ink of a blind pig before? I put a case of apple in de cellar. Dat make de kid happy. Flory show no sign dat she is not happy, but I can see she have no interest in my idea.*

"Papa sure was good to get all those apples, eh Maman?"

"Yes, very good. He bought a roast and now he tells me he's ordering oysters from Edmonton."

Lord, forgive me. I am a hypocrite. But he is staying home more, and he isn't staggering home for everyone to see.

* * *

It couldn't have been more than two months later when someone knocked at the door.

THE BLIND PIG, ROSE'S VISIT

"Come in, come in."

"I didn't come to stay, Armand. I came to tell you that I got word the searchers will come. I don't know when, but if I were you I'd get everything out of sight right away."

"Gee cripe, tank you. Tank you very much."

"Flory, if some man come to de house and he ask to search, you say go ahead an' search. Gee cripe, dere is always somet'ing, eh?"

"Armand, you first told me they would play cards. Oh, I saw it all."

"Yes, of course, and you know dat card player drink, an' you know dat me Armand, would have a drink wit dem once in a while. You are not a fool, Flory. No, you were wit' me all de time. Now I get hell from you."

"It's good for you. I'm glad the searchers will come. Feeding them raw oysters, and all laughing about *Monte en haut Rose Lagune.*"

"Ah, you also have big ear, Flory."

"Oh, I was a fool to sell my soul for a paltry bit of food for the children. Every day I felt ashamed. It's a load off my mind, and my conscience."

"Do not holler from de kitchen. I have work to do. Do you want me to pay a fine or go to prison, or would you radder keep your beautiful mout' shut?"

* * *

There was great excitement at the school. St. Jean Baptiste Day celebration would soon be here. Sister Superior chose all those who would be angels. They had to have a white dress made. Yards of cheesecloth would drape over their heads and fall in saintly folds. They would be placed evenly on each side of the street, kneeling with praying hands. Young poplar trees would be cut. Holes would be dug and each tree planted to make an avenue of trees. Four of the older girls were chosen from the angels, and they would carry boxes of crepe paper roses and fresh-picked leaves. They would have to walk backwards facing the first car where the Bishop would ride, scattering roses toward the slow-moving cars.

"I have chosen the older girls as this is a most difficult task. Those of you who do not have a white dress will have to have one made. There will be a concert in the evening. Father Gerald will announce it in church. All of you will help to make flowers and cover the boxes. We must all work together to make this a success. Class dismissed."

A MATTER OF COMPULSION

"Maman, I have been chosen to be an angel. Sister Superior asked me. She wants us all to be angels for St. Jean Baptiste Day," Juliette said.

"What do you mean she wants you all to be angels?"

"Other girls and me, and Maman, I have to have a white dress and some cheese cloth to look like an angel. The sisters will drape it over our heads. Can you make me a white dress? Will you Maman, please?"

"I'll make you a white dress, dear. Don't you worry, and you'll have the cheese cloth as well."

Flory picked out the whitest flour bags and lay them on the sewing machine.

The mail rig pulled in. Flory looked out. It so puzzled her that she set her sewing aside and stepped out on the porch.

Rosie stepped down from the rig holding a baby in her arms. There was another child, older, more the age of Baby. Flory screamed, "Rosie, Rosie! Dear God you've come back."

They cried. They laughed. They reminisced about the farm days. The children were happy to have a cousin named Lila and a new baby named Constance. The house was alive. Alive with a thousand memories and a thousand sorrows.

"Flory, I'm so lonesome I could die. You'll never know how I've missed you. I can hardly stand the thought of having to go back."

"Tell me everything, Rose."

"I never should have married Steve, but I was young and alone. I never did have a boyfriend or a young man to flirt with. When Steve came along it seemed like the natural thing to do. He said . . . well, he said he could support me. I had no home, so I said yes. Mother made me a hat and sewed a pretty flower on it. I walked to the church alone. Oh, how I needed a friend."

"Where was mother, Rose?"

"Working, and as I came along the street, right close to the church, young girls were playing jacks. They were having a lively time. I wanted to join them. They were young, just like me. I did, Flory. I knew I belonged with them. I knew I shouldn't be getting married at my age. Steve was waiting for me at the church entrance. I looked at him, then I looked at the girls playing jacks. Flory, I lowered my eyes in sorrow. Then I noticed the manure on his shoes."

"I was too young, Flory. I'm sure Steve had no one to care for him either. We were, I guess, both searching for something. I know I was. I slept with my clothes on. I slept with him for weeks fully dressed, until I thought of you letting your hair down in your flannelette nightgown, like you were going out to a special party. I did. So I put on my nightgown, but I lay and I shook. I couldn't face him."

"When he finally touched me I cried, and I didn't speak to him for days. Poor Steve. What did he do in his life to deserve that? I got pregnant for Lila of course, the first time he touched me. If that's what it took, I wondered how the world could have so many people."

"Rose, they're beautiful children. They both have brown eyes, and you know how mother likes brown eyes."

"It has nothing to do with the children. I'm just not happy with Steve. I have no feelings for him. I don't love him. Flory, when I left you on the farm, my hopes were high. I was going to do so many things. Mother had Lillian and Leonard to support, so I had to go to work, not to school. All the schooling I had was on the farm when I went to school with the grey nuns. I never had a childhood. The only girlfriend I had was Edna Massey. We went to school together. She was the only friend I had."

"What did you do, Rose? What work?"

"When mother took me back to North Bay, I never went back to school. I scrubbed floors, hauled water, did laundry and ironing. I felt like a little old woman at twelve years old."

"Then I got a job at the Feed and Livery Store. They had a son called J.R. He was a terror, but oh, they thought he was an angel. He was the apple of their eyes. I slept in a little outside cottage. That's what they called it. The chipmunks would come in. Oh Lord, I was scared, and if that wasn't enough I shivered all night with the cold. I felt so alone in the world. Then they accused me of stealing money. Money! Why, I was too scared to ask for an extra blanket, let alone steal! It must have been their precious son who took the money. I was lucky, and found another job at a summer resort doing . . ."

"Oh Rose, I never wanted you to leave. I cried so much. You'll never know. I didn't mind mother and MacLeish leaving. I was pregnant and tired. You understand. But I was a long time getting over losing you. Every day I expected you to walk in from school. We didn't get out much, but weren't we happy, and didn't we laugh?"

"We did, Flory. I never had a home after I left you. Maybe that's why I married Steve. I truly don't know what love is about. Are you in love, Flory? I'm asking because mother said you had a young man friend in England before you met

A MATTER OF COMPULSION

Armand."

"Oh, mother would say that. She thought he was 'a bit of all right'. No Rose, my heart didn't give a turn. Not until we came to Canada. The minute I set eyes on Armand, I knew. I could barely touch his hand. It was electric. I can't explain. It was like a current or a surge that made me feel higher than life. A divine feeling Rose, as if we were part of one another. I had a great desire to breathe in deeply the very breath he exhaled. Can you understand how easy it was for me to become pregnant for Elizabeth? Yes, and then how I was looked down upon by certain members of our family."

"You are lucky. It's terrible not to love the man you marry. Steve is impossible. If I get serious about anything, ordinary things, he laughs and does a little jig. Then when I'm happy, or if I sing, he sulks. He won't open his mouth. It's so long from day to day. I have two children now Flory, and I don't want any more. I can't bear for him to touch me, but how can you live with a man and not let him touch you?"

* * *

Baby Constance cried a lot. She was put in the big pram and wheeled back and forth on the veranda. The girls did everything to keep her happy. Nothing worked. That afternoon Juliette was rocking the pram gently up and down when suddenly Constance threw up.

"Come, Maman! Aunt Rose, come quick! The baby vomited a lot and it is black."

"Oh God Rose, she's white and lifeless."

"I've got to go to Edmonton, Flory. Help me get ready."

Rose quickly bundled the baby, while Flory ran to the Beauchamp's for help. Rose boarded the train to Edmonton. Lila was happy to stay behind and play with Venice and Baby.

Rose came back two weeks later with empty arms.

"No, Rose! Oh God, no! Is she in hospital?"

"Constance died. I haven't cried. I can't. I have no tears."

"Cry Rose, cry. Cry, my dearest sister." They held one another until the flowing tears mingled on their cheeks.

ST. JEAN BAPTISTE DAY

Father Chapelle was called the Vicar. He wore a long black frock with tiny black buttons down the front. The young Vicar was one of the catechism teachers. Juliette was one of his pupils. She liked him because he was never strict. If something deserved a laugh, he laughed. Then all the children laughed.

He drove out of the churchyard and stopped. "How would you like to come for a ride? I need two more trees for the church entrance."

"Can I truly come?"

"Yes. I wouldn't ask if I didn't mean it."

Juliette stepped up and sat beside him. He drove past the farm and around the corner toward Diligence, where the young poplar trees grew in abundance. "Come help me pick two trees with the roundest, fullest foliage."

What fun, running like wild deer from one tree to the other, trying to make up their minds which of the trees was the most beautifully shaped. The two first-prize trees were anchored in the back, one on each side. The boughs hung out of the window and rustled in the wind.

"Would you like to help me plant them? I'll dig the holes, then you can hold the trees straight while I bank them with soil." She looked up and smiled. She felt special. She felt needed, and suddenly she felt grown.

* * *

Sister Superior had told the girls not to move or fidget while kneeling.

"Bow your heads, and it wouldn't hurt any of you to say a prayer of thanks for this special day."

The cars were barely moving. It seemed they'd never get over the hill. Juliette's knees ached until the pain was unbearable. *Why did I choose the sidewalk instead of the grass? Now I can't move and I can't leave. We're evenly placed on each side of the road. Everybody at school would know. Oh, I can't stand it any longer! Please hurry!*

The cars were closer now. She lowered her head. *Dear Jesus, make them hurry or make the pain go away. It's my bony knees.* Now the cars were nearing the church. Nothing mattered anymore.

A MATTER OF COMPULSION

* * *

"Oh Maman, was I ever glad when it was all over. I could hardly get up."

"It was lovely dear, but you don't have to cry about it. You were out of your mind with joy when you were chosen to be an angel."

"I'm not crying. I feel sick to my stomach. Have you ever had to kneel on a sidewalk for hours without moving, with pieces of sand, gravel, and clay stuck in your kneecaps? Don't forget, I was kneeling in front of Docket's garage. Look at my knees! Where's the salve?"

"Oh you darling. Never mind, tonight is the concert and we are all going, except for your father of course."

* * *

A special booth was built for the occasion. It was filled with surprises. The nuns had made a large white duck with a bright yellow bill. Anyone who had a nickel or a dime to spend only had to put it in the duck's bill and down it would go to retrieve a gift.

"Maman, can I have a nickel? You should see the big white duck with a yellow bill. All you do is give it a nickel. Then it comes up with a wrapped gift. Can I?"

"I'll give her a nickel, Flory. Here you are dear, and I want you to come back and show us your gift."

Juliette took the nickel from Rose and put it in the duck's bill. Down it went, then back it came carrying a small package.

"You can open it Maman, and we can all see the prize."

Flory carefully unwrapped the parcel, then removed the lid. There, on silky paper, lay two small white candles. Both Rose and Flory looked blank. They looked at one another with raised brows. Eventually though, not to show disappointment, they put on smiles of approval.

"You don't like my gift? Well I do. I never have five cents to light a candle in church, so now I have my own."

"They're lovely, aren't they Rose? You'd better hurry or you'll never find a seat, dear. It looks as if the concert is about to begin."

After bobbing her head from side to side looking for a seat, Juliette was about to turn back when she heard someone call her name. He was right there, right where

ST. JEAN BAPTISTE DAY

she had decided to turn.

"If you're looking for a seat, there's room for one more."

When she saw the Vicar her heart skipped a beat. There was no one she'd rather sit with. He was her catechism teacher and she had helped him choose the trees. She had even helped him plant them.

He told her so many things about the concert, things others wouldn't have known. The players were from St. Albert and had been trained by the nuns. Then when she remarked on how lovely the parlour was, with all the fancy curtains and furniture, he told her it was a stage made to look like a parlour and that after the play was over everything would be moved and it would become a plain stage again.

She felt sad that everything had to be taken away. It was all so beautiful. The long avenue of trees, the white angel dress that Maman had made with yards of cheese cloth that fell to the floor, the big white duck with the big yellow bill, and now tomorrow would come with no avenue of trees. The road would look gloomy with all the scattered roses gone.

"Did you enjoy the concert?"

"I did. They must have worked very hard to make it look so real. I've never been to a concert before. It's my very first one."

Now they were clapping, clapping until everyone stood to leave. He smiled and said goodnight. It was all over. One glorious day of happiness.

* * *

It was all too interesting, especially the clearing of the stage, with its long drapes, bookcase, rugs, and even a sofa. To stay a while, just to see how it was done, wouldn't hurt. Surely Maman would understand.

* * *

"Rose! Rose, get up! My Juliette isn't in her bed. She could, oh God, she could have been kidnapped. Get your things on. We're going to the rectory. She was sitting with the young Vicar when I last saw her. At her age? At one o'clock in the morning?"

Flory knocked hard on the door. Father Giroux opened it. He frowned. Flory thought he must be wondering why she had brought her sister along.

A MATTER OF COMPULSION

"Father Giroux, my Juliette didn't come home after the concert. I last saw her sitting with Father Chapelle. See if he is in please, Father."

He nodded, then slowly walked up the stairs.

"Oh Lord, Rose. Do you think he's in? He took her in his car. They drove to the country for trees. She told me all about it. What's taking him so long?"

"Don't you start crying. After all, he does have to get dressed. He's there Flory, or the Father would be going crazy by now."

Father Giroux, then the Vicar, slowly walked down the stairs.

"Mrs. Pilon, Father Giroux told me your daughter Juliette didn't go home after the concert. I'll take the car and we will find her. Who are her friends?"

"Oh dear. The Billet girls and the La Baies, but she wouldn't go anywhere to sleep. Never, without my permission."

Neither family looked happy to be wakened at one o'clock in the morning.

"Flory, can you tell me why we're looking in the country? She could be right next door. Why, just the other day she was telling me about the music teacher and her daughter Marie Anne and how she played the piano. Or she could be at Robert's. She always plays with Yvonette."

"She wouldn't sleep anywhere Rose, especially not at Robert's. She could be kidnapped and on her way to Montreal right now."

"Go to Yvonette's father. If she isn't there I'll phone the police from somewhere."

Father Chapelle, Rose, and Flory went to Robert's and called three times before he came to the window.

"Yes, what is it?"

"Have you seen my Juliette? She never came home after the concert."

"Yes, Mrs. Pilon. Juliette is sleeping in Yvonette's bed."

"Thank God. Thank you. Thank you Father Chapelle."

"Go home. Sleep well. You will see her in the morning, Mrs. Pilon. Goodnight."

"Why would she do such a thing, Rose? It's not like her, or any of the children. She didn't ask me, and I know darned well Mme. Robert didn't ask me either."

"Maybe not, but she didn't ask you if she could go and chop trees with the Vicar either, did she?"

"No she didn't, but she told me all about it when she came home. I'll have one good talk with her tomorrow and she won't soon forget it!"

ST. JEAN BAPTISTE DAY

* * *

Yvonette's room was so pretty. It had two dressers, a large stuffed chair, and there in the centre was her bed, facing her very own balcony. Mme. Robert had turned the bed sheets down.

"We keep the balcony door open just a little for air. If you feel cold pull the comforter over you." She closed the door a little, then said goodnight.

Why doesn't she like me? Maman keeps us clean. I'm not a bad girl. We've been playing together since we moved from the farm. I wish we were rich. She'd like me then, I know.

Juliette tiptoed to the window and looked across at her own house, which was in complete darkness.

They're all sleeping. No one knows I'm not home.

The mystery of the balcony had no real meaning anymore. She longed to be in her own bed with all her sisters close by. Yvonette had never had a sister. *Maybe she feels lonesome. Her brother Arture is so much younger. That's why they built her that playhouse. I'll bet it is!*

Juliette lay very still. She remembered how, just days before, Yvonette had invited her to see the parlour with its fancy piano. It was safe to be there because her mother was at the store. *Oh, if Maman could see that room. Poor Maman, with all those bundles of wire and the cream separator in her parlour. I sure am glad Mme. Robert never comes over.*

While they had been in the parlour Yvonette had heard someone open the kitchen door. She had panicked.

"It's my mother! Hide quick!" Then she had disappeared. Where she hid was a mystery. Juliette stood alone. The only place she had seen to hide was under the high dining room buffet. Her heart pounded faster as she saw Mme. Robert's legs coming toward her.

"Get out! Get out and never come back here again."

Scared. Why am I always scared? When Yvonette left me standing there why didn't I sit in one of her puffy chairs and say, "Hello Mme. Robert. Yvonette wanted to show me the piano but when she heard you coming she was so scared of you that she ran and hid." I wish I could be like that. Now here I am sleeping in Yvonette's bed.

It must have been very early. There wasn't a sound of life anywhere. Ever so quietly she walked downstairs and out the door. No one was up at her house either, so she sat on the sidewalk and with a stick she dragged the gravel and dirt into patterns.

The third time she tried the door it was open. The girls ran to hug her and tell her how happy they were that she hadn't been stolen.

"Yeah, and you could have ended up in the slave traffic!"

"What happened? Did Mme. Robert invite you in?"

"No, of course not. If she had, I would have refused."

Flory looked over her glasses. "Whatever possessed you to do such a wicked thing without first asking your mother? Rose and I had to go to the rectory and wake Father Giroux. Then he had to wake the Vicar and it was the Vicar who took us out in the country knocking on doors looking for Juliette Pilon. Yes, at one o'clock in the morning! Sleeping at Yvonette's and worrying the insides out of your mother!"

"Why don't you ask me what happened, Maman?"

"And one more thing. If you ever get in a car with anyone again, the butcher, the baker, or the priest, you'll not be able to sit down again!"

"Yvonette wasn't home. Both she and Arture went back with their cousins to Diligence. They went right after the concert. Where's Papa?"

"Your father came home drunk. God knows what time he went to bed. And don't change the subject."

"Oh Maman, it was all Papa's fault. He was on the porch. I could see his light shirt. It was real dark and he saw me coming. He hollered, 'Is that you, Juliette?' I didn't answer. I was so afraid I thought I would die, so I ran across to Robert's, hoping the door was open. Then he ran after me. He ran after me all around their house. Oh, he was getting close. I ran up the stairs, tried the door, and it was open. I called M. Robert. He came running. He turned the light on. Then Mme. Robert came down. She said my lips were blue and M. Robert gave me some water. He said I could sleep there."

"Did you tell him your father was chasing you?"

"I didn't want to, but I did."

"I am sorry, darling. Your father is a bad man, but could he have thought you were too young to be out that late? Why didn't you come home with us?"

"I stayed a while longer to see how the stage was all cleared away. It was fast. You should have seen it."

ROSE'S MARRIAGE, CECILE'S ABSENCE

"Do you mean to tell me you would go through all this hell with Armand when you could have Napoleon Demarne?"

"I would only be exchanging one problem for another, Rose. It would break Maman and Papa Pilon's hearts, and their girls', and yes his brother's as well. Sometimes I feel strong because I put up with it, but I'm sure I put up with it because I'm weak."

"Don't cry, Flory. I can't stand to see you hurt. I remember on the farm he didn't drink much. Not too much then. He was funny. He'd make me laugh so hard. I always liked Armand. He's been so good to me."

"Yes, but now he's getting worse. He's mean and says terrible things to me. Then I lose my temper and he becomes violent, bad enough to make the children run and hide."

"It must be hard on you, loving a man that much. Isn't it strange? I would be forever grateful if Steve had some of Armand's qualities. Most of them, really. It's that terrible drink, Flory."

"Yes, that's the biggest problem. The second is, he never will work for anyone. The closest he ever got were those wonderful first years on the farm when everything belonged to us. I still have the picture of Leonard, you, and Edna Massey. Remember? Oh, he went to the village and had his drink, but he was never mean then. And do you know Rose . . . well I could never tell anyone but you, and now I wonder if I should."

"If not me, Flory, who will you tell?"

"I'll tell you, of course. It's no great story. You'll probably laugh, but at the time it was far more than a laughing matter. If Armand had a couple of drinks and he came close to me, close enough that I could smell it on his breath, all he had to do was look at me with shining eyes. I'd melt. It really stirred me up, Rose. Of course I was young and innocent. I never ever dreamed it could get out of control."

"Did you tell him that you enjoyed passion with him when he had had a drink?"

"Of course not. We were always passionate with one another. But this was different. I used to run away from him. It became a game where, when I was completely exhausted, I was corralled."

"It sounds exciting. All Steve did was a little jig. Speaking of jigs, it is time for me to go. I came back to you after Constance died. I wouldn't have, you know, not

A MATTER OF COMPULSION

so soon, but Steve said I should come back to you. I'm sure he knew I would be happier here."

"No one is all bad, Rose. He certainly tried to be a kind, thoughtful man."

"Yes, but he knew I had to come back anyway for Lila."

"I'll miss you. Do write to me when you get time."

"I'll be back, Flory. You know, it's time I had a little enjoyment in my life."

"With your voice, you should never have to go to work. Even Armand said you were wasting your life. He did, and he's no fool."

"Oh, I wish I had more faith in myself. I was asked to sing at the Rialto Theatre. That's a lot different from singing in the church choir. Can you see it? Hundreds of people, and me on stage alone? No, I need some training. What a dream! I've never had a chance at anything in my life."

"Oh Rose, I'm so sorry. I can't help but wonder what life would have been like if we had stayed in England. It is strange how father dreamed of coming to Canada. For years, mother said. Then when his dream was realized he passed away. Do you think he knew he would die? Why, it was as if he brought us here and left."

"I was too young. I only know what you and Madge tell me. Mother was one who never said much."

* * *

"Don't you think my Cecile is pale and thin? I do worry about her. Anna Seigner was telling me that it could be pinworms. She said she had them when she was young. I've been worrying for some time. She seems so gloomy and sullen. Rose, I'm going to take her to the Royal Alexandra Hospital."

"What could be the problem is the worry and fear they all have when Armand comes home drunk. All of them look frail, except the boys."

"But Rose, Cecile is growing so tall. Whatever it is, I've made up my mind."

* * *

Cecile was in the hospital for one month. Never a day went by without one of the girls bringing up the subject and asking Maman clever questions. It wasn't easy, since not one of them had ever seen a hospital.

"How big is the hospital, Maman?"

ROSE'S MARRIAGE, CECILE'S ABSENCE

"It's bigger than a big hotel, dear."
"Wonder what she had to eat today."
"Oh, they feed her well."
"When she has to go to the privy, does she go out alone?"
"No dear, the toilets are all inside."
"When is she coming home?"
"She's coming home this weekend. She won't be used to noise, so I don't want you hollering questions at her."

When Rose and Lila left, Flory felt empty inside. She looked forward to seeing Cecile again.

* * *

It was more than a surprise when Cecile came home. Her long ringlets had gone. Now her hair was bobbed, short and curly. She seemed to have grown taller still, and had gained weight. Her face had filled out and she looked as pretty as a picture in her soft blue and grey plaid dress. It didn't seem possible at her age, but she was wearing silk stockings and patent leather shoes. She told of happy experiences and of a very sad one.

"There was a little Negro girl who had been helping her mother wash. I don't know how it happened, but a pail of boiling water tipped and spilled all down the front of her. I don't know why I was allowed, because they were very strict, but I saw her stomach and it was like you could see inside. Maybe it wasn't the inside, but it looked like it. They'd put fresh bandages on, and oh Maman, she suffered and screamed. I cried. They weren't very kind to her. They'd scold her if she cried. It made me sick inside of me. I hope she gets better. I keep thinking of it, and I know Maman, I'll never forget it for as long as I live."

"Time alone smoothes the sorrows in life, dear."

PICNIC AND PLAYHOUSE

Armand was an early riser when he didn't have a hangover. A pot of hot tea was pushed to the side of the stove. The oven door was open and the younger ones stood in their nightgowns to enjoy the heat. Slices of bread were toasted on the stovetop until they turned golden. Then they were placed on the reservoir to keep warm. Maman walked in, her hair perfectly combed and braided.

Papa sometimes made his special loaf of crackling and cheese. It was a favourite recipe they all enjoyed. The pork rind was put into the roaster. As it roasted, Armand kept pouring the fat off until the crackling was golden and crispy. Then he put it through the meat grinder along with large chunks of Ontario cheese. Then he patted it firmly into Maman's bread tins. It could be sliced or spread on toast or crackers. There was no flavour like it. It was a simple and delicious appetizer. If there was garlic, Armand was in his glory. It needed nothing else. The cheese provided the salt.

As simple as it was to make, Flory never made it. In fact, she never made any of Armand's recipes. She was a great believer in boiling beef. It went farther. That way she was never without bouillon for cabbage soup. There couldn't have been another family in the village of Legal that slurped more cabbage soup than the Pilon family.

"Flory, I was t'inking. My crackling and cheese, to me it taste like not'ing I ever taste. I believe, Flory, dat would sell like hotcake in a *salon de bierre*. People like to have some little taste wit bierre. I believe so. Gee cripe, it taste like nut."

"You would think of it, Armand. Would you deliver it to the hotels?"

"Maybe one day I will, Flory. You never know."

He filled his cup with black tea and went to his parlour workshop with its lace curtains. He sat twisting wire one way and the other, looking at it from all angles. He thought of the snowmobile. He was happy he had removed Wop May's propeller. It worked very well without it. It should not look like an airplane and it should not look like an automobile. *It have to look like a snowmobile, an' have a look dat belong to it alone, wit' no frill. Clean-cut to travel trough de bush.*

There was a loud knock at the door.

"Come in, come in."

"Mr. Pilon, I hate to be the one to tell you, but old man Boules shot your dog."

Armand stared back, stone-faced. "What you mean, he shot my dog? *Christ de*

A MATTER OF COMPULSION

Calvaire!" He ran to Boules' and pounded on the door.

"Where is my dog, you no-good bastard?"

"Your dog is over there on the grass. I told you before what would happen if she killed one more of my chickens."

Armand ran toward Queenie. She was stretched out, long, sleek, and golden. Blood had trickled from her ear and mouth. He saw how the grass had been pounded with her last fight for life. Tears filled his eyes. He thought of how he had built and measured the snowmobile to hold Queenie and Blackie, and now it was too late. He should have listened to the old man when he had complained.

"You know M. Boules, I believe if I phone de policeman dat he will take you away. I do not know why I call you Monsieur. You are no gentleman. Non, an' you are not a sonofabitch. Dat is too good for you. If my dog Queenie give birth to you, she would kill you. Many people say dat you are an old fool. Wait until dey see what you have done."

"I warned you when your dog hung around my chicken coup. You didn't believe me, eh? Well phone the policeman. See what he says."

* * *

The boys helped Papa carry Queenie home. They buried her behind the barn.

Armand went to the hotel. "I am broken. Gee cripe, I feel if I have a gun today I would have killed. *Sacré Bleu!*"

"Killed who, Pilon?"

"Old man Boules. He shoot my hunting dog, Queenie. When I see her on de grass wit blood dat come from her mout' and ear it make me see de colour red for old Boules. He say she kill two of his chicken. It is my fault. I never believe dat she kill. I feed dose dog very good. Dey never go hungry."

That night Armand was carried home and left on the porch. The boys carried him to bed.

* * *

"I was never happy with your father buying dogs in the first place. No, he kept saying they weren't ordinary dogs. They were hunting dogs. Well Queenie hunted all right, and she was killed for it. I do feel sad, though. She was a lovely dog.

PICNIC AND PLAYHOUSE

Romeo, I'm wondering if she got enough to eat. She did have all those pups to nurse."

"There was plenty of horse meat whenever I looked. I guess she was a hunting dog."

* * *

For two days Armand stayed in his bedroom, too ashamed to face the family. He would send Venice to the store for Chanticlair cigarette papers and his fine-cut tobacco.

"It was all too good to last. He couldn't stay away from that cursed hotel."

"Maybe he would have stayed home Maman, if old man Boules hadn't shot Queenie."

"He was trying dear, and wasn't it lovely while it lasted? I do believe he has his drinks of moonshine, even when he's home working on his clothespin. How he disappears so quickly, then appears as though nothing has happened. Oh dear God, if he keeps on drinking, I'll jump off the High Level Bridge!"

It was sad for Maman and all of the children when they worried day after day as to whether Papa would come home drunk. Now the children had another worry, wondering when Maman would go to Edmonton to jump off the High Level Bridge.

* * *

Only one of Queenie's pups was golden. Juliette chose it for her own and christened it Finesse. It didn't seem that long ago that she had run to Papa, crying out in a French frenzy, "*Papa, Papa, la chienne va véler.*"

"Not so loud on de street. Queenie is not going to have a calf, she is going to have *petits chiens*. Puppy is de name."

No wonder all the children ran home from school like there was no tomorrow. Something different happened every day. It could be very happy or it could be very sad. There was nothing in between. You either laughed or you cried.

* * *

A MATTER OF COMPULSION

Sister Superior announced that a school picnic would be held at the old cheese factory down by the creek. "All of you must bring your lunch to school. We will have our usual French lesson in the morning. When the noon bell rings, we will take our lunches to the hill."

"Oh Maman, there is a very special picnic tomorrow. We're all going to the old cheese factory! Everyone has to take a lunch to school! I've never been to the old cheese factory, have you, Maman?"

"No dear, not yet I haven't. I'll make your lunches, don't worry."

Five lunches, she thought. *I wonder what I could give them that's different. I must do something to make them happy. I can see them tomorrow getting up before it's time, especially my excitable one, Juliette.*

* * *

"Now before you leave for school, I must tell you that mother bought each one of you a banana. I don't want any of you eating that banana first. If you do, you won't have anything to look forward to. Do you hear me?"

"Yes, Maman. Thank you, Maman."

* * *

Sister Carreveau was calmly going about her duties, walking down the aisles to see how the students were doing, just as if it were an ordinary day. This was very disturbing. When suddenly the clang of the bell sounded, everyone quickly closed his or her books. In no time the desks were cleared. The children were up on their feet and ready to leave.

"We are not animals! All of you be seated until I am ready. Now you may stand, file out in line, go to the cloak room, get your sweaters and lunches, then file out like human beings. Also, the trail is very narrow. I do not want any of you running wild."

At the very bottom of the trail ran the creek and on the other side was the old cheese factory.

"You may sit wherever you choose. Do not touch your lunches until we have rested for a while. Then I will let you know when to bow your heads and give thanks."

PICNIC AND PLAYHOUSE

The girls did as Maman had said. They knew now that she was right. They ate their sandwiches with their eyes on their bananas. This was far better than eating their bananas with their eyes on their sandwiches. Juliette was caught smelling the inside of the peeling. Her friends laughed. "Juliette is trying to eat the peeling. Don't you know you can't eat banana peelings?" She laughed and said she liked the smell of it. She wouldn't dare tell them it was the first banana she had ever tasted.

Sister Superior announced that if they were careful they could go down the hill to the creek. Everyone started down the hill, going in different directions, when suddenly Sister Carreveau was rolling down, tumbling round and round like a large spool of black and white thread. Everyone who saw her rushed to help. She lay still for just a moment, then stood up, brushed herself off, smiled and said she felt fine. How her habit stayed in perfect condition was unbelievable. Even the little side puffs on her cap were as fresh and perky as before. Sister Superior decided that Sister Carreveau should be back at the nunnery. She must have been far more shaken than she had let on.

The picnic was all very wonderful, but it was sad that it was over so soon. "What are you going to do when you go home?"

"I don't know. Why, Yvonette?"

"My playhouse is finished. Do you want to come over and play?"

It was a real playhouse with a peaked roof. It was painted cocoa brown with white trim. The windows were curtained in a delicate white fabric. Dishes, toys, and anything her mother didn't need went to the playhouse.

They decided to build a chapel with apple and orange crates, draping it with a large tablecloth. A smaller box was placed in the centre. It would hold the holy sacrament.

"We don't have a good curtain to hide the chalice."

"I'll make one, Yvonette. Look at this gold velvet vest. Wouldn't it make a lovely one?"

"That vest belonged to my uncle, but my mother can't want it. Anything in the playhouse is mine, so you can take it home and make one. Can you sew?"

"Yes I can. I made myself an apron just like Sister Carreveau wears, with exactly the same stripes and colour. It even has a bib like hers."

"Where did you get the material?"

"Maman gave it to me, but she wouldn't let me use the sewing machine so I sewed it by hand. Even Sister Carreveau saw it."

A MATTER OF COMPULSION

"Did you take it to school?"

"No. One day after dinner I put my coat on and ran to school. I forgot to take it off, so I kept my coat on and asked if I could run home and come right back. She asked me why. I told her I forgot to take my apron off. I was shy, Yvonette. You would be too. Then she opened my coat and saw my apron, exactly the same as hers. She raised my chin and gave me a lovely smile. She said she liked it very much, but that if I didn't feel comfortable wearing it I could put it in my coat pocket. Maman said it was very well done for a girl of my age. So I know I can make a curtain to hide the chalice."

The bottom of the small curtain was scalloped in three half circles. The one at the church had fancy letters in the centre, but Juliette didn't know what the letters were, so she cut out a Y and an R for Yvonette Robert. Yvonette liked it.

The next day Yvonette showed her mother the velvet curtain. On Monday when they met at school she told Juliette how furious her mother was. "She said it wasn't yours to cut and she said I shouldn't play with you any more."

"But I did ask you, didn't I? Did you tell her it was just as much your fault as mine?"

"Yes, I told her, but she knew I wouldn't think of such a thing on my own."

"Did you tell her it was you who took me into the parlour to show me your piano?"

"Well she didn't slap you, but she slapped me."

"Can you play the piano?"

"No. I took lessons for a while but I don't like it."

"Well I'm going to play," Juliette said. "I went to Carrier's and Cecile Carrier, she's grown up, let me play on a real doll's piano she had when she was small. I never played before so I hid behind the swinging door and played there. I sang too. And you know what? They have a big piano like yours as well. Mrs. Carrier said I could play the big one sometime. And something else, Cecile Carrier took me upstairs to her bedroom and showed me a whole big box of pretty handkerchiefs. Oh, they were beautiful. Can we play together again, Yvonette?"

"I'll ask my mother. Maybe she'll say yes."

Juliette felt like a broken bird. *Why should Yvonette have so many things, like a piano, a playhouse, pretty clothes, and a whole store full of good things. Maman was right. Why should I have to pick the apple peelings they throw out? Why do I always have to ask if I can play with Yvonette?*

PICNIC AND PLAYHOUSE

* * *

"Yvonette, I have a big secret to tell you."
"What is it?"
"You won't tell? You promise?"
"No, I won't tell."
"Well, up in our attic we have a beautiful little store. It's small, not much bigger than your playhouse. It has shelves all around with one shelf for candies. It's very handy for Maman."

Yvonette didn't move a muscle. Then with penetrating eyes she said, "If you have a store in your attic why didn't you tell me before?"
"Because I'm not allowed to tell, that's why."
"Can I see it some time?"
"I'll have to ask my mother."

Now Yvonette had something to think about besides her own spoiled little world. *I'm not happy about lying to her, but it will heal. Somehow I feel that she likes me more.*

* * *

"Flory, if you are baking, don't forget to burn a few crust of bread. I got some good grain of different kind. It is time dat we have *café de crème*."

The grains were put in a pan and slowly roasted until they turned a rich brown. Everything was brewed together in the big blue coffeepot, even the burnt crusts. The cream was heated until a light skin formed on the top.

"*Le goût*, eh Flory?"

When Armand did thoughtful things Flory would look at him with pure adoration. She wondered what life could ever be like without him. These were the happy moments the children never forgot. The times when Papa played his violin, the times he ran after Maman until she laughed so hard she would fall onto the bed, trapped and with no strength left. Then the bedroom door would slowly close.

The times he made *patte de cochon*, standing at the stove with a hundred-pound flour sack tied around his middle. The pork hocks were browned. Onions, bay leaf, different spices, and always a few big sticky raisins, were added. The flour would be browned, lifted over and over so it wouldn't burn. When it turned the colour of maple sugar, Armand thickened it, stirring until it was as smooth as cream. It was poured over the hocks to make a thick gravy. Then, holding the spoon to her mouth he'd say, "Taste, Flory. Tell me how you like it."

"Oh, Armand. It is good."

It must have been good, because not one of the children ever forgot the flavour.

ROSE'S ARRIVAL

It was snowing when the mail rig pulled up to the door.

"Children, it's Rose and Lila! Oh Rose, you've come at a lovely time."

Everyone was happy when Rose came to visit. She could make Flory laugh so heartily that she had to hold her stomach still.

"Are you going to stay for Christmas?"

"Yes, I plan to stay for Christmas."

"Oh Rose, there's a basket social at the church. I've never been to one. What do you say we each make a basket? Armand would never go. With him, it's either you think or you drink."

"I've never been to a basket social either. When is it?"

"Next Saturday, so we have lots of time."

* * *

"Do you know Rose, that Mme. Morin always had meat hanging? Every winter when we were on the farm they'd have pork hanging in their shed. This afternoon let's take the boys' sled and go. We can have a nice visit with her and Cecile is home to mind things."

Dear Mme. Morin made hot tea and served her special doughnuts, which she seemed to make as regularly as Flory made bread. Her house still smelled of carbolic. They bought a young pig for one dollar and fifty cents and pulled it home on the sled. They slipped, they laughed, and they fell. It was as though they had never been apart.

"Don't you think roast pork sandwiches would be nice for a man to enjoy? And you could make a cake. Mother said you made the best cakes she ever tasted."

They bought a roll of white crepe paper and one of pink. One box was covered in white paper with pink bows, the other with pink paper and white bows.

* * *

"I saw a dress in Edmonton, Flory. I'll never forget it. It was made for us. We are getting stouter, and it would flatter us. I know you could make it. It was simple, but oh, the petticoat was blue silk, two shades lighter than the lace that covered it.

A MATTER OF COMPULSION

It hung loose. We should each have one."

"It sounds wonderful Rose, and one day I'll make them, but we can't have them for the basket social. We'll have to wear what we have."

Rose had brought wonderful-smelling face powder that had golden puffs all over the lid. She set it on the dresser. Flory put on her navy dress with the lace trim. Rose put on a black dress with a rose pinned below the waistline.

"Put a little powder on your face, Flory."

"Powder? I've never used powder."

"Well you're going to use it tonight. It gives your face a velvety look and it smells good. It has a pink tone to it. Here, let me put a little on your face. Now look at yourself!"

"Oh my. It is lovely, Rose."

* * *

"I don't know a soul. Aren't you nervous, Flory? I mean, whoever will buy our baskets?"

"Don't worry, Rose. Someone will. They may not be as fancy as a lot of them, but they are pretty with all those bows. It was Anna Saigner who told me all about it. She said last year one basket was shaped just like the church and another one was made to look like a tiered wedding cake. You know Rose, the wives hide their baskets from their husbands. That's the fun of it. You don't know who your partner will be. And of course the highest bidder gets the basket. Anna said it was all very innocent, so we won't worry about it."

"Oh, aren't the baskets pretty! Look what they're bidding on now. Why it's a red polka dot handkerchief filled with a lunch and tied on a stick and it's resting on his shoulder."

"Kind of reminds me of Beatrice. Remember her, Rose?"

"Yes, I remember. I always thought you loved her more than you loved me. Flory, it's my basket. I can't look, I'm so nervous."

"Going, going, gone. Sold to M. Gil Blais."

"Mr. Who?"

"M. Gil Blais bought your basket."

"Wonder who will buy yours, Flory. There's a pretty one. There's a huge rose covering the whole box. That's what you should have done. Oh Flory, I'm so

ROSE'S ARRIVAL

excited. I don't even know Gil Blais. Look, look. There's yours. They're starting to bid."

"Going, going, gone. Sold to Napoleon Demarne."

"Flory, did you trick me? You knew, didn't you?"

"Yes, I had a few hints. We'll sit together, Rose. They'll come to our table after the bidding is over. I only wish I had brought a bottle of wine, but I wouldn't have had the nerve. Anna said that most women did."

"I wouldn't know what wine tasted like, Flory."

"Oh, it's lovely Rose. Armand made parsnip wine on the farm. I hated to admit it, but I can tell you I did enjoy it. Don't say anything. Here they come. Just smile and be happy."

Never could it be dull when Rose was around. What Flory didn't know was how Rose could flirt. Mother did say that Rose was like their Aunt Rose, who supposedly married a gypsy prince. Aunt Rose also had velvet brown eyes that could melt any man's heart.

Flory thought of how lonesome and boring Rose's life must have been with Steve, and what a hard life she had had after she left the farm.

It was an evening that would remain one of their most memorable. There was no age difference now. They were young, they were together, and Rose was free. Never would she go back to Steve.

"Isn't Napoleon a handsome man with his trimmed moustache parted in the centre, his pin-striped suit, and the shiniest shoes I ever did see. Do you like him Flory?"

"Of course I like him. He's the dearest man, the dearest friend I ever had. How do you like Gil Blais? He's a darned good looking man, Rose."

"Yes he is, but he's so shy. I'd have to get to know him better, and he's a Catholic, Flory. I'm not divorced. I don't imagine I'll ever be. We just went our separate ways. Steve doesn't care if he has a divorce any more than I do."

"Well the two of you were sure gazing into one another's eyes, and I heard him laugh. He can't be that shy."

"Yes, and I saw Napoleon hold your hand under the table, and you were also doing a bit of gazing. Oh Flory, it's good to be back."

"Rose, you can stay forever. At least we understand one another's problems."

* * *

A MATTER OF COMPULSION

They felt young again. They cleared a big patch outside the left side of the kitchen door for a skating rink, hauling pail after pail of water to flood it. They had two old pairs of skates that dear Mr. Massey had given them. One pair had black boots, the other pair had brown.

Neither Flory nor Rose could skate. They hung onto one another, their skates turning inwards and outwards. They were like young girls, falling and laughing so hard they'd wet themselves.

To see Maman acting so young and playing as if her heart was happy, with not a problem in the world, made the children love Aunt Rose even more. They never wanted her to leave. With Rose there they forgot all about the High Level Bridge.

* * *

"Now we're going to get a Christmas tree, and I want all of you to collect all the comic strips you can find."

"How many, Aunt Rose? We'll save ours, and maybe M. Robert's, and I'll bet M. Demarne would give us his, and Anna Saigner too. Would that be enough?"

"That should be plenty, dear."

"What are we going to do with the funny papers?"

"We're going to decorate the tree. All it takes is scissors and some paste."

"When can we start?"

"You can start when you've gathered the comics."

By the time the tree was hauled in they had yards of coloured chains. They started at the top of the tree and scalloped the whole tree down to the bottom. It was the most beautiful sight they had ever seen. They could hardly leave it to go to bed. It was the very first tree they had ever had, and they decorated it themselves. Under the tree Aunt Rose placed a tiny wrapped gift for each of the girls.

"Rose, what are you doing? How can you afford to buy gifts?"

"Don't worry, Flory. They're just little trinkets I picked up at Woolworth's and The Five and Dime. It isn't much, but they'll love it, I know."

"Rose, Armand got apples, oranges, and nuts. They're in the cellar. Now if we put a lovely roast of that pork in the oven with dressing, wouldn't you like to invite Gil Blais for Christmas dinner? I know he's crazy about you."

"No, Flory. It's all too soon. He's a nice young man, but his clothes smell old, his coat sleeves are too long, and he never says anything. He just looks at me with calf eyes and I get feeling sorry again. It reminds me too much of Steve. I'd be jumping out of the frying pan into the fire. And what are you going to do with Napoleon Demarne?

"I'm sorry, Rose. I have been anxious about you. I do want you to be happy."

"Flory, there were times when I lay awake wondering why mother would take me away from you, then send me out to work at eleven years old."

"No Rose, you must have been twelve, going on thirteen."

"I don't care, Flory. I had no home. I was out there working while everybody was playing. Flory, I'm going back to Edmonton where I can find work."

"Why don't you sing, Rose? I've told you a thousand times what a beautiful voice you have."

"Yes Flory, and I've told you a thousand times what beautiful hair you have, so what can you do about it?"

"Oh Rose, I know you have to go. How I wish I could help you. You have been blessed with a God-given voice. All I can say is that our home is your home, anytime you need it."

FLORY'S STORE, LENNY'S HAND

This idea, the more I think of it, the more brave I become. I know Mme. Robert has gone to Diligence with her two children. I would say it's the perfect time.

Flory slipped on her best house frock and boldly crossed the street.

"Hello M. Robert. Can we have a little talk, you and I alone?"

"Yes, yes Flory. What would you like to talk to me about?"

"M. Robert, you do know that Armand took my parlour to build his snowmobile? Yes, you do. He also rented it to the Morencys. Then he brought boarders in when I was pregnant for Baby. You should know, you are her godparent. Then he ran a blind pig in my bedroom. You know, because you had liquor and oysters there. He bought expensive hunting dogs against my wishes. Now he has moved the cream separator into my parlour to work on his clothespin. Oh yes, he also has sold liquor or moonshine. I know that you have bought the odd bottle."

"Yes, Flory. What is all this about?"

"M. Robert, I want to start a small store in my parlour. I want something of my own. Can you understand?"

He looked at her in disbelief. "Are you serious, Flory?"

"Yes, M. Robert. I've never been more serious in my life, and I know I can make a go of it. It won't be a big store that would hurt your business."

"Flory, it would be good for you. I wish you luck."

Tears filled her eyes.

"Don't feel sad. Smile, Flory."

He gently flicked a teardrop from her cheek and hugged her. He was a small man. She remembered when he was at the house having a drink with Armand, how he put both arms around her neck, and how she swung him from side to side like a pendulum.

Yes, I've always been fond of M. Robert, and thank you dear God for giving me the gumption to speak out.

Spring would come soon. The farm would be rented to M. St. Martin. *When Armand comes home, I have to be smart, especially if he has been drinking. After all, he would have to move the cream separator, the wire, and everything else to the shed. Then he would be expected to give me the money from the rent of the farm. God, my stomach is beginning to turn. If I weaken, I'll never be good for anything.*

She decided to wait until he was in one of his very special moods. *It may take a*

A MATTER OF COMPULSION

while, but I'll get to him.

* * *

Leonard walked in holding both hands behind his back, one under the other to catch the blood.

"Maman, I don't want you to cry. It doesn't hurt. I had an accident." He held out a hand with fingers that looked like fresh sausages split down their centres.

"Good God in heaven. What happened? I feel faint."

"I was helping Yvon make a fence and he hit my hand with a sledgehammer."

"We can thank our stars we have a new doctor in the village."

While Dr. Reopelle looked at Leonard's hand, Flory quickly told him how Leonard had been hit with a sledgehammer.

"I don't think so, Mrs. Pilon. It doesn't look like a hammer hit. It looks like a gun shot."

"A gun shot? Look at me Leonard! Look at me and tell the truth."

"We were playing at the creek. Yvon saw the gun. It was stuck in the rocks. We thought we could shine it up and sell it. We even cleaned the inside. He got some shells. At first it wouldn't fire. We tried again, and it shot me."

"Dr. Reopelle, it's the same gun that shot my brother Willie's hand. My husband was furious and threw it in the creek when the water was high. We were on the farm when it happened. I can't believe it. I truly can't believe it."

Whenever Lenny's hand throbbed with pain he went to the doctor to have small pieces of the primer removed. He'd bring the pieces home to show the kids. Flory would wrap them with the other pieces she had kept.

"For a smart man, you weren't very smart, Armand. Why, it could have killed him."

"Non, Flory, I was not smart. I was mad. I never t'ought somebody would find dat gun. I should have break it."

"Lord, it was close to killing him."

"You said dat. You want me to commit suicide? *Non?* Den be happy dat he is alive."

When Lenny's hand healed it looked exactly like Uncle Willie's, with slanting fingers and a deep hollow in the palm.

* * *

FLORY'S STORE, LENNY'S HAND

"Are you ready for some news, Flory? M. St. Martin have rent de farm. Dis year I feel dat I would like to buy a car. A Model T Ford."

"A Model T Ford?"

"A truck. I could do a lot wit a car like dat. What you t'ink?"

"Well Armand, I'll tell you what I would like. Oh, I've thought about it for a long time."

"What is it?"

"I am going to start a small store in my parlour. It's my turn, Armand. I thought about it when Robert's store burned down, but you went to Brownsburg, and when you came back you started on your snowmobile and we didn't have five cents. I learned to have patience, but there wasn't a day that went by when I didn't see that store in my parlour."

"Flory, do you forget dat Robert have a store across de street? Gee cripe, are you crazy?"

"I went to M. Robert to ask him if he minded, and he wished me luck. He is a dear man. I know you won't mind moving the separator to the shed. There's plenty of room, and you'll have peace and quiet there. Wouldn't that be better, Armand?"

"It do not sound bad Flory, but can you do it?"

"I was a very young girl when I worked, Armand. I also watched my mother in the shop. I have enough brains and experience to sell ordinary things to ordinary people. It's been a dream of mine. Ever since I was a young girl I've wanted to own my own shop."

Armand wasn't saying much, but he was doing plenty of thinking. *She surprise me. Gee cripe, dat is a big job to tackle. Yes, maybe we can pay de loan on de house. She have gut, I say dat for Flory.*

* * *

"Children, your mother is going to Edmonton on business. I'll be taking Baby with me. You will play in your own yard, understand? Your father will be home, so there's no need to have Mme. Benet here."

* * *

A MATTER OF COMPULSION

"Cecile, what about the High Level Bridge?"

"No Juliette, she wouldn't be taking Baby with her if she intended to jump off the bridge, so we don't have to worry about that. Let's decorate the whole kitchen to surprise her. Remember how happy she was when Aunt Rose put up our first Christmas tree and we made chains to decorate it?"

They hung the chains from the four corners of the kitchen and crossed them above the centre table where an extra cluster was hung for a bow.

Without Maman around, the house was empty. Papa behaved himself. He may have had his little sips, but he was still drinking cups of black tea. When he saw the kitchen decorated for Maman, his eyes lit up and his nostrils flared.

After three days, Flory came home. Her coat smelled like trains, a different smell that wasn't in their everyday lives. It was a worldly smell of greater things.

"We did it for you, Maman. It's a surprise. Do you like it?"

"It's all very nice dear, but it will have to come down."

They did expect a little more enthusiasm after all the hours of love put into it. Just looking at it and saying, "It's very nice. It has to come down," wasn't the jolt they expected. Anything would have sounded better than that. Even, "It's beautiful. We should have thought of it before. Now the flies will have some place to land besides the kitchen table."

"Now all of you sit down. Mother has something very special to tell you. You know where the parlour is? Well that is where I'm going to have my store."

"What store? M. Robert has a store across the street. I'd like to see you put that in the parlour."

"Don't upset your apple cart, Leonard. I told you, I am going to have a store. It won't be a big store. It will be a little store. A handy store. That's why I went to Edmonton. The shelves and counter will be started this week."

Her own words kept ringing in Juliette's ears. "A little store with shelves all around and one shelf for candy. A little store the size of your playhouse, Yvonette. A little store in the attic that's so handy for Maman."

Each child's happy face looked up at Maman and smiled.

* * *

"Do you want to come to my playhouse, Juliette?"

"I'll come. What will we play?"

FLORY'S STORE, LENNY'S HAND

"Oh, we'll just play. You told me a lie when you said you had a store in your attic because my father said your mother was going to have a handy store. I heard my father tell my mother."

"Don't say that, Yvonette. It just got crowded with stuff up there. Candles and little lamp globes. Now it can be moved downstairs."

"I bet you're happy, eh?"

"I am, but most of all Maman is happy, because when she lived in England they had a shop. She missed it very much. Now she's going to have a handy store. Not a big one like your father's. It just wouldn't fit."

The shelves were put in and contained two large bins along the bottom. The counter held the scales and the gold-scrolled cash register. Stock came in with odd-sounding names like Réveillon, Ira Wannacot, and The Great West Saddlery. Boxes of cookies were set in the bins. There were marshmallows topped with white or pink coconut, and chocolate cookies. There were round, square, and diamond-shaped candies, licorice pipes, and chocolate bars called Wildfire, Eatmore, and Sweet Marie.

"Children, I don't want you taking candy or cookies from the store. You got along very well without them before. Once in a while mother will give you a treat."

* * *

"Armand, the children are taking cookies. Oh, I know. They're not fooling me."

"How you expect dem not to taste de sweet? Dere is too much temptation. When you want something and you are forbid Flory, you want it more. It is human nature. It is as simple as dat."

"I was strict at first, but they got around that. No, I can't let them eat the profit. I've only just started. I do give them something once in a while."

"Once in a while is no good. Let dem eat a little every day. Give dem somet'ing when dey come home for dere dinner. Dey will get use to it. Soon dey will not take your candy and you will not have to worry."

None of his big ideas. I'm not going to let him ruin the best thing I ever had. Selling a leather jacket on credit and not asking me! No, I'd rather not have him in the store. If I know him, he'll give everything away.

A MATTER OF COMPULSION

* * *

On Saturdays the girls wore black sateen bloomers. They were made full with elastic drawn through the hems. It was easy for Cecile and Juliette to put a tin of sardines in each leg of their bloomers. It was the canned corn Juliette often had to give up. Cecile, being taller, could handle a tin of sardines in one bloomer leg and a tin of corn in the other. Not Juliette. She was too short and had skinny legs. The weight of the corn fairly pulled her bloomers down. If Flory had come along and said, "You look terrible. Pull your bloomers up," they surely would have been caught.

Slices of bread were buttered. Nothing else was needed except for a can opener, two forks, and one of Maman's flour sack tea towels. Maman didn't mind them going, but she didn't know about the sardines.

They walked far behind Saigner's old farm, where pools of water went in and around bright emerald green islands. The bottom of the ponds looked untouched, with rosy terra cotta-coloured sand. Tadpoles jetted and spurted from one bank to the other, while long-legged mosquitoes skated on the crystal-clear water. It was like a maze leading from one small island to another, perfectly hidden with a border of poplar trees. It was the calm and peaceful beauty that only Nature could mould.

"Let's go bathing in our underpants. Look how shallow it is. All we have to do is stay close to the bank." The bottom was not as firm as it appeared to be. Their feet sank. The water turned into a reddish mud and the girls sank into it. They had to lie flat and ever-so-carefully pull themselves along until they could reach the bank. It was a scary experience.

"If Maman knew what we did, Juliette, she'd have a carroty fit."

"Yeah, and it looked so beautiful. You know, I bet if Maman ever found out we took sardines and corn she'd never ever trust us again, would she?"

"No, I guess she wouldn't. We're going to have to change our ways. If Lenny, Romeo, Venice, and Baby each took something, Maman wouldn't be able to afford the store."

* * *

"Armand, you won't believe what happened to me today. A man came into the store. He started to order things, but every time I looked up, he was looking at me.

FLORY'S STORE, LENNY'S HAND

I thought maybe he knew me, so I asked him where he was from. Then, when he paid me, he said, 'I would like to . . . ' Oh Armand, it was terrible."

"What was terrible, Flory?"

"He said, 'I would like to . . . ' Armand, it's a bad word. I can't say it. It starts with *F*. I told him to leave and never come back. He had a heavy black moustache and red gums, and spoke broken English with a guttural voice. I could barely understand him."

"I have a moustache and my English is not so good, Flory."

"Not like that. Don't be soppy. I was alone and very frightened."

"You do de right t'ing, but you lose a good customer. You should have said 'I am a slow t'inker, but I will t'ink about it dis week.' You were not very smart dat time. What was his name?"

"I'll never forget it as long as I live."

"So what was his name?"

"His name was Len Small. That's what he said. It doesn't sound foreign, does it?"

"Wit a name like dat, what can you expect? I am de only one wit good news today. M. Montpetit want to buy de farm."

"Good heavens! What would your mother and father say?"

"We are grown people now, Flory."

"We may be grown but it was their wedding gift to us. It's a cruel trick to play on them. We only had it for a few years and oh, I do love it."

"My parent would be happy. Dey know by now dat I am not a farmer. I read about a place named Cold Lake. It is in Alberta also, so we would not be going to the end of the world. Flory, I always want to live beside a lake. For a long time I am t'inking about it. I hear de fish is very big. I read fifty and sixty pound. Also, it is a summer resort and de American go crazy to take a trip to fish in dat lake."

"You're serious, aren't you?"

"You bet your boot. I mean every word I say."

"Why did you never tell me that's what you want?"

"What would be the use, Flory? We have de farm. It rent. I never t'ink to put it on de market for sale, but M. Montpetit, he come to me."

"What about my store? Will I have to sell it?"

"Ah Flory, you can always have anudder. I always t'ink if I live beside a lake, I buy a boat. I can see you wit your braid let down and your hair float on de water.

A MATTER OF COMPULSION

Life don't wait for nobody an' I feel life could be easy for us. What you say we take a gamble, Flory?"

"It wouldn't do any good if I said no, would it Armand?"

"Non, it do no good. My soul is hungry. Can you not understand?"

"Well then, you'll have to get on with it, won't you?"

THE GOODBYES

The farm and the house in the village with Flory's little store, were sold. Until they left Legal they rented a small two-story house close to the farm. It had a barn where Blackie would feed and sleep until he was sold. Now there was nothing for Flory to do but wait.

The new place was a sad and dreary little house with a dark kitchen. A narrow, steep stairway led up to the bedrooms. It was a place in which to ponder for a while.

The news of Pilon selling his farm, house, and store travelled as far as the Fortesque Hotel. It was no surprise that Armand went there. He always did, when he had something important to tell.

It was early evening when Armand staggered into the house, running his hand up his fly to check things out.

"Oh how I wish I had never laid eyes on you. You've let me down at a very sad time, Armand. I gave up the farm, the house, and store that I loved. I even gave up Napoleon Demarne, and now I'm going to a place called Cold Lake. What for? What's it all for? To go through the same things over and over again? I should leave you now. Yes, it would be a good time, maybe the perfect time."

"Leave, leave! I don't give a goddamn. Take all de kid wit you. Go back to England. You try to rule me like Britannia rule de wave."

The girls ran out to the barn and up the ladder to the hayloft. They looked down at the dog snarling and growling over a long horse shank that had the sickly smell of marrow. Old abandoned tools splotched with rust lay useless on the ground. It was getting darker now. They took turns going down the ladder to listen. The coal oil lamp was lit, but not a sound came from the house. That was far more frightening than the hollering.

"It's all right children. Your father has gone to bed. You should have taken Baby with you. She was jumping up and down on the bed, screaming and pleading with your father not to hit me."

"Did he hit you?"

"No, but I believe he would have if it hadn't been for Baby's screaming."

Oh, thank God we are leaving that cursed hotel and all his cronies behind. It's the only thing left to do, sell everything and go. Who knows, maybe he'll be a better man if he buys a boat and goes fishing. I wonder what he'll do for a living? I'm not

A MATTER OF COMPULSION

going to worry now.

Armand stayed home for days, packing things. He had a lot of business to attend to. Also, he was waiting for a very important delivery. He hollered, "Flory, are you dere? Come here!"

"Yes, Armand?"

"Where would you like to go in our new automobile? Come on. Bring de kid. Get a blanket for dem to sit on. Bébé can sit in de front. Where would you like to go?"

"I would like to see Mrs. Pepin. I like her. Whenever she came to the store we laughed a lot and always had so much to talk about. She's English, you know."

Where Armand learned to drive she never knew, unless it was the night he took off in his snowmobile. Now he was on his way to George Lake just as if he knew the way.

Mrs. Pepin opened her arms in welcome.

"Come! Do come in, all of you. You kept your promise, Flory. You said that one day you would visit me."

"We are so many. Surely the children can play outside. We can't all be treading on your floor."

"Nonsense. All sit down and it won't be long until we have tea."

Nothing seemed difficult for Mrs. Pepin. In no time at all she was folding cake batter over and over with a wooden spoon. How all the ingredients she threw together could blend like thick cream, was unbelievable. Then quickly she poured the batter into two round cake pans and put them in the oven. The whole time she worked, she chatted with Flory and never missed a beat. When the cakes had cooled, the egg whites were beaten, and a pinch of salt was added.

She had long skinny arms with two little mounds of muscle sticking out hard. She could make that egg beater work faster than Maman ever could. She kept throwing in scoops of brown sugar and vanilla, whipping it until it rose above the bowl. She took out the wild strawberry jam and spread it thick on the bottom layer. Quickly she placed the top layer over the strawberries, then mounds of icing were swirled into high, nodding peaks. Juliette never turned her eyes from the performance. It remained forever a picture in her mind.

* * *

THE GOODBYES

"You'll never know how I enjoyed this day. Don't you think she is a dear woman? She'd bring eggs to exchange for something she needed. I always had tea and cookies, but nothing like the cake she made. Oh wasn't it good, Armand?"

"Yes, it was quite a cake. She make it like a magician."

"I do feel that Mrs. Pepin would have been a dear friend to me. There were so many times when I needed someone. Now we are moving away."

"I also like M. Pepin. He is like me. He marry an English woman. Do not worry, you will meet many new friend. I will to go to Cold Lake tomorrow. I want to see it before I make a move, eh?"

"Will you promise me that you won't drink?"

"Do not worry yourself. Also, I do not know how long I will be away. It depend on de property for sale. Many t'ings, Flory, come into de picture."

* * *

A long two weeks had gone by with Flory not knowing where Armand was. There were so many worries she could think of. He could have run off the road and into a tree or ditch. He could be hurt, or he could have met someone he knew and gone on a spree.

Flory heard a noise. She ran to the door.

"You didn't expect to see me, did you?"

"No. I thought it was Armand. He went north to a place by the name of Cold Lake. That's where we are going to live. I'm happy to see you, Nap."

"I heard you sold everything, even your little store. Also, I must confess, I knew about M. Pilon going north in his new car. You see, I wouldn't have driven in if the car had been here."

"It wouldn't have made any difference. Armand's known about us for a long time. He never was a jealous man. He's the type who would invite you in and pour you a drink, if he had one. Yes, and then he'd thank you for being kind to me when he went east and had so many, many things to do. That's Armand."

"You would have left without saying goodbye, Flory?"

"I don't quite know if I'm coming or going. It has all happened so fast. Maybe it will be better away from here, close to a lake. That's what he loves. He said it himself. He even wants to buy a boat. Yes, away from here he may be a better man. I don't want to cry, but I can't stop the tears."

A MATTER OF COMPULSION

"Call your girls. I'll take you for a drive. You'll forget your troubles and smile again. Ah, I can see you are surprised to see my new car, and it isn't what you think. I bought this car before Armand bought his."

"Oh, it is lovely. Why it looks as if the Queen of England should be riding in it, with that fancy buff top and all. What is the name of it?"

"It's a Maclachlan Buick. I'm sorry I didn't have it to drive you to my place."

"Don't say that. I enjoyed our rides. There were so many lovely talks. Early morning should never be rushed, and what nicer way to share the time than by horse and buggy? That will always hold very special memories for me, Nap."

The car was roomy. The seats were wide and soft. It had the smell of wealth, like Maman's coat when she came home on the train. Baby sat in the front. Cecile, Juliette, and Venice sat in the back. Juliette wondered what Papa would think if he saw them in the car. Cecile and Venice never stopped talking. Juliette never said a word until she called out, "Stop! I'm going to vomit! Quick, stop!"

Napoleon braced himself, put on the brakes, and came to a full halt. Juliette just made it out of the car in time and managed to hit the side of the road.

"Oh, I am sorry for the inconvenience. I do apologize, but there isn't a speck anywhere. I've inspected every inch of the car. She isn't used to a car. She even felt sick when we drove to Mrs. Pepin's and she was driving in the open back."

"Don't worry about it, Flory. Leo gets sick too. It takes getting used to after a horse and buggy, especially if the roads are winding."

"Now wasn't that a lovely drive? Thank you. Say thank you to M. Demarne, and before you play, go to the barn and see if the boys have fed Blackie."

"Napoleon, you helped me a lot when you told the Galatians around Diligence that I sold things cheaper. I truly will miss you. I enjoyed being with you. I couldn't wait for Saturday mornings. You made me feel needed. You treated me like a woman, and for that I'll be forever grateful. I'm sorry, here I go again, crying like a big baby."

"Forever grateful isn't what I wanted. I hoped that one day I would have you to share my life with. Look at me, Flory! Don't look down. Look me straight in the eye and tell me."

"He does make my life miserably unhappy when he drinks, but I can't help myself. I love the man and I hate him for making me love him. Can you understand?"

"Understand? How could I not understand what love is, Flory?"

They held one another silently, hearts connected. Then, the last kiss. Flory

THE GOODBYES

walked toward the house. They were the longest steps she had ever taken. She prayed she would never regret the biggest decision she'd ever had to make. She neared the door, then turned to face him.

"If you ever change your mind Flory, I'll be waiting." He drove down the grassy road and turned to the left.

COLD LAKE

"Flory, where are you? Your husband is home."

"Is that you, Armand? Where have you been for so long? Did you like it?"

"Not so fast, not so fast. I want to breathe."

"You've been breathing fresh air all day and I've been worrying my insides out."

"Put de kettle on de fire. We'll have some tea. Gee cripe, you will like dat place. Ah yes, it is a beautiful country to live in. It is what all men dream about. You should see de lake. It make you feel like you are in paradise. I come home because I want to take you to Cold Lake. How about we leave in one week?"

"Oh, I'd love that. And we won't have to eat in hotels. I'll pack food. Whatever we need we can buy on the way. The children will go crazy with happiness. You know how they love picnics."

The children wondered how Maman could have known they were going somewhere. She had made Venice, Juliette, and Baby each a new coat and new dresses with matching bloomers. Miss Gray, the new housekeeper at the Rectory, had a new coat that was too small for her. It was a beautiful tweed coat with a black velvet collar.

"Try it on, Cecile. Let's see how it looks. It was made for you dear. It fits perfectly. Oh, you do look lovely, and you shall have it."

Leonard and Romeo were to stay home, take care of the house, and feed the dog. They didn't complain. In fact they seemed happy about the whole arrangement.

It was early morning on July 15th, 1926. The weather was warm. Everyone was happy. A new life lay ahead, with wondrous dreams that couldn't help but come true. Armand would holler, "Hold tight, I am going to go fast! It is no danger, Flory. Do not be frighten. A fire smoulder along de roadside. Still, de road could be hot anyway eh, and de car runs wit gas. A good cup of black tea would taste good to us an' I am sure de kid are hungry. We will have to wait until we come to de river where we will take de ferry across. Dere is a place where we can sit. Dere is a special place where we can make a fire an' boil water."

They lingered ever so long, resting and enjoying their tea.

"You are happy, Flory?"

"Of course I'm happy. I'm happy it's all behind us. Now we have a chance for another new beginning."

"Yes, I feel you will be happy. I feel it in my bone. An' now de ferry is coming."

A MATTER OF COMPULSION

That night they slept at the Lamont Hotel. In the upstairs lobby was a big piano like Mme. Robert's. The girls looked at it longingly, but didn't touch a note.

"So you like de piano?"

"Oh Papa, can we have a piano one day?"

"Not so fast. We will see about dat later." He sat on the piano stool. His fingers glided over the keys. He looked up. His nostrils flared. He gave them a wink.

"When did you learn to play, Papa?"

"I learn when I am a boy. I compose dis myself."

"Did you take lessons?"

"Non, non. I never take lesson. I learn myself. Anybody can play if you have a good ear for music."

Now the children knew that nobody, no other father, was as smart as Papa. And no one could smile with his nose like Papa.

They drove through villages with quaint domed churches, unlike the one in Legal with one long steeple. Papa said they were Galatian churches. At Mundare they shopped for food. Flory picked out two huge round loaves of bread. Armand got a thick wedge of cheese, milk, and homemade Galatian sausage.

"De man say he make de sausage himself an' his wife make de bread Flory, and he say it is de best. Now we will drive to a place dat is cool. We will enjoy and relax for a while."

Papa sliced the sausage, Maman sliced the bread.

"I tell you, I never taste not'ing like dis in my life. Dey must bring de secret of dat from dere own country. Ah yes, I decide that I will buy a sausage machine. My mind is made up for dat."

"Oh Armand, you are so right. I can hardly stop eating. And the bread, well it's different, isn't it?"

"Yes I am sure de Galatian people have *recettes* dat are different den our own."

That night they stayed at the Lafleur Hotel in St. Paul de Metis. The Lafleurs were French. It didn't take long for Armand and the Lafleurs to discover that they were second cousins. Much laughter and many stories were shared that night, with Flory joining in to tell stories of her own. Armand had drinks, but he did behave. After all, it wasn't every day that someone came along who was your second cousin, and miles away from home. It was a good time, and when they were leaving, everyone saying their farewells, it was certain that the Lafleurs and the Pilons felt strongly related, and would never ever lose touch with one another.

COLD LAKE

* * *

"We are getting closer, Flory. We are now on our way to Bonneville. Later we will stop to eat. You are happy? I can feel dat, but non, you are too almighty to smile an' tell me. Listen to de kid singing your English songs. Dey are happy, eh?"

"Yes Armand, they are. I am too, but it frightens me. Every time, when I'm happy, I end up crying."

"T'ink happy, den you will not be sad."

"Turn in here, Armand. I feel we must all have to go to the privy. We have some of that sausage left. There isn't much, but I'll make it go far with sandwiches of cheese."

It was a sheltered spot with green, thick grass that welcomed them to sit.

"Do you know what we did, Maman?"

"What did you do, dear?"

"Well at Mme. Lafleur's, the sheets on our bed were all torn, so we pinned then on the wall."

"What are you talking about? You pinned what on the wall?"

"In case Mme. Lafleur didn't know, we pinned the sheets on the wall so she could see them and mend them."

"You are wicked children - little cats, to do such a thing! Why, that's your father's second cousin."

"Where's the first one, Maman?"

"Bébé, dat is a good question. Do not look at me like dat, Flory. I laugh because it is a good question. Can you not laugh at a good joke?"

"I don't care. Pinning torn sheets to the wall isn't exactly a joke to me. She probably thinks I did it. You should be ashamed of yourselves! Just when I met someone I could like."

"Ah Flory, you always miss de point. Now we go to Cold Lake. Forget your problem."

"Is it far?"

"Non, not too far. Maybe forty miles. We will be dere in good time for supper."

"I see water. Is that it?"

"Gee cripe, you do not sound too happy. Wait until we arrive, den you see de lake. It is not a big town, so do not excite yourself. I will drive straight down to de

185

A MATTER OF COMPULSION

fish wharf. It will be a surprise for all of us."

* * *

"Hello. My name is Armand Pilon. I would like to buy a fresh Cold Lake trout to feed six people, an' I know we will each want two piece. An' please could you cut it in large slice? Are you de man Martin, who rent de boat, because I would like to rent a boat to take my wife and kid for a ride an' maybe to fish."

"Yeah, you come when you are ready. Maybe in the morning."

Halfway up the hill Jean Renard had a store. Armand stopped for two loaves of bread and a pound of butter. Further up the hill was the Beauregarde Hotel. Directly across from the hotel, gentle sloping stairs led down to the water.

Rounded stones were placed in a circle and dry wood was gathered from the timbered shore. Armand lit the fire. The iron frying pan just fit and the butter bubbled half way up. He slipped the slices of trout into the pan.

"Flory, are you not happy? All around dere is beauty, eh? You are sitting on dat big stone like de Queen of England. You are happy? What are your dream, Flory?"

She looked up, smiled, and nodded. What he didn't know was how far away her thoughts were. Time had stopped. Everything lay still. Only the haunting cries of the loons echoed across the calm waters. *Here I am, sitting on this sun-warmed rock, my children gathering pebbles on the beach, with Armand. Yes Armand. The love and curse of my life. A whole new beginning could be ours. He is a good man, Lord. Please help him stop drinking. Lord Jesus if you do, I'll cut off my hair. It's the only real thing I have to offer.*

"Call de kid, Flory. You have de voice for dat. De fish have bone. Dey should use dere hand. We do not want a catastrophe."

"Did you enjoy de Cold Lake fish, Flory? Kid, say somet'ing, eh."

"Armand, it was better than all the cockles and mussels I ever tasted."

"It sure was good, Papa. Can we go now? They jumped from stone to stone and down to the golden sand.

"You see, Flory? Dey are happy. Everybody have to be free. We were born to be free."

"Yes Armand, I truly love it all, the lake, the smell of the air. I have never felt such peace."

COLD LAKE

"Now we call de kid and we go. I want to show you somet'ing."

He drove down the hill, turned left, then parked right opposite the Catholic church.

"Why are we stopping here, Armand?"

"I am stopping here to show you our place. Yes, dis will be your home, Flory."

"Good heavens!" A huge building was being erected on a large lot. "A home this size? Whatever possessed you?"

"It is not all a house. It is a . . . you will be surprise, I warn you. It is a dance hall, and a butcher shop, and here on de left side is de home. It is all-in-one."

"A dance hall right opposite the Catholic church? Are you out of your mind?"

"Don't excite yourself. People have no place to dance. De tourist come and dere is no amusement."

"You're not all there, and if you thought you were going to surprise me, you did. I feel I'm going to faint."

"Wait, Flory. Dere is plenty of time to faint when we start our business."

"You took me to the beach. Oh, you are a devil. You wanted me to love it all. You knew the children would go wild, and you kept on looking at me, wanting me to tell you how much I loved it. Oh Armand, what will I do with six children to raise in a dance hall?"

"You will do a better job on de kid in a dance hall. Do not fret. Dey will learn about life. Also, I buy a lot from Bedard. It is on de beach and face de water. It is very beautiful. I show you. I rent a boat for tomorrow. You Flory, and the girls, will go on your first fishing trip. You like dat?"

"I've never been on a fishing trip. Is it safe?"

"It is safe. We will take a lunch an' enjoy ourselves."

*   *   *

What a calm and peaceful day. Papa with smiling nostrils and Maman sitting tense and rigid as she stared down the fishing line and into the water.

"Armand, are you sure there are fish in this lake?"

"Yes, but you cannot sit with a frown looking for fish. Dey are not going to follow our boat. De fish are deep swimmer. Give me your line and I will telephone dem. Hello down dere! I am telephoning you to let you know dat my wife have come many mile to get here. So could you be a sport and welcome her please? Now Flory,

A MATTER OF COMPULSION

hold your line tight. It will not be long."

"Oh Armand, you are a soppy man. Armand! Armand! The line is jerking! What do I do? Help me!"

Armand pulled in a huge trout. He looked at Flory with the assurance of a thoroughbred.

"You see, Flory? Anyt'ing can come true, if you believe it can."

Martin cleaned the fish. The meat was a deep salmon colour.

It was a happy day for all of them, and Maman said, "No children, there is no one quite as smart as your father."

*　*　*

Armand rented a small log house which years before had been a hospital. It belonged to George Hill. Now it would be their home for a while.

Armand went back to Legal. It was a quick trip to pick up the boys and give Blackie away. He put as many of his things in the back of the truck as he could, leaving enough room for Leonard and Romeo.

All he could think of was the dance hall. It was the biggest, most important endeavour of his life.

*　*　*

"Flory, you tell me last week dat you were sorry you did not stop at Edmonton to buy dishes and a new bed. Why you do not go dis week? You will also need some sheet. While you are in Edmonton you can take de train to Legal. It is not far, eh? You see, dere are two crates dat hold my important papers and my drawing of my inventions. Also all my tools."

"It's too bad you couldn't have brought them with you when you got the boys."

"Dere was no room. You see de truck, how loaded it was. If you see me go like wild man from one place to de udder to try to sell Blackie and de pups, you understand. I never stop. For two, tree day I go steady. I have to see Montpetit. Dere were many t'ings left on de farm. All we take was de cream separator. It will be easy for you. I have put my name an' address on de crate. Joe Beauchamp, he will take you and de crate to de train. He charge very little. You know dat I am needed here. Dere is no time to waste. Dis dance hall have to be ready for de Grain

COLD LAKE

Growers' Pique-nique Dance."

Flory did go to Edmonton. She ordered four new beds, sheets and blankets, and striped bedspreads. She didn't mind going back to Legal. Although it did give her a strange feeling of emptiness when she walked close to the barn where she could see the shack that Armand helped build. It was their first love nest alone and away from the prying eyes of her family, especially the ones who kept on staring at Armand.

"Our Flory, marrying a Frenchman! Can you believe it?"

"No, I can't believe it Madge. She probably fell head over heels in love with him when Mr. Pilon bought him that black horse and buggy. You've got to admit we never had anything like it in England."

"Maybe not George, but I wouldn't marry anyone, not anyone, but a blue blood."

Yes, how well I remember. I had five children in that shack. I loved him. I waited for him. I'm still waiting. Now things could get worse, with six children to bring up in a dance hall.

She opened the barn door. The dogs were gone. Stripped bones lay bare and stained with the stink of life and death. Against the wall were the crates, addressed and marked for shipping. In a dark corner the snowmobile waited for its master. Flory lay her hands on it and felt it. He had made it long to hold Queenie and Blackie. She looked at the seat where he sat so bravely that night when he said, "Are you going to wish me luck, Flory?" Tears washed down her face. She spoke out loud. "You were made in my parlour. I didn't like you then. It was like everything else he did. I knew you would go the way of all things, but you were brave that night. You never let us down. Don't you know how proud I was? Where will you go now? Will you rust away like all the old tools and be forever forgotten, or will someone find you and make you live again? Oh, Armand Pilon, how could you leave it? How could you be so cruel? All the years of sacrifice, then to lose everything we believed in. And you Armand, sitting by coal oil lamp drawing your dreams, three sheets to the wind."

She thought of Napoleon. *It was here, right here, where we held one another. Wasn't I strong, and wasn't he? Why, we would have made a perfect couple, I think. Strange how Armand trusted me to come back here alone. I could bet that he never gave it a thought. He's so excited about his new venture. "Ready for the Grain Growers' Picnic Dance," he said. Oh Lord, how am I going to cope with it all? If my family could see us now. I'm disappointed that some of them thought I married him*

A MATTER OF COMPULSION

for the horse and buggy. Time will tell what happens.

* * *

Armand had a very large tent pitched in the shade of the poplar trees. It was on their own property, and close to the log icehouse they had built. They moved out of the rented house and into the tent. It held four double beds with a walking space down the centre. There was storage space where Flory kept her metal flour tin that held a hundred-pound bag of flour. Flory took out the blue enamel bread pan and made enough dough for six loaves of bread. While it was rising, a ham simmered on the open fire.

It was the first time she had ever cooked outside, except for when she had made soap on the farm. The days were warm and sunny. She thought it might be a beautiful way to live forever, just like the Indians had lived. *Maybe they prefer their lives uncluttered with useless and pretentious things, and maybe they get on with their lives with things that are important to them.*

The loaves of golden bread were set on the table and covered with flour sacks. The ham was left to cool in its own juices. She could hear the workers hammering and decided to walk over to see how her new home was coming along. The partitions in the living area were up. She liked the idea of the four bedrooms in a row. She was happy she had stopped over in Edmonton to order four beds and the bedding.

"I do find the kitchen long and narrow, Armand."

"It look that way because it is not finish."

"Armand, why did you tell the carpenters to take a break and go for a beer?"

"Don't get excited. Dey pay for dere own beer."

"They *should* pay for their own beer with the wages you're paying them. We should be careful. We have no way of knowing if this so-called dance hall will make a living for us."

"Complain, complain. Flory, dere was one time when I love you very strong. I could eat you. Now I am sorry dat I did not. In one week I go to Edmonton on business."

"What business, Armand?"

"Do you not realize dat you cannot have a dance hall wit'out having a piano? You expect me to play my violin? Non. Do not tell nobody. I would like dat to be a surprise for de kid."

THE DANCE HALL

The piano was ordered. Also, a huge sausage machine, scales, hooks, and everything that was needed for a butcher shop. The dance hall floor was laid and Armand waited for the piano to arrive.

The children couldn't believe the wonderful things that were happening in their lives. Sleeping in a tent and eating outside was like a picnic every day. A new house was being built with a big dance hall, and there was a lake to swim in. But best of all was the day the piano was delivered.

It was a Willis roller piano. Armand slid the small doors open and set in a roller that looked like white paper with a hook on the side. He hooked it, then started to pump with his feet. The sweetest music came out of the little slots and dots. It was all unbelievable. There were boxes of rollers. The first one he played was called *When Your Hair Has Turned to Silver*. The second one, he said, would make them feel happier. It was called *Turkey in the Straw*.

"You see Flory, de word are on de roller an' de kid can learn de song." He turned to the children. "Now you watch Papa. I show you how to operate de piano."

The music was heard all through the village. When people heard that the Pilons had a roller piano with buttons and pedals, they wandered up the hill to ask if they could see it. The native people never asked to see it, but would stand outside the doors to listen.

The days were long and sunny, and right there from the porch you could see the beautiful lake, twenty-five miles long and twenty miles wide. The water was crystal clear, so clear you could see a small nickel floating down to settle on the white sand. In long rows the golden sand lay scalloped, pure and untouched. The rocks were round and smooth, as though they had been polished by a master jeweller. The water gently washed over the pebbles that lay sparkling like gems. The children played in the shallow water, wading out a little farther every day, until finally they could do the dog paddle like the other children.

The four new beds had arrived. They would have to be put in the dance hall until the bedrooms were finished. The children slept there. There was a heavenly smell of new lumber that lulled them to sleep. When the workmen started hammering, they awakened fresh and alive, ready for all the excitement of a new day.

The dance hall had large windows with wooden shutters that could be hooked to

A MATTER OF COMPULSION

the ceiling to provide cool, fresh air for the dancers. The windows faced the lake. If it was cold, they could be let down.

Finally, Pilon's dance hall was ready. The St. Paul Orchestra had been hired and preparations were being made for the first Grain Grower's Picnic Dance. There were many tourists, good fishing, and now there was a dance hall for amusement. The Beauregarde Hotel was built the same year as Pilon's Dance Hall. The beer parlour was a real refresher for tourists and fishermen.

"De St. Paul Orchestra have arrive, Flory. Gee cripe, look at de size of de drum, eh?"

"Oh Armand, I do hope everything goes well."

"You worry for not'ing, Flory. It's easy. I stand at de wicket an' take de money, de orchestra play, de people dance. It is very simple, and you will see some dancing tonight, I can tell you dat!"

The younger girls wore the dresses Maman had made, with bloomers to match. Cecile wore a pale yellow dimity dress with narrow frills that were bordered with a delicate black stitching.

"You all look lovely. Do you know what your mother always wanted? I always wanted a lace dress, a loose one that slips over a silk petticoat. I wish I had it for tonight."

"Wear your navy one with the lace trim. Papa said you looked slim in it."

"I'm not going to worry, dear. I may glance in once in a while."

"Have you ever danced with Papa?"

"Once. Just once. We went to a *soirée* when we first met. My face was as crimson as the stripes on that towel. I finally had to sit down. I never danced in England. Oh, it didn't bother your father. He thought it was a big joke."

Armand stood at the wicket taking the money. He had something to say to each guest. As they walked away they were either laughing or just plain happy. Flory watched. *Look at him. He does have a winning way with people.* She thought that maybe he had found his calling. Not working on a farm or in a store, but doing something happy like music, being the centre of attention. *I should have known it years ago when he borrowed my braid ring to show off.* She noticed how he ran his hand up his fly and wondered where he hid the liquor. She had to admit, though, that he was in control of things. The hall was filled to capacity. The long benches that wrapped half-way around the hall were for non-dancers and onlookers especially.

"Armand, the children should go to bed. I don't mean Cecile and the boys, but

THE DANCE HALL

the younger ones"

"It is an experience. Let dem stay a little longer."

When the last of the dancers had left and the players were packing their instruments to leave, Armand called to Flory.

"Come on de porch. I want to show you somet'ing beautiful. Look at de sun come up. Look at de lake. Do you not feel dat we make a good move? Dat was de best dance Cold Lake ever have. Yes, an' de best music. Dat was a good orchestra, Flory. You know, I feel I do somet'ing for dis place."

Flory was in deep thought the whole time. *To even mention the word "liquor" this evening would be the worst thing I could ever do. I wonder where he got it? It isn't beer. I know that smell.* "Yes Armand, it was lovely. A big crowd and a good orchestra."

"I have one good idea. Dere could be some money to make. We are built on a slope, eh? De back of de hall stand on beam. If we dig deeper, we can make living quarter down dere."

"Haven't we got enough space, Armand?"

"But Flory, we can rent de room up here. Also, at midnight dey get hungry. We should serve a meal. We should build a counter and some shelf in de hall. Yes, I will plan for dat. Also, I meet Jean Renard today. He have de store up de hill where we stop for bread and butter? I tell him I want to build some cabin to rent. He say it is a good idea. Not everybody want to sleep in de tent, eh?"

"You should keep your ideas to yourself. By the time you think about it, he'll have some of his own built."

"What I want to do first is build a log summer kitchen wit' a good slanting roof for de tourist. No window. All open. De tourist can cook dere meal even when it rain. I also decide wit' dat lovely park we have, wit' all dose tree, we should have a camping groun'. It will hold fifteen or more tent. Dat's not'ing to cough about, Flory."

"I don't know where you'll get the money. You're ordering barrels of pickled pigs feet and giving them away, and what did you order all the dill pickles for?"

"Gee cripe, what have pig feet and pickle got to do wit' cabin and camp groun'? Not'ing!"

"Money, Armand. It has to do with money."

"When I have good idea you have to put stick in de wheel. Bullshit! You never tell me I am right. Never! You see de dance we have, yes? But you tell me I am crazy

A MATTER OF COMPULSION

to build a dance hall. I will show you dat I am not crazy!"

"Look at me, Armand. You're drinking again. People see you going to Gilbert's hotel every day."

"I don't give a damn who see me. If dey look at demself first, den look at me, it will not bodder dem."

"What do we do between dances? How many dances are there going to be during the cold winter months?"

"By dat time de coolers will be build for my butcher shop. We should make money. I am only one. I have not stop since we arrive."

The counter and shelves were put in at the front of the hall. On dance nights large containers of ice cream were brought in and set in chipped ice. A huge glass barrel-shaped container with a tap was kept full of thick, pure, mission orange juice. Chipped ice was added to each ten-cent glass. The shelves held cigarettes, matches, gum, and chocolate bars. Most popular were the boxes of kisses. Each box held a prize. It could be anything from a chic lady's compact to a man's pure leather belt.

That winter the hall was rented to Mr. Zigler. It was Cold Lake's first picture show on a large silver screen. Armand had a projection room built directly above the front entrance.

Flory had made one stipulation. If Armand was to pay for the projection room, her children must be allowed to attend the shows free of charge. Mr. Zigler agreed. He said he would rent the hall every summer.

"We are not doing it right, I can see dat. You be surprise to see de tourist. Some are swimming, some go fishing, some are on pique-nique. Yes, an' I saw some picking berry behind Bedard's place. We do not have to wait for Saturday night to have a dance. Remember, you tell me dat in England dey ring a bell an' holler loud, 'Murder, bloody murder!' Well I will hire de young Ryder boy. His name is Raymond. He will ring a cow bell all over de village an' holler, 'Dance tonight at Pilon Hall', an' also for de picture show he holler. Dat should bring de people, eh Flory?"

After the picture show a dance could be held with little cost, if local musicians were hired. Adolf Rockstaad was George Ryder's helper when the hall was built. He never went anywhere without his violin. Adolf knew other local talent, so Armand hired Adolf and trusted him to show up.

Raymond Ryder, the bell ringer, had a natural loving nature. Everybody liked him, but he was gifted as well. He could imitate a violin so perfectly that you would

THE DANCE HALL

never believe the haunting melodies had come from a young man with lips perfectly relaxed. You could be fooled into believing the music came from his expressive eyes, and not the trickery of his mouth.

"You can do it, Juliette. Look. You rest your top teeth very gently on your bottom lip. It will tickle at first, like blowing through silky paper set over a comb. Not every one can do it if they haven't got the right shaped lips or teeth, and if you can't sing, don't try." It didn't take long before she could make the rich violin tones that Raymond made.

The moving picture screen hung from the ceiling far enough down to hide the stage. Venice and Juliette were very quiet. They could hear much talking and laughing as people took their seats. After all, it was a big occasion to watch a movie on a huge silver screen. Venice was sitting at the piano on the stage and Juliette was ready to play her make-believe violin. The laughing and talking stopped. There was complete silence.

Everyone thought the music was part of the show, like a scenario. Abe Zigler, Mr. Zigler's son, was the projectionist. He was young, good-looking, and only had eyes for Venice. He walked onto the stage and whispered in Venice's ear that the show was about to begin. The three of them walked out from behind the screen. He said, "I liked that. What is it called?"

"It's called *When Your Hair Has Turned to Silver*."

"Who was playing the violin?"

"It was Juliette."

"You mean you can play the violin?"

"I can't, Abe. I play it through my teeth. You know the boy who rings the bell, Raymond Ryder? He taught me."

* * *

Armand made a business trip to Legal. When he returned he told Flory he had hired a man, and that he would arrive some time in September. She looked at him over her glasses.

"Don't look dat way. I told you we are going to dig under de hall to make living quarter."

"Yes Armand. I know all about it. I can slowly see it coming. Spending money like it's water and hiring men. You'll regret it one day."

A MATTER OF COMPULSION

"You regret. You regret. Goddamn! I believe, Flory, you would be happy if I fail."

"Can you tell me what we'll do in September, October, and November Armand?"

"Dere will always be a dance, every Saturday night, be it rain or be it snow."

"I won't say a word, Armand. Get on with it."

A NEW WAY OF LIFE

Closer to the lake was Charbonneau's store. It was a two-story building with living quarters upstairs. It was handy for Flory. All she had to do was step out of her door, walk past the Lakeside Hotel, and into Charbonneau's store. They had become friendly enough that she rather looked forward to walking down to buy what she needed and to having a visit with Mme. Charbonneau.

"Mrs. Pilon, my husband and my son are going away for a while. I was wondering if your Cecile would come and work for me. You see we live upstairs, and I cannot work in the store and mind my children. I will be happy to pay her."

"I'll ask her, Mme. Charbonneau. I'm sure she wouldn't mind. I'll let you know tomorrow." Cecile wasn't happy about it, but when Flory said it would help if she could make a dollar or two, she willingly went. What Flory didn't know was that Cecile would have to live in, in order to be up with the children, clothe them, and give them breakfast.

The outside stairway that led to the Charbonneau's living quarters was long, steep, and narrow. There was no yard for the young ones, so they were confined to the stuffy rooms all day. Cecile was so lonely, and home was so close she felt she could touch it, and yet she couldn't get away.

Stores closed late at night. Mme. Charbonneau stayed in the store after the last customer had left and read the Edmonton Bulletin. Only then, two or three hours later, did she lock up. Cecile felt she deliberately stayed down in the store to be alone and away from the children. Mme. Charbonneau also had a daughter named Cecile. She went to school each morning, which meant one less in the confined quarters. When Sunday came Cecile was allowed to go home.

"Maman, I don't know how much longer I can stay there. I hate it! Hate it! I can't go out in the fresh air and I hate to take a deep breath. I'm sick and tired of smelling pee."

"There can't be that much pee, dear."

"No? Well I'm awake half the night. I'm sleeping with two of the children and they both pee the bed. There's always one peeing up my back. The bed smells terrible. Mme. Charbonneau told me to dry the sheets by the stove. She said it was only babys' pee so it wasn't dirty. They're grey flannelette sheets and you can see big pee rings. Oh Maman, they stink so bad and I'm tired."

"How long have you been there now?"

A MATTER OF COMPULSION

"I've been there for two weeks and that's a lot of pee. She's always in the store and I'm stuck upstairs smelling pee."

"When you go back dear, tell her I need you home. I do, you know. Tell her you will stay until she finds someone else. It wouldn't be fair to leave her with the children and the store to care for without giving her some notice."

Three days had gone by and Cecile hadn't come back home. Flory needed a few things and decided to walk down to the store. When Mme. Charbonneau saw Flory she quite lost her temper.

"Mrs. Pilon, I don't think you need Cecile. You are being cruel to me. You have two other girls who can help you, and you don't work like I do in this store!"

"My daughters go to school just like yours do. My Cecile is not sleeping well here, and for a growing girl it isn't right."

"Ha! Not sleeping well? Excuses! Yes, you are making excuses! She sleeps like the rest of us."

"Mme. Charbonneau, I had a store and six children to care for. I managed it myself. It was mine, and Armand let it be mine. So don't talk to me about your work in the store. I understand that your husband is away and it is difficult for you, but I also have a daughter who I understand, and . . . "

"Oh my God, what next? What other excuse have you got now?"

"No excuse, Mme. Charbonneau. The truth is, I didn't want to hurt your feelings. You see my Cecile isn't used to sleeping with babies."

"Ha! Now you say you do not want to hurt my feelings! You are a cruel woman."

"As I was saying, your two young ones have been peeing up my daughter's back for two weeks and the bed smells awful."

"You say I am dirty?"

"I'm not saying one way or the other. All I am saying is that I want my daughter at home."

Flory walked out. That evening Cecile was home. One thing was certain - Flory would never go back to Charbonneau's. When something was needed she sent one of the girls up the hill to Jean Renard's.

Jean Renard had a goatee. If you happened to walk in when there were no customers, he was sitting behind the counter nervously twisting strands of hair into corkscrews, each one sticking straight out from his chin. He was a thin man who always wore the same trousers with deep creases and bulging knees. If he did have

A NEW WAY OF LIFE

two pair they looked no different. The Pilons did as others did, and called him Old Man Renard behind his back.

Germaine, his wife, appeared solemn, as though she carried a deep, dark, secret. Annette Pawlic lived with the Renards. No one seemed to know how they were related. It was said she was adopted. Then in later years the story was that she was their foster daughter. Whoever she was, she remained dedicated to the point of obedience. She had two children, Fiona and Clyde.

"I hear today dat Renard is dickering wit' Charbonneau."

"Dickering for what?"

"He want Charbonneau's store. Yes, his mout' have water for dat."

"He has a store. Why would he want Charbonneau's?"

"Ah, Charbonneau have a good spot, right on de corner. It is close to de wharf. You get de tourist an' de fisherman. No walking up dat steep hill. Old Renard is like a fox. Many people have tell me. He will get it, just watch."

"I wondered why Mme. Charbonneau and Mme. Pawlic were suddenly as thick as thieves."

"How you know dey are t'ick like t'ieves? You do not go to Charbonneau no more. Do not tell me you spy on dem."

"Spy on them? What do you think I am? The girls know I don't see Mme. Charbonneau anymore so they told me she and Mme. Pawlic are always going for walks together. What do I care? It's just very strange. There was no friendship before, because Old Man Renard had his store on the hill and Charbonneau had his store down here. Yes, I'm sure you guessed it, Armand. Old Renard will get Charbonneau's store."

* * *

"De man I hire is here. Gee cripe Flory, I never t'ink dat he would come."

Flory started for the kitchen. She stepped through the doorway and stopped suddenly. Her blood curdled. The man looked crude, and as he smiled broadly his red gums showed from under his heavy moustache. How well she remembered. She turned and walked back to her sewing. *Oh God, how could Armand have done it, bringing that man all the way from Legal. Wait until I get him alone. Just wait. Of all the men he could have hired, why would he hire Len Small? If he thinks I'm going to make his supper, he has another thought coming.*

A MATTER OF COMPULSION

It was no problem for Armand. He had moose steak from Stanley Nest, and it was so tender you could almost pierce it with your finger. He chopped potatos and fried them with onions. Then he made gravy from the drippings.

"You sit down wit' de kid an' have your supper. I have to see a man."

Flory had decided she wouldn't sit at the table with Small, but when she heard gagging and choking she hurried into the kitchen. In Armand's hurry to get out, he hadn't bothered to trim the edges. Moose meat especially, can be sinewy. Len Small must have been famished. He swallowed a mouthful of meat, which connected to a long sinew that hung from his mouth. There was another piece of meat hanging from its end. He didn't know whether to pull it out or push it back in. The children ran from the table when his eyes rolled back and his Adam's apple shot in and out.

Flory briskly walked away. *Let him get on with it. If he throws anything up Armand will clean it! He's the one who brought him here.*

* * *

"Now will you tell me why you hired that man? I don't like him, Armand. He put so much food in his mouth he almost choked to death. The children ran from the table."

"I can see dat you enjoy yourself because you want him to suffer. Why, Flory? Because he is a man? He say words to you in Legal. Maybe you do not understand his language. He maybe ask you for knife and fork an' not what you t'ink. Don't be a *bébé*. Get dose idea out of your head. Besides dat, he was de only one dat would come for de price."

"I don't care. I don't like the man. I'll put it in the back of my mind Armand, but I'll make darned sure he never sees me smile."

When the girls came home from school they enjoyed watching Len Small dig. Shovel after shovel of dirt filled the wheelbarrow. Then it was hauled away and dumped. When they asked him questions, they never understood his replies, but he did smile a lot.

One day Len Small said, "I horse. You ride." He lifted Venice onto his shoulders, then holding on to her legs he ran around and around in circles.

After class they'd watch him dig and fill the wheelbarrow.

"Len Small, are you going to play horse today?" They never called him "Len." That seemed too friendly. "Mr. Small" didn't seem right. In fact it didn't suit him

A NEW WAY OF LIFE

one bit, so he was called "Len Small." He'd gallop and buck as he ran down the path to the icehouse. It was the most fun they could have, sitting so high, with their arms tightly round his neck.

Unfortunately for him, Len Small played horse once too often. He hung on to one leg only, and used the other hand to reach where he shouldn't have. Juliette told Maman what he had tried to do. "He dug his thumb in my private and it really hurt."

They never did know what Maman and Papa said to one another that night, but the next morning Len Small was gone.

* * *

"Why don't you and the boys finish the digging?"

"Non, Flory. De boy have to get jack pine. We need wood for de winter. Not a little wood, but many load. It have to be bucked and ready. De hall will take a lot of firing."

Not long after Len Small disappeared, Armand hired two German men. They spoke very little English. Heinz had a proud walk and was always clean-shaven. Karl was much huskier than Heinz, with a full head of thick, black hair. From his build you could tell he was the better worker.

Autumn was long and glorious, with not a breeze to disturb the golden leaves that covered the winding paths.

"Indian Summer, Flory. De most beautiful time of de year. Ah, it will not last and very soon de snow will come, an' when it come it will stay for a long time."

Heinz and Karl had finished the living quarters under the hall and Armand had them build another counter in the dance hall. This one was on the opposite wall, facing the window. Armand's thought was to put a cot behind the counter where a mother could sit to nurse her baby.

That first year they came from as far away as St. Paul, Bonneville, Fort Kent, and Chocolate Valley. They brought their babies bundled up and tucked into large fish boxes, where they were hidden out of sight behind the counter. It was at one of these dances not long before Christmas that Leonard met Rose Bertrand. A few days before Christmas a huge box was delivered. Everyone gathered round as Flory opened it. There was a gift for every member of the family, each one signed "Merry Christmas, from Rose Bertrand."

A MATTER OF COMPULSION

"Whatever would she do this for? Why, I've only met the girl once. Oh I could see she only had eyes for you, Len."

"Yeah, she's crazy about me and she sure can dance."

"Well you be careful now. I don't like her sending all these gifts. You don't know where she's from or what she does. Why, these gifts must have cost her a small fortune."

"She's a waitress in Bonneville. She's a nice girl. Hell, I didn't ask her to send these presents."

"Maybe not, but it's strange how she knew all our names."

"Yeah, well maybe she asked me. Maman, can she stay next Saturday night? She doesn't have to work Sunday or Monday."

"Goodness knows where she'll sleep, unless you bring in the small cot from behind the counter. We can put it in the hallway. I'll make it nice and comfortable for her. That's the best I can do."

That Saturday Flory was curious and watched how closely Rose and Leonard danced. Her hopes were that he wouldn't go too far with her. By the looks of things they were a bit too close already.

* * *

Juliette opened her eyes and wondered what time it was. She thought of how Rose had bought each one of the family a gift, even though they weren't related. She got up and quietly tiptoed toward the cot. There was no one there. The bed looked the same as when Maman had made it. She turned down the top blanket and saw the sheets covered in blood. She ran to Maman's room.

"Are you awake, Maman? Something terrible has happened! Rose isn't in bed and the sheets are covered with blood. Somebody must have killed her!"

"Saints in heaven!" Flory stood like a statue looking down at the blood.

"She didn't die. The hussy had a miscarriage! The nerve of her coming here to my home. Why she even left her bloody pants. Everything is soaked. Oh God, what did I do to deserve this?"

"What's a miscarriage, Maman?"

"She was going to have a baby. She was pregnant and she lost the baby. Go and tell Leonard to come here at once."

"Yeah, what happened now?" asked Leonard.

A NEW WAY OF LIFE

"Your so-called dancing partner left this. Isn't that lovely? She was up and gone this morning, leaving it all for your mother to clean. Sending all those gifts! Trying to get on the right side of me! I can see what she wanted. Did you touch that girl?"

"No, I didn't."

"Look at me, Len. Did you touch her?"

"I am looking at you. No I did not, but I liked her a lot and I might have later."

"You can thank your lucky stars . . . what do you mean, you might have later?"

"Well I'm older than Romeo, ain't I?"

"Never mind. Romeo just brags."

Flory feared what could lie ahead, with all the temptations a dance hall would bring.

It was very strange how this girl could have taken the chance and decided to stay overnight instead of going home. I can't help but feel sorry for her. Where did she go, and how did she get there in her condition?

Rose Bertrand never came back for another Saturday night dance.

* * *

The little French school had one big room with rows of benches and one big blackboard at the front of the class. There was a small cloakroom at the entrance. M. Pierre was the teacher. He was French, yet he came to teach the French kids how to speak English. If anyone said "dey," "dere," or "de," he would give them a fixed look. Then loudly and clearly he would say, "It is 'they,' 'there,' and 'the.'"

One day, for whatever reason, he made Venice sit on a high stool that faced the class, then placed a dunce cap on her head. The pupils were dead silent for a split second, then the snickers and giggling started. Romeo walked to the front of the class and without a word he swatted the dunce cap across the room and calmly returned to his desk. The classroom was dead silent. M. Pierre picked up the hat and replaced it on Venice's head. Romeo walked back and gave it such a swat that the pointed hat flew across the room.

"Nobody's going to laugh at my sister! Come Venice." He took her by the hand and led her out the door. Then flinging her onto his shoulders, he started down the road, taking the shortcut home.

Maman was very disturbed. Cecile, who wasn't in school anymore, decided she'd walk to meet M. Pierre. No one knew whether the words exchanged were good, bad, or indifferent. It didn't matter. Romeo never went back to school. He went to work. He learned all about winter fishing with jiggers and nets, and even how to keep the fish from freezing by covering them with snow and water. It made them look like small igloos.

He played poker with the fishermen, fish buyers, and trappers. Moonshine became rampant, and many a time at the Saturday night dance there were fights, with flying fists and bloody noses.

"We have to do something to keep de peace or we could be close down by de police. Leonard, you are big and you are strong. When you see a fight, I want you to break it up. Do not strike nobody yourself. You pull dem apart. Beer and moonshine do not mix togedder."

Leonard didn't half mind. He was six feet tall with broad shoulders, and when he was mad he even looked like a bull. He would pull the fighters apart, and holding them firmly he'd say, "Do you want to go out the door, or do you want to dance?" He was a good bouncer, and he felt he had a very important job.

LIVING QUARTERS

Living downstairs didn't please Flory. She made up her mind that Armand had never intended the upstairs to be her home. The way it was planned puzzled her, though. Where her kitchen used to be now held a big furnace, and her front parlour now held two double beds. Armand wanted to keep an eye on things, so for a while he and Flory occupied the back bedroom. Now there were five double beds that could be rented out. One had to walk across a small terrace and down three steps to get to the privy. During the winter months it would have been unfair to waken from a sound sleep and have to step out into the bitter cold to relieve oneself. It would also be unfair for anyone to fill a pot with anything more solid than urine. A fish buyer from St. Paul rented a room for one night. The next morning after he had left, Juliette walked into the room, turned, and walked out.

"Come and see, Maman. There's caca all over the curtains and the pot is full of caca too!"

"Did you say my lace curtains? The dirty dog! He knew where the privy was. Armand always tells them."

"I've been melting snow so you girls don't have to haul as much water, then taking the clothes off the line as stiff as boards and hanging them anywhere around the kitchen stove to dry. God, I'm tired. No, your father never finishes anything he starts. He's always thinking of new things and never finishes one of them. And he always has money for drink. Cursed drink!"

Flory was crying. Juliette knew that when things went wrong Maman always reverted back to Papa and his drinking, turning her problems into bigger ones.

* * *

Many nights they were awakened by gun-like shots. They were told it was the heads of nails that were blasting off from the frost and cold.

Each morning the first one up was Papa. He would break the ice on the water pail and fill the kettle.

At the end of May the ice on the lake split open. You could hear a thundering crunch as it moved. When the wind shifted the ice heaved up and over into mountainous peaks that lasted for days. One morning Baby looked out and the ice had gone. She hollered excitedly, "The ice is gone. It's all gone. It left in the night.

A MATTER OF COMPULSION

Where did it go, Maman?"

"It blew to the opposite shore. It could be thirty feet high, and could last well into July, or so your father said."

It was a long, cold winter. By the time they got to school, the lunches packed in Gainor's lard pails were so cold that when it was time to eat the sandwiches they were speared onto pointed branches and held over the school's oil drum furnace.

That spring Armand advertised for an orchestra. The musicians were to be provided with free bedrooms. There were many replies. It took some time to make a final decision. The last letter he received was the most explicit. It stated the towns where the band had played, what instruments were played, and also that all four musicians were single and would enjoy being at a summer resort. The good news was that the price was right.

* * *

The log summer kitchen was being built with a cement slab to hold the stove. A long sign was hung high above the road that led to the park. It simply read "Camping Ground."

* * *

A large parcel arrived from Eaton's. It was taken to Maman's room. The girls gathered round with the same excitement they had felt when they were small. The blue silk for the petticoat and the heavy lace that would cover it, were for Flory. Cecile got the pongee silk and the black satin. Venice, Juliette, and Baby each got a navy reefer coat. Flory had one happy afternoon of feeling the quality of the fabric.

The previous summer many young tourists had come to holiday. Young teachers, university graduates, and doctors spent the days fishing and the nights dancing. It was the year for party dresses, and there were some beauties. Flory could copy anything, so she paid particular attention to the party frocks. She knew exactly how to make the pongee silk and the black satin. For days the treadle Singer sewing machine was open. The blue silk petticoat with the loose lace was made exactly as Aunt Rose had described. It was like the one she had seen in Edmonton. It became Flory's favourite dress. It was so special that she later made one for Rose, and another for herself.

LIVING QUARTERS

Cecile's dress took thirty petals rounded to a peak, each four inches across and self-lined. Fifteen petals on each side for the pongee dress, which was to Juliette the dress of the year. The black satin was made full, with a very large butterfly bow at the back waist. Nothing pleased Flory more than having her girls dressed just a little better than anyone else.

* * *

"Don't you think it's time to get rid of the hired men? What are you paying them for? You have two sons who should be working. God only knows what they'll be good for."

"Because dey are big for dere age it don't mean dey can build. I will need de men about one more week, den I will tell dem to go."

"I'll say this, Armand. I don't like the girls hauling all that water from the lake. Venice and Juliette hauled twenty pails up the hill yesterday. Where were the boys? Playing poker with Ray and Willis Bedard."

"How do you know?"

"Oh, I know all about it. I'm not blind. Yes, and the girls had to saw wood and haul it in. Two sons and two hired men!"

"Yes, you have said enough Flory. I will see dat de boy haul water and buck de wood. We have to prepare de hall dis week. De moving picture will be coming. Dat is why I need de hire men. Dere is a lot of sweeping to do to pick up de sand dat come in, also de summer kitchen to finish, and de boy will go to get jack pine so de camper have wood. Gee cripe I cannot do everyt'ing myself. It should be a big dance after de show Flory, I am sure of dat."

"We've got to be careful, Armand. There's no money coming in and too much going out, and you are drinking again. Please, please Armand. Be careful."

* * *

Mr. Zigler and his son Abe arrived. The projection room and the dance hall were in ship shape, with rows of benches set up for the picture show. Willis Bedard had come early with his new lady love, and was anxious for Armand and Flory to meet her. She wore a grey suit with matching grey pumps. Taffy coloured hair swept above her brow and across her highly coloured cheekbones. Her name was Edith

A MATTER OF COMPULSION

Lampson, which was pronounced "Edit'" with a long "e." She was the daughter of Jean Paul and Germaine Renard. Years before, Edith had lived in Cold Lake as a young girl. She loved the water, and could swim across to French Bay. Now she had returned, along with her young daughter Marcelle.

There were very few evenings when Edith and Willis didn't come to visit. They would all sit on the long bench that faced out over the lake. Flory was happy that Edith had come that night. She was good company, and there was no need to keep looking over her shoulder, wondering where Armand was.

After the show Baby asked Maman if she could stay up to see the people dance.

"You may watch three dances dear, and tonight mother will let you sleep on the small cot behind the counter."

"It's not fair! You let Venice stay up."

"Not for very long, I don't. I could take you downstairs and put you to bed. I thought you'd be happy to sleep on the cot."

"Yes, I'll sleep on the cot, but someone will have to carry me downstairs afterwards."

"Yes, of course dear."

Both Edith and Flory were proud, serious women, unlike what they had been in their girlhoods of secrets and idle chatter.

"Baby, what are you up for? You were asleep when I looked in."

"I want to tell you something, Maman. I have to whisper it in your ear."

"Yes dear, what is it?"

"One of the hired men woke me up."

"Yes, what for?"

"He tried to feel my tiddly wink."

"What do you mean, tiddly wink?"

"Well that's what Lila called it. She fell down once and hurt her dicky, only she called it her tiddly wink."

"Which one?"

"She only has one, Maman."

"Which man was it? There are two!"

"I didn't know what you meant. It's the big one with black hair."

"You go to your bed, dear. Don't worry, I'll be watching."

Flory excused herself, telling Edith she had to find Armand.

Oh how thankful I am I kept her up here. When I think of what could have

LIVING QUARTERS

happened, I shudder. The beast! The wicked, wicked man!

"Armand, are you through with your hired men?"

"Well yes, it will not be long. Why do you ask?"

"For a very good reason. That big dark-haired one, Karl, who never said a word, went behind the counter and touched my Baby's private! First it was Len Small, and now Karl!"

"You say de big one touch Bébé? Gee cripe, I fix dat. Tomorrow dey will not be here. Also, what did Bébé say he do?"

"She came to me and said she woke up when he touched her. She sat up and saw him. Then he quickly disappeared. Oh God, who else will you hire?"

"Are you going to give me hell every time dat somet'ing go wrong?"

"Oh Armand, I can't help it. They're my daughters. I would die if anything happened to them."

"Flory, you should be happy dat dey are here at home where dey have picture show an' all de entertainment. Dey are safe where we can keep our eye on dem."

* * *

That summer tourists flocked to the lake. It was a beautiful place to live and many who had come to holiday returned to live permanently, just as Armand had done. In that one year of living in Cold Lake many wonderful things came their way. All the children knew how to swim. They learned to skate on Bedard's pond. They could sing and harmonize. They played the piano and they could dance. They were in a position where they could meet people from all walks of life. On the other hand, this caused many of the local girls to be jealous.

That summer the Morris girls came to Cold Lake. They were from North Dakota. Hearing the orchestra practising one afternoon, they became curious and wandered over to the hall. Armand gave them a real welcome and invited them to the Saturday night dance. They listened to the music for a while, then asked Armand if they could dance. Armand said, "Dat's what we are here for."

The Pilon girls watched, wide-eyed. They had never seen anything like it. The Morris girls held hands, one with the other, their trained legs flying in all directions.

"What you call dat dance? It is not de turkey trot, I can see dat for sure."

They said it was the very latest dance called the Charleston. "It looks difficult,

A MATTER OF COMPULSION

but it isn't really. Come," one said, taking hold of Baby's hand. To everyone's amazement Baby did the exact steps. Seeing the smile on Papa's face, she knew she had done well.

"Tell me, will you come to de dance on Saturday night? I would like de people to see dat. Gee cripe, dat is different from all de dance I have seen."

"We'll be happy to come every Saturday because we are going to live here."

They did come on Saturday nights. In fact they never missed a dance during the week either.

Two weeks later, crudely made signs were posted up on the telephone poles which read, *Don't Kick at the Basket, Kick at the Ball. No More Charleston in Pilon's Hall.*

"Can you understand dat, Flory? Maybe de people dat dance straight up and down do not care for dat. What can happen next?"

"It's probably because they can't do it Armand, and they're jealous."

"Maybe, but it sound like I forbid people to dance de Charleston. It also sound like I commit a mortal sin if I let dem dance it."

"How could you forbid it if you encourage your own children to dance the so-called Charleston? And how can you commit a mortal sin when nobody can dance the darned thing anyway? The signs have been taken down by the boys so we should forget it. We can drive ourselves crazy if we let that get to us. One day we'll find out who did it."

"I build dis hall to make people happy, to bring somet'ing to Cold Lake dat dey never have before. You tell me Flory, dat de farmer who bring dere bébés in fish box last winter are not happy?"

"Forget about the happiness you brought to Cold Lake. You built the hall to make a living. Edit' told me about the troublemakers in the village, and she should know. At most we only have four months in the summer. There's nothing in the fall, and not enough dances in the winter. With eight mouths to feed we'll have to send the boys out to work, and you too Armand."

"Dere is no work. What you want me to do, build a skating rink on Bedard's slough? It do not matter if I have fifty fishnet, de fish only open in November and December. August de tourist go back home to put de kid in school. For seven month of the year we have no big dance. I was t'inking maybe I go south for de t'reshing and de boy will come wit me."

"What would you do, Armand?"

LIVING QUARTERS

"Do? Cook for de t'resher, dat's what I do. Flory, we are not going to worry about our problem now. We should have a good summer ahead and dere is plenty to do."

* * *

The butcher shop was ready. Armand stood proudly in his white butcher's apron. He was happy, but that didn't last very long.

"I figure dat de butcher shop will lose money. Dere is too much fish. De farmer raise dere own beef and chicken. Also, what about all de wild meat? Non, it is too big a gamble. I can make two, t'ree room out of dat butcher shop, rent dem to de tourist in de summer and de fisherman in de winter. Don't worry Flory, winter is not here yet. I will manage it for a while. I am only t'inking ahead."

* * *

"Guess what, Armand! I received a letter from Rose. She's coming with her new gentleman friend, Gordon Armstrong. Oh, I'm so excited. I wonder if she's found someone to love her. She so deserves it."

"Wit a gentleman friend? Good. We will need help for de Pique-nique Dance. I decide we are going to serve meal. We have all dose table for playing card. We will make use of dem. I will hire Mme. Armitage and Mrs. Hunter to cook and bake pie. And Rose's gentleman friend Flory, we find work for him too."

"Why didn't you tell me, Armand?"

"I am telling you now. I just make up my mind. Dat is not soon enough for you?"

"Here you go with your big ideas again. What if no one comes?"

"If. If. Dere is no if, Flory. We do it."

* * *

Gordon Armstrong was a tall, slim man with protruding teeth and a lisp. When he walked his knees touched. He was well-dressed and fresh-looking in a crisp white shirt. At mealtime he sat alone, always at the same table. Mme. Armitage and Mrs. Hunter did the cooking. Aunt Rose and Cecile were the waitresses.

A MATTER OF COMPULSION

Flory didn't think Gordon was the man for Rose.

If he loved her, he certainly could wait until she was through with her chores. Then they could dine together. Why, even Willis Bedard never ate without Edit', and he was a country boy! Willis certainly doesn't wear his Sunday best every day of the week. Poor Rose, if she knew what I was thinking it would break her heart. She's so crazy about him, telling Cecile that she wanted to wait on her Gordon.

Flory enjoyed having Rose with her, but the thought of having Gordon Armstrong stay until fall bothered her. He never even asked if there was anything he could do to help. When there was water to haul, the woodbox to fill, or the hall to be swept, he was nowhere in sight. When everything was done, along would come Gordon, dressed in his Sunday best.

"Cecile, have you noticed our star boarder? He's seated at the table waiting for Rose to wait on him. I don't think I've ever known a lazier man who could eat so much. He's been here for over two months and hasn't done one thing but eat three meals a day. I thought your father was lazy, but at least he has something to show for his efforts."

"What can you do, Maman? Ask him to leave? You know that Aunt Rose would follow him."

"I'll think of something, dear."

* * *

"Rose, if Gordon could find work and pay his board I wouldn't mind, but there's a long, bitter, cold winter ahead of us, and Gordon is no fisherman."

"We've talked it over Flory, and of course wherever Gordon goes, I go. As much as I want to stay I can't, for fear that one day I may regret it."

"He isn't for you, Rose. I've seen how you wait on him hand and foot, ironing his shirts, always there at his beck and call. Why he's far more demanding than Steve ever was. He never says two words either. What do you talk about?"

"Oh yes he does. And he wasn't foolish enough to buy a homestead in the wintertime when everything was covered with snow, like Steve did. We rented a place in Edmonton and waited for spring. When we went back, the farm was nothing but big rocks. I never saw so many stones in my life. It could never be farmed, so we left it. That was Steve."

"He was green, Rose. It wasn't his fault."

LIVING QUARTERS

"You're right, he was green and he still is."

"Rose, who has stranger ways than Armand?"

"Well, I'll say this for Armand. He's proud and smiles when the kids do something smart. And another thing, he talks to you. Whatever his thoughts are, he tells you. If it weren't for his drinking and all his big ideas Flory, Armand wouldn't be half bad."

"Yes Rose, but if it weren't for his drinking and his big ideas he wouldn't be Armand Pilon. Where will you go with Gordon?"

"He wants to go back to Toronto. If it doesn't work out it won't be because I haven't tried. Believe me, I'll try Flory."

* * *

"I did hope Rose would stay, Armand. How she can love that man I'll never know. Why, the big sop couldn't even hook the shutters."

"Don't worry. I feel we see her again. I see de way she look at him when she sing her song. I was t'inking if we make a café out of de butcher shop it could make more money den to have room to rent. Yes, I will t'ink of dat when I return from t'reshing. Edit' and Willis say dey are going sout' also."

"Well Armand, they must make money. The Vadeboncoeurs went thrashing last fall, and the handy things they brought back! Remember the lovely doll they bought Juliette, with a china face and a white kid body. Now they wouldn't do that if they hadn't made money, Armand. They are dear people."

"Forget de sentimental, Flory. I buy two small pig and de boy and I will build a log house for shelter. De girl can feed dem every day. We will fatten dem for winter. We start to build a pigpen tomorrow wit a good roof. After de pen is build, we will move you upstairs where you will be warmer. You like dat?"

"Are you going to take your suit, Armand?"

"Non, non. I don't take my suit an' I don't take my banjo. I am not going to a party, I am going to work."

"I have very little money. I don't know how I'll manage, let alone feed the pigs."

"There will be mash for de pig. Mix dat wit potato peeling, anyt'ing you have. I am not going for de winter. I will be back in a few week. I will send you money when I see de colour of dat."

"Armand, I have an idea. I'm going to bake and sell my own bread. I can't lose. I have to make it anyway, and what doesn't sell, we'll eat."

"Who will buy bread?"

"Bachelors. Why even the teacher. I'll put a sign out. You see, Armand? I won't be doing anything I don't ordinarily do."

THE TRIAL

"That was one of the hardest decisions your father ever had to make. He swallowed his pride and went to work. It's the first time since he worked at Robert's store. I do hope he's found something in the line of cooking."

"He will, Maman, and he won't be drinking because he'll have too much to do. Maybe he'll want to go every year. He does like to cook."

"I wouldn't bet on it. Now Cecile, I want you and Juliette to feed the pigs. Mix the potato peelings and pork rinds with the mash. Venice and Baby will bring in the wood. Then there's water to haul."

I can still see him walking around like he was lord of the manor. All his big ideas and his drinking. I told him time and time again that the money would run out, but no, he had to have hired men and do everything in a big way. Grandmaman Pilon knew when she came to the farm. I can see her standing in the doorway. I'll never forget her looking at my three babies and a new one in my arms. Then she looked at me and said, "misère noir," and it was just that, black misery.

Close to the pigpen was a shortcut that crossed the property. Armand always left the big gate open for trucks or people who wanted to take a shortcut home. While the girls were feeding the pigs, they heard laughing.

"Listen, Juliette. Don't make a sound. I hear Cecile Charbonneau's voice. I'd know that laugh anywhere. Wonder who's with her. Don't move, I'll peek. I thought so. It's Fiona Pawlic and Betty Ryder."

When they got closer Fiona's voice was clear and loud. "And do you know what? Juliette Pilon came to grandpa's store and stole ten pounds of sugar, and . . ."

Before anyone answered, Cecile stepped out and quickly picked up a stick.

"What did you say Juliette did?"

Fiona had lied, and couldn't repeat it. Cecile hit her, and with each stroke she hollered, "Liar, liar!"

On the way home the girls decided that Maman had enough on her mind without worrying about who else Fiona Pawlic had told this wicked lie to. They would not tell Maman what had happened.

"You know Juliette, I walked out too soon. She was going to tell the girls that you stole a lot of other things. Did you see the look on her face?"

"You know Cil, I never told anyone, but once I went to Old Man Renard's for something. You know the big beam with dippers, frying pans, and everything

A MATTER OF COMPULSION

hanging from it? Well did he ever go after me. He tried to feel my titties. Well I got too close to the beam. Dippers, enamel cups, oh, all sorts of things were falling down. It was awful. He knew that Germaine Renard would hear it so you know what he did? Her called out in French, '*Germaine, ici, ici. Dépêches-toi,*' and she answered, '*Je viens. Je viens.*'"

"When she rushed in he appeared very annoyed. 'The nails have to be longer. It could be very dangerous if an iron pot fell on a customer's head.'"

"I ran home, but wouldn't you think he'd be worried? I could have told Germaine, but I just couldn't. Besides, if he ran after me, why wouldn't he run after Fiona Pawlic?"

* * *

"Are the pigs all right, children?"

"Yes, the pigs are all right. What are you reading, Maman?"

"I got a letter from your father. He says he's cooking in a buck's car. What does he mean? He could mean a box stove like the one in the front room. He says that Leonard is with him and that Romeo went somewhere else to thresh."

Suddenly the back door flew open and in walked Mme. Charbonneau and Mme. Pawlic. Flory was startled. No one just walked in without knocking. Her first thought was that something terrible had happened to Baby or Venice, who had gone to the lake for water.

Flory stood to receive them, when suddenly Mme. Pawlic punched her against the wall. "What have I done? Oh God in heaven, what have I done?"

"Your Cecile beat my Fiona with a stick! This is to teach you a lesson."

Mme. Charbonneau was next. She slapped Flory across the face. "You said I was dirty? Well I'll go in your bedroom and see how dirty you are!"

She walked into the first bedroom where Cecile and Juliette slept. She threw the bedclothes down. There, on the white flannelette sheet was one red spot of blood. "Annette, come and see the dirty blood on the sheet!" They started to laugh hysterically, like witches.

"Get out of my house! I'm going to call the police!"

"Ah, it will do you no good. My Cecile is a witness, and so is Betty Ryder."

"Yes, and my Fiona has the bruises to prove it."

When they walked out Flory's knees buckled and she fell to the floor in a faint. In

THE TRIAL

a panic the girls threw water over her.

"Oh God, you did overdo it. I'm soaked."

They helped Maman to a chair, and with tears in their eyes they said, "We didn't want to tell you, Maman. We thought you had enough to worry about."

"Now take your time and tell mother what happened."

"Well, we were feeding the pigs and I heard voices so we listened, and Fiona Pawlic was telling Cecile Charbonneau and Betty Ryder that Juliette stole ten pounds of sugar from Old Man Renard's store. I picked up a stick and hit her and called her a liar."

"I'm going to the post office to phone the police. I'm all right. I won't be struck again. I'll make it there, you bet I will."

They watched Maman take the shortcut through the churchyard until the bushes hid her.

Suddenly Flory saw someone coming out from behind the trees. Old Man Renard was waiting for her. *I'll walk right on by. I'll show him a thing or two.*

He pounced on her, knocking her to the ground. Flory got up. He hit her again, and grabbed her shoulders to hold her back.

"You are going to phone the police? Oh no, you will not!"

"You can kill me if you like, old man, but I will phone the police if I have to crawl."

How Flory got to the post office, no one knew, but when she got home her face was ashen. She didn't do anything that day, nor the next.

M. Pierre, the teacher, would be picking up his bread. He came every day after school. Flory had also set two large loaves aside for the shoemaker.

Flory called from her room, "Children, your mother is very sick and I need your father. Cecile, get Papa's letter. Take the address and go to the postmaster. Ask him to phone your father. Tell him I'm sick, very sick. Tell him it's urgent."

Cecile got a nurse from the hospital who was kind enough to stay at night. She slept on the cot by Maman's bed. With broken hearts full of worry, Juliette, Venice, and Baby went to school.

These were the longest days of their lives. They constantly looked at the clock slowly ticking the minutes away. At recess they stayed together and away from the others. Fiona Pawlic, Betty Ryder, and Cecile Charbonneau were surrounded by other girls who laughed loudly enough to be heard. When school was out they would run as if they were fleeing from a fierce burning fire.

A MATTER OF COMPULSION

Cecile was washing. It wasn't an ordinary wash with warm sudsy water. It was cold water and clear red blood. The girls ran to Maman's bedside. She lay pale, and spoke in a weak, soft voice. "I want you to kneel down and pray for your mother. Do it now, like good children."

Cecile lay a throw on the floor. Juliette drew down the green blind as low as it would go. They knelt in a row, resting their arms on the bed, and with clasped hands they prayed in the sombre green darkness.

"Cecile, why is Maman so sick? Why was the water red like blood?"

"Venice, Maman was going to have a baby. She was so weak from all the beating that she lost it."

The policeman from Bonneville arrived to question Flory. When he was led to her bedroom the nurse was holding a small teapot of water to Flory's mouth. All Flory said to the policeman was, "They beat me. They beat me. I had a miscarriage. I lost my baby."

He turned to Cecile and questioned her. She told him what had happened. He kept nodding his head and saying, "Yes, yes." He finally said that since her mother was so ill the trial would have to be held in their house, and that they would be notified as to the date and time.

In all their years, they had never needed Papa more than they did now. The misery and fear that he caused Flory and the children didn't matter. There was a part of him that they loved and needed. If anyone the world over could help Flory and make her well, it was Papa.

"Are you sure the postmaster telephoned, dear?"

"Yes he did, Maman. I saw him. Nurse, do you think if we helped mother sit on the commode it would be better than the bedpan?"

"I don't think she's strong enough."

It took some time urging Maman to shift her legs to the edge of the bed. They helped her up and managed to lower her to the commode.

"God in heaven, where are you, Armand?"

"He'll come, Maman. Please sit for a while."

"I'm going to faint. I've lost my insides. Please, please put me back to bed."

The nurse and Cecile saw the heavy clots of blood. They looked at one another. Not one word was spoken.

Cecile was hurt to the core. *Why hit Maman? They should have hit me.* Part of her felt she did the right thing in protecting Juliette, and part of her felt she was

THE TRIAL

wrong.

The dreaded letter came, saying a trial would be held at the Pilon residence. It was to be in the evening in the middle of September.

"If your father isn't here I don't want anyone setting foot in my home. Do you understand, Cecile?"

"Don't worry, Maman. I was thinking the same thing."

Flory was still in bed and only drinking soup and liquids from the small teapot. She was pale, weak, and so completely drained of energy that her words came out in slow breathless tones.

Leonard drove the Model T Ford down the side road and parked in the back yard. Armand jumped out and Leonard followed, rushing to the back door. When Flory saw her husband she broke down, sobbing deeply and saying over and over, "You'll never know, Armand. You'll never know."

"Do not cry, Flory. I am home. Tell me what happen."

Leonard, Cecile, Juliette, Venice, and Baby stood at the foot of the bed. Only Romeo was missing.

"Children, tell your father what happened."

"Non, non. One at a time. I cannot hear all of you. Take your turn. We begin wit Cecile."

The story was told from beginning to end.

"The policeman came, Armand. Cecile, show your father the letter about the trial."

"*Sacré Bleu!* What kind of wild animal are dey? I hear story about Jean Renard, plenty of story, and I believe every one of dem. I will sue dat goddamn old man. You children should have grab de iron pot and strike Pawlic an' Charbonneau on de head."

"It happened so fast Armand, as though they would think of such a thing."

"If I be here I would strike dat old man and also take my carabine. Why strike you, Flory? Why they did not strike Cecile and Juliette?"

"No, Armand. Mme. Charbonneau had a lot to do with it. She was very angry when Cecile left and she was happy to get back at me for saying her bed smelled terrible. I wasn't going to tell her, but she kept on sneering and telling me I was cruel and was only making excuses. I couldn't bear it any longer, so I just spoke out and told the truth."

"The trial is tomorrow, Flory. You cannot get out of your bed?"

A MATTER OF COMPULSION

"No, I won't get up. I couldn't if I tried. If you hadn't come home Armand, we wouldn't have allowed anyone in the house."

* * *

The big gas lamp was filled. One new mantle was put on it. The policeman was the first to arrive. Not more than ten minutes later the pack walked in. Annette Pawlic led the way with the evidence, a pole five feet long and bigger than any man's wrist. Old Man Renard followed close behind with Fiona Pawlic at the rear.

Nosy people came to see and hear. Armand must have known, because he had extra chairs for seating. Then came Mme. Charbonneau with her daughter Cecile and Betty Ryder. All you could hear was whispering.

"How could she do this?" Cecile asked Juliette. "I hit her with a branch, not a pole."

"I didn't see it, Cil. It happened all so fast. When I came out of the woods they were running away. If you had hit her with that she would have been screaming. I mean look at the size of that pole. Surely you would have broken her back."

"What is your name?"

"Annette Pawlic."

"What happened on the afternoon you entered Mrs. Pilon's home?"

"My Fiona and her friends were taking the shortcut across the Pilon property. Cecile and Juliette Pilon were hiding in their pigpen. Cecile Pilon came out of the pigpen. She picked up this piece of wood and hit my Fiona with it. My Fiona came home crying with the pain. Mme. Charbonneau was at my place. When we saw what she did to Fiona we decided to make a visit to Mrs. Pilon."

"What happened in Mrs. Pilon's home?"

"I was heartbroken at the way Cecile hit my Fiona"

"What did you do?"

"I gave Mrs. Pilon a push and told her she should teach her kids not to be so cruel."

Armand's insides were churning. *Sacré Bleu. Look at dat old bâtard Renard playing wit his barbe. He look like a devil. Yes, I hear dat she is his second wife. I never pay too much attention to dose story, but tonight I can see dat for de trut'. I wonder what he will say when he is call to give his story.*

"Cecile Pilon?"

THE TRIAL

"Yes, I am Cecile Pilon."

"What happened that afternoon?"

"Papa went south to thresh so Juliette and I had to feed the pigs. I heard girls laughing. When they came closer Fiona Pawlic was telling the Charbonneau girl and the Ryder girl that my sister Juliette had stolen ten pounds of sugar from her grandfather's store. I knew she was lying. I just, well I just ran out and picked up the first branch I saw and I hit her with it."

"Mme. Charbonneau?"

"I am Mme. Charbonneau"

"You were with Mme. Pawlic when you went to the Pilon house?"

"Yes, I went with my friend. When I heard what Cecile did to Fiona, I asked my daughter and Betty about it. They both saw what Cecile had done."

"What did you do at Mrs. Pilon's?"

"Uh, I didn't do anything but push her. Mrs. Pilon is a cruel woman. I know her well."

Armand was standing against the wall with his arms folded. With one quick step forward he said, "Excuse me, M. Policeman. I am Armand Pilon. My wife Flory was going to have a bébé. Mme. Pawlic and Mme. Charbonneau come to my house. Dey do not come like civilize people who knock on de door. Non, dey come like wild animal. Dey strike my wife until she fall to de floor. Den when she go to de post office to call de policeman, dis old man Jean Renard strike her and she fall to de groun'. Dese animal were trying to kill my wife! She get very sick and lose de bébé. She have to have a nurse from de hospital. I went sout' to cook for de t'resher. I get a telephone call to come home. I give up my job to come. We not only lose de bébé, I almost lose my wife and I almost lose my son and my car when de train come from behind a big sign."

Everyone shifted nervously. The policeman stood and said they should take a short break. The first one to walk out was Jean Renard, followed by the Pawlics, Charbonneaus, and Betty Ryder. Most of the on-lookers remained seated for fear of losing their seats. The family went to Maman's room. Her eyes were red from crying.

"Ask them all to get out. I don't want any more of it, Armand."

"It will not take long now. I do not know why dey take a break. He only ask t'ree people some question. He cannot be tired, eh?"

When they walked back in the policeman questioned Betty Ryder. Betty had a hearing problem. When the policeman asked, "What did you see?" her answer was, "I didn't say anything." The policeman shuffled a few papers then said, "There is nothing I can do. It's one word against the other. We have many calls from people who live in small villages. It's always the same. One says one thing, the other denies it. This court will be adjourned."

Annette Pawlic, still holding the pole, was the first to walk out. The others followed close behind. Jean Renard looked at Armand, his small eyeglasses resting low on his nose. He looked as wicked as the old pictures of devils.

"You are not finish, you old *bâtard*! I will sue you for one t'ousand dollar. You will pay for my wife's sickness. You are de devil come back to dis eart'."

Renard, with a sneering, jeering laugh, walked out.

A few days later Armand received a letter. In it was a cheque that read, "Pay to the order of Armand Pilon, 1000 pills, one thousand pills." A heavy stroke was drawn though the dollar sign. It was signed P. Jean Renard. On the bottom of the cheque he had written "Paid in Full." Armand decided not to tell Flory until she got stronger.

OLD MAN RENARD

The story of Leonard's collision with the train soon became known to all the family. Because Armand had been cooking for the threshers, he had needed a few things and had asked Leonard to take the Model T and go to town.

"You take dis road and go as far as de railroad track. You cross it and turn left. Do not forget to post my letter to Flory and do not forget my tobacco."

On the way home, and just approaching the tracks, Leonard was slow to see the train. He looked up and saw the iron numbers on the huge black engine. It picked up the truck and Leonard, sweeping it off the tracks and into a heap.

Leonard didn't know how long he lay on the gravel. He opened his eyes and slowly moved his arms and legs. There was no pain, just a numbness through his whole body.

He slowly pulled himself up and walked to the car. The car had turned and rested on its side. The top lay in a heap. Nothing covered the motor, and only three spokes were left on the steering wheel. The few things he had picked up were scattered everywhere.

What will Papa do? Oh why? Why? Then he remembered Papa's tobacco. He would not walk back to the cookhouse without Papa's tobacco. He searched in a daze until he found it.

Slowly he walked away from the wreck. Every part of his body felt disconnected. He walked for what seemed like hours. He pushed the door open and stood motionless.

With a blank, futile look of failure he said, "Papa . . . "

"Gee cripe, what happen? You are white like ghost! Sit down, sit down. What happen, Leonard?"

"The train ran me off the track."

"Come, come. What you mean? If de train run over you, you will not be here."

"There's a sign. I couldn't see the train, then it was right there."

"Where is de car, Lenny?"

"It's by the track and it looks pretty bad. I don't know why I'm here. When the train was right there, I reached for Baby. I don't know why. It was like she was sitting right there beside me. I had to save her."

"Tell me Lenny, can de car be fix? We must have de car. I get a message today dat Maman is very sick. Ah, mon Dieu. What can happen next, eh?"

A MATTER OF COMPULSION

"The motor's bare. There's no top on the car, and only three spokes on the steering wheel."

"Never mind de top and de spoke. It is de motor we worry about. You walk to town, go to de garage, get a man to come to pick up de car. Tell him we have to get home, dat Maman is very sick. Are you too tired for today, Lenny? Eat some food before you go. I have to feed de t'resher."

"I'll go, Papa. I'll go. I'm not hungry."

As he walked Leonard had to fight the temptation to lie down anywhere.

The money they had earned went for repairing the Model T. It took them home safely on three spokes, a bare motor, and no top.

As Armand sat beside Flory's bed telling her what had happened, tears filled her eyes.

"Oh Lord in heaven Armand, it's the third time Leonard's life has been spared. First at the Ottawa station where he could have been electrocuted, then with the gun, and now with the train."

"It was not his time to go Flory. Everybody have a time."

"And the car, Armand? It can't be of much use."

"Do not worry about de car. I have one good idea for dat. Flory, you are not eating enough. Dat is why you feel weak."

"I do feel better, but I have no strength left in me. Oh thank goodness it's all over with. Now I'm beginning to feel angry. I can't believe what they did to me. I was too sick to care before. I wonder how well they sleep at night."

"Ah, I am sure Old Man Renard sleep well. He has paid me in full."

"Paid what?"

"I get dis cheque after de trial."

Flory took the cheque from the envelope and read it. Then she read it again, not raising her eyes.

"I am sure you get de message, Flory. Yes, I only feel I can kill two men in my entire lifetime. De one who shoot my dog Queenie an' Old Renard. De world would be a better place witout dose two."

"Don't you think it strange that a wicked man like that could be Edit's father? I know she dispises him. I always wondered why. Now I know he's capable of doing anything vicious to his own family."

"Yes, Edit' hate him, but de one who hate him de mos' is Renard's son René, de artist who paint picture. I do not believe any of his kid care about him."

OLD MAN RENARD

* * *

"Now I decide to make a saw out of de car. People have to have wood for de winter. We need wood ourself. We cannot lose wit dat. You will help me Leonard, and we will hire Christopher Gleeson and his team to get de jack pine."

"How do you know it will work? Hell, I like that car and I could fix it up."

"You like dat car for what? To drive around wit no food in your belly? Non, dere is not'ing to do wit dat car. It was a car, now it will be a saw."

Every morning they were up early. Leonard liked the idea of working with Papa, and agreed that a saw could make them money. It was the first time they had ever done anything together. Flory could hear the motor reverberating over and over, all day, until dusk.

* * *

"Oh Romeo, you're home! You were a good boy to write. I just this day got up. I've been sick. You'll never know, dear."

"Don't tell me, Maman. Papa told me, then Lenny told me. I always knew Renard was an old son of a bitch. Yeah, the Bedards were living there when the Renards came years ago. Just ask Ray or Willis. They know so much it would make your hair stand up. The old crook. So Len had an accident?"

"Yes dear. How he still lives, God only knows."

"Well we had a Model T, now we have a Model T saw!"

"There's enough noise out there. Have they got it working yet?" Flory asked.

"Yeah, it works like hell, and I've got a little money to help pay Christopher Gleeson to bring the logs in. Everybody needs wood, even the farmers. If they can't afford to pay us we can barter, maybe for a small pig or some eggs and butter."

"Yes dear, but I know your father. He's a marvel at starting things."

"How can we lose? We need wood to heat the hall for card games and anything else that goes on this winter, like the school Christmas Concert and the New Year's Dance. If we never sell a damned stick we'll still be ahead. It's not like a bucksaw. You should see how it works. The old man is pretty smart, just the same."

Flory watched Romeo as he walked away, and thought how like his father he was.

A MATTER OF COMPULSION

* * *

Edith and Willis returned from the south. After hearing a few distorted stories, they wasted no time going to Flory and Armand's house.

"Oh Edit', I am happy to see you. We've had so many problems. I don't think you could ever believe what we've gone through."

Armand broke in, "Yes, an' you know Edit' if I would strike Jean Renard's wife an' she lose her *bébé*, I would be in de prison today. I believe dat. Also I feel somet'ing go on. De trial end too soon."

"Ah, he is cruel, a demon, and he is my father. You don't know one half of the story, eh Willis?"

Willis nodded.

"Ah, we have heard a few. De udder day at de hotel, yes at de hotel Flory, I hear he go bankrupt and he hide his yard good in de steeple of de church. In de night a big wind blow, an' de yard good are blowing out of de steeple in long stream. Cripe, I laugh at dat one."

"It is true. Yes, he is my faher, but I have deep hatred for him. I cannot begin to tell you what he has done. My mother has a fear of him, so she never talks much. It is the law that she obey him. When she was young she was very religious. She still is. Always she carries her bible. He, ah *mon Dieu*, he rules her with a hand of iron. Worse, she will never speak out for what is right and I do not like her for that. To me he is a hypocrite."

"Edit', he is an animal and I am a broken man today. You see, I wonder why an old man bodder wit woman problem and kid problem. It is very peculiar. What have Flory ever do to dat man? She have not step her feet in his place an' she have never buy anyt'ing at his store. Maybe we send de kid to buy somet'ing, but Flory? Non, she have never seen his face."

"Flory, we all need a good cup of tea. Come with me," Edith said.

When Flory and Edith left for the kitchen, Willis spoke in low tones. "Armand, I have something to tell you. Someone told me that Old Renard gave the policeman money."

"What you say, Willis? Who tell you dat? *Sacré bleu*! Tell dat to me again."

"When they took a break, the policeman and Renard stood at the side of your place where it was dark."

"Who tell you, Willis?"

OLD MAN RENARD

"I cannot tell. I gave my word so do not ask Armand, but I didn't give my word that I would not tell you that Renard paid the policeman off."

"I know. I know. Gee cripe I have dat thought when de policeman did not ask him one question. He never even ask him if he strike Flory."

"A man who could steal his own daughter's horses has no conscience. Yes Armand, he stole Edit's horses many years ago. I don't think you should tell Flory at this time. She is not very strong."

"Non, I will not tell her until later. You see, dere is not'ing I can do. I have no proof. So de old *bâtard* crook pay off de policeman. I have a feeling it all end too fast."

CORSETS AND SHOES

The girls walked in with a huge parcel sent by the aunts from Québec. There was also a parcel from Eaton's, which always held a grab box. The girls stood around Maman who sat on her bed, scissors ready to snip very carefully. Everything was saved of course, from paper, to string, to box.

No matter how tempting a coat or a dress looked you held your tongue, not because you were asked to, but because Maman had a rule. With every parcel from Simpson's or Eaton's a grab box was ordered for her four girls. The contents held a rarity of dainty things such as a small powder puff, coloured buttons, a few yards of lace or elastic, a small bar of scented soap, and a tear-drop bottle of perfume. Someone must have known Maman had long hair, because there were always added a few hairnets and hairpins.

Every grab box was different, except for the package of little golden safety pins. Never did Maman fail to divide them equally among her four girls. Nothing came easily. The grab box was always set aside until Maman examined and felt the quality of Papa's blue shirt, how big the tops were on her mercerized stockings, and especially the long fleece-lined underwear with the double crotch for her two boys. It could be a long afternoon of feeling the quality, to the point of the children taking every article of clothing and with great interest rubbing it between their own fingers and saying, "Oh, it is good quality Maman, and so soft, and I like the colour too." Anything to please her so she would set it aside and get to the grab box.

* * *

"What you t'ink about a good idea I have, Flory? It take too much money to hire orchestra from outside, so I decide to form my own orchestra. We have a family. I hear dem play. Dere is no reason why dey cannot play as good as anybody else. Hector Muron can play a violin. I tell you, he can play! De first time I hear him, I know he was born for dat. I have a talk wit Hector. He say he is ready any time."

"How long will it take, Armand?"

"Do not expect miracle. De two main dance is de New Year Dance and de Fisherman Ball. I have to hire an orchestra from St. Paul or some local musician to play wit Hector."

"Armand, you are a dreamer."

A MATTER OF COMPULSION

"Yes Flory, I am a dreamer."

* * *

"I want you all to listen to Papa. We are going to form our own orchestra. We can save money. No more hiring. Leonard, you will play de saxophone an' sometime de banjo. Juliette, you will play de piano. Romeo, you always say you like de drum, so you play de drum. Hector Muron will play de violin. He knows how to read music."

"Papa, are you going to buy a set of drums?"

"No, Romeo. Not yet. In de meantime you will play on your mudder's brass jardinière. You will use your mudder's knitting needle."

"I won't! I'm not playing that piss pot with knitting needles. Do you think I'm a jackass?"

"You will play dat piss pot or I kick you in de ass. You unnerstand?"

"Who said you could have my jardinière, Armand?"

"Tomorrow we start to practice and we do it every night for two hour and wit no fooling around. Juliette, Papa will teach you some chord. If you cannot play de piece, you chord. I expect all of you to be here at seven o'clock sharp."

At seven o'clock sharp, Hector Muron and Armand started tuning their violins.

"Juliette, do not stand like you do not know what is going to happen. Sit at de piano. Romeo, de chair is dere wit de piss pot an' de knitting needle. Sit down an' take dem in your hand. Leonard, take dat saxophone and hold it like you mean business."

"Hell pa, I can't play that good."

"What you t'ink we practise for? Not because you are a professional, eh? What you want to play?" Armand asked Hector.

"How about *Let Me Call You Sweetheart*. It's a nice slow one."

"Good. You play Hector, an' I want you all to listen. Ah, dat's beautiful. Now Hector, play it again. Now we all play de best we can."

Romeo sat with a far away look, holding the knitting needles as though he was ready to start knitting but had forgotten the yarn. Hector started again. They all followed, a slight pause behind.

Juliette forgot to change chords at the right time. Armand hit her across the fingers with his violin bow. "Juliette, you do not dream! Dis is serious business!

CORSETS AND SHOES

Keep your mind on de music."

Juliette hated Papa for doing that. Her heart was thumping as she held back the tears, not daring to lift her eyes from the keyboard. *How could he humiliate me in front of Hector? I wouldn't give a damn in front of my own family.*

When the practise was over, the boys headed for the poolroom. Hector put his arm around Juliette and kissed her on the cheek and with a hearty laugh he said, "You sure did jump when your father brought that bow down on your fingers."

"So you think that's funny? You're as mean as he is!"

"I'm sorry, *Poupée*. You were like a defenceless child. I saw it. I know how you felt. How would you like me to come over? We can practise as long as you want. You'll learn all the pieces I play."

"I would be happy. I'd much rather play the whole piece. Once I know the tune I can play it easily."

*   *   *

It was getting colder now, so the piano was moved into the wide passageway where practising was more comfortable.

In November and December the fishing season opened on both Primrose and Cold Lakes. Fishermen and fish buyers had all left for the lakes. Romeo, Leonard, Hector, and all the young men left in hopes of making a fortune fishing. Romeo was especially happy, because he had heard rumours that Ralph Ryder, their next door neighbour, had said that the Pilons had a tin pan orchestra. He was determined that after the fishing season he would have enough money to buy the best set of drums this side of St. Paul. Never, never, would he play that piss pot again. He would show that S.O.B. neighbour a thing or two.

"Do you have to hire an orchestra this winter, Armand? Why don't you have our own family play? They sound as good as anyone I ever heard."

Armand's nostrils flared and his eyes sparkled. "Non Flory, not until de summer season come. Den dey will be ready to make dere debut. It should be a good winter now dat dere is a fish packing plant. It will give work to many people. Many fish buyer will come. De hotel will do business. Also, people will have food. I was t'inking, maybe we should move down to de lower quarter. We can rent de room up here. Yes, de boy will do dat. Don't look at me like I commit a sin. We have to go while de going is good. Do not worry, Flory. I will get Mrs. Hunter to help."

A MATTER OF COMPULSION

"I'd rather have Edit' Lampson. I do know her better than I know Mrs. Hunter and she is good at anything, Armand."

"Yes, I believe she is, but Edit' would not come. You know dat she is not going to be your maid. Friend are friend when dey are needed, but not work for us. Non, Willis Bedard, he want her for his woman. Now dey are going to build a place by de lake. I don't believe Edit' like a big city. She was happy to come back here where she could be free."

A long sign was hung above the big front window which read, "Lunches and Meals at all Hours." Four booths were put in and now the butcher shop was a café.

"My department is in de kitchen. Your department Cecile, will be to wait on de customer." Cecile hated Papa when he drank, so she was hating him most of the time.

The family members were at no time to eat in the café. Whatever food was left over was taken downstairs to their quarters. Mrs. Hunter now occupied Flory and Armand's old bedroom, which was called the "back bedroom." Armand asked her to keep an eye on things. The long bench that sat out on the front porch all summer was painted a fresh grey and put in the passageway. The fish buyers from the south could sit to warm themselves, or to dry their clothes. Rows of mittens and socks circled the big furnace.

"Juliette, do a favour for mother. Go and see how the fire is doing in the passageway."

Juliette walked across the hall and into the passage. Mrs. Hunter was sitting on the bench with a man on each side of her. Juliette quickly walked out.

"How was the fire, dear?"

"The fire must be all right but something funny is going on. Mrs. Hunter was sitting on the bench and two men had their arms under her skirt. I couldn't see their hands. She looked sleepy, like she was drunk."

"Be a love. Go downstairs and see if Baby is tucked in."

"Do I have to?"

"I said be a love and go." After she was gone Flory turned to Armand,. "Did you hear what Juliette said?"

"Non, I cannot hear everyt'ing dat go on."

"She said that Mrs. Hunter had two men fondling her private."

"What you mean 'fundling'?"

"Juliette said they each had a hand up her skirt and she said Mrs. Hunter looked

CORSETS AND SHOES

drowsy, like she was drunk. Do you think the men are giving her liquor for favours?"

"I be go to hell! I ask her to take care of t'ings. She waste no time to do dat, eh?"

"I don't want her in my home, Armand. How can I tell her?"

"Well de best way is to tell her you don't want her in your home."

Flory didn't go into detail and was very calm when she told Mrs. Hunter that Armand did the cooking and with the help of her daughters, they could manage the rooms.

"Business isn't that good," she said, "and we really can't afford hired help." Mrs. Hunter must have known why, but she didn't say a word, and never came back.

"Oh I am sorry you hired that thieving woman! My lovely new silk knit underpants are gone. Both pairs! She took them, Armand. Mrs. Hunter stole them. Do you hear?"

"How do you know it was Mrs. Hunter dat take dem? Maybe it was one of de fish buyer."

"They were there just before she came. You know I opened my drawer the last time we slept there, and you know why I opened it. I saw my pants then. I never had a chance to wear them and they were the first silk pants I ever had."

"Do de catalogue only have two pair? Non, I am sure you can order more silk pant. De boy tell me Mme. Hunter sell dat for twenty-five cent."

"Twenty-five cents for my silk pants?"

"Non Flory, twenty-five cent for what is inside de silk pant."

* * *

Hard liquor had to be trucked in from St. Paul. When it was scarce the bootleggers reaped the rewards. The beer parlour was buzzing with life. Also, poker playing became serious business. The Fisherman's Dance was a huge success, being the major social event of the year. Fortunately there were enough local musicians to take turns playing until early sunrise.

It was a bitter, cold winter so the back kitchen was used for storing food and hanging meat. Armand had a partition put up that didn't quite reach the ceiling. It made the café a little smaller, but much cosier, as the heat from the kitchen stove drifted over the top and provided an even temperature. Nothing otherwise had to be altered. The booths remained where they were, with enough space at the front for four small tables if need be.

When school was out Juliette ran straight to the café before reporting to Maman. Paul Montpellier, the mailman, and Jean Montmartre, a trucker, were steady boarders. Paul was about the happiest man in the village. He even had long, happy creases that almost touched his sideburns. You could hear Papa's utensils clatter different sounds while the tantalizing aromas drifted in from the kitchen.

"Juliette, show Montmartre how you can do the splits and kick the back of your head," Paul Montpellier asked her.

"Oh Paul, it goes like this." Doing a quick split to the floor, Juliette quickly stood and kicked the back of her head. The rubber sole of her shoe flew over the partition and into the kitchen. No one had said a word, but suddenly Papa's voice boomed, "Juliette, come into de kitchen!"

He was ready and waiting. He slapped the rubber sole across her face, chicken gravy thick and rich splashing all over her.

"Get downstairs! Never, never do the split in de café. Dis is not a t'eatre. I will deal with you later."

Juliette didn't dare turn to look at Paul, but kept on running down the stairs.

"What in heaven's name happened to you?"

"Oh Maman, if I had worn my moccasins today it would never have happened, but I didn't. I just wore my rubbers over my socks. All the girls do when the snow starts to melt."

"Is the kettle warm? Look! My hair has gravy in it! Papa's mean. No one had to know what happened."

"What are you talking about?"

"Well Paul Montpellier asked me if I could still do the splits and I said yes, that's all."

"What has that got to do with chicken stew in your hair?"

"I kicked the back of my head and my rubber flew off. It went over the top of the partition and landed in Papa's chicken stew. Will he hit me again when he comes in?"

"How lovely! Can he serve it? Oh, you are a naughty girl! No, I don't expect he'll hurt you, but he may not allow you in the café again. I remember when Romeo cut up the horse harness. When your father came home and saw what Romeo had done he said, 'Wait until Romeo comes home. I'll give him something that he'll

CORSETS AND SHOES

remember for the rest of his life.' When Romeo came home your father asked him why he had done such a wicked thing. Romeo only said that the horse had died and couldn't wear the harness, so he cut it up to make one for the dog. I'm sure your father was more amused than angry. Yes, I'm sure he thought Romeo was a genius to have thought of the idea."

"Well he sure hit me. My ear feels deaf, and he hit me across my fingers with his violin bow. That hurt! He humiliated me in front of Paul Montpellier and in front of Hector when I hardly knew him."

"Well you know him now. I never see one of you without seeing the other."

* * *

The snow was getting slushy, with touches of black earth peeking out of it. It could be dangerous walking. The girls had to stomp their feet to pack the snow. Baby had been playing with Gail Ryder when she fell. Someone rushed into the house, carrying her. She had blood over her face and scarf. Her mouth was gashed from her nostril to the end of her lip. All you could see was blood and teeth.

"Good God! My Baby! Run to the poolroom Armand, and get anyone with a horse and sleigh."

Luckily Christopher Gleeson was there. Flory bundled Baby in a blanket. All the way to the hospital she kept on repeating over and over, "Oh, my baby."

"Dear God, who will fix it without a doctor. She'll have the scar for life. The nurses can't do it, can they Christopher?"

"No, they can't."

"Oh dear God, I pray they can."

Miss Hale was the nurse in charge. She told Flory the best she could do was tape it. Flory watched and prayed. Miss Hale started from the corner of Baby's mouth, taping to above her nostril. Then she covered the whole length of the gash with wide tape. Her head and half of Baby's face were bandaged. She was to be kept quiet, with no crying or laughing, and drink thin soups from a teapot. Later on she could have mashed vegetables.

When the tapes were removed the scar was red and sore looking.

"Oh Armand, she was a beautiful child. Do you think the scar will fade?"

"She have not change. I make you a bet. In a few years you will not see dat scar, an' in a few week she will sing *Petit Pinson* for Papa."

A MATTER OF COMPULSION

* * *

The ice had shifted to the far shore now and the lake was a blue-black colour. Boats were being repaired and painted. Everyone was preparing for the tourist season. Edith and Willis dropped in for the evening. It was always enjoyable company, with good talk and much laughter.

"Armand, we sold a lot to a man, eh? Well he started to put up a pretty big building. I thought it might be a garage, but yesterday I found out it is going to be a dance hall."

"Who is dis animal?"

"He is a bachelor. His name is Fritz Hermann."

"So he is one, and we are eight to feed! Dere is not enough business for two dance hall. What dat bloodsucker try to do to me? Gee cripe Willis, I have enough worry!" Armand hit his forehead hard with the palm of his hand. "Nobody get Pilon! Nobody! I was de first an' I will be de last. Did you not know when you sell your property dat he was going to build a dance hall?"

"No, Armand. I thought he was going to build a garage. Then when I saw the size I asked Ray. Ray knows everything, you know. Do you know the man, Armand?"

"Non, I do not know de man, Willis. I hear he is German, and he build a garage. Dat is all I know, an' all he know is dat I am a Frenchman and have a dance hall. We can be happy dat we have our own orchestra an' don't have to hire, but now de crowd will be split. Gee cripe, just when I form my own orchestra somebody have to crucify me. Yes, crucify!"

"Crucify! That reminds me Armand, Father Powell came this morning. He wants to rent the hall for a card game next month."

"Good! We will have to fire up de place to take de chill off. You get chilly when you do not dance. When you play card you have to be comfortable."

"The girls said he would announce it to his parishioners this Sunday."

Venice and Juliette attended church. When mass was over, Father Powell made an announcement.

"We have decided to make a change. The card game will not be held in Pilon's Hall. It will be held in the new hall, as we were able to get it at a more reasonable price."

Venice and Juliette lowered their heads. They felt all eyes shift toward them. It

CORSETS AND SHOES

was customary when outside the church that everyone linger to visit for a while, but this time no one dispersed for an hour or more. The church was directly across from the Pilon home, so it was easy to look out the window and see all the interest and wonder amongst the congregation. Father Powell renting a Protestant hall was something unheard of.

"How was church? Did Father Powell announce the card game?"

"Yes, he announced that the card game would not be held in Pilon's Hall. That it would be held in the new protestant hall because he got it cheaper. Look out the window at their arms flying, Maman. I'll never go to church again!"

Armand overheard the conversation. "You are sure you heard it right? Mon Dieu! What next?"

There was a knock at the door. It was Hector Muron.

"Come in! Come in! Did you hear, Hector?"

"Yes, I heard. Everybody in the church heard."

"If he had come to me like a man and tell me, I would have give it to him cheaper, much cheaper. Non, Fadder Powell is a Fadder Rat. I can see dat."

"Armand, you've had the card games since you built this place. Why wouldn't he at least give you the right to refuse?"

"I do not know. I have fired dis hall from early morning to have it comfortable for de evening card game, which last quite late. Also, I have to burn all de gas lamp I have. It cost money Hector, an' he expect dat we all go to confession and communion? Non, he take de bread out of our mout' an' make a fool out of Armand Pilon before all de people. Dat hurt, Hector, an' I don't give a goddamn if it is a protestant hall, a cat'olique hall, or any hall. Yes, I serve dis community very good, and what can de farmer do? Not'ing. Dey have to follow de priest like sheep."

"It's just the beginning, Armand. If the card games are held there, think of what could happen when the tourist season comes? He'll just be laughing up his sleeve."

"Who is laughing up de sleeve, Flory?"

"This Fritz Hermann with the new dance hall. Two dance halls in a place this small?"

"Let him laugh. Dat blood sucker will not get me. We have our own orchestra an' we do it ourself."

"Oh Armand, it may be a lovely place to live but there's no steady work for the boys. If we had a little money coming in it would be a great help, but the farmers have

A MATTER OF COMPULSION

their own sons to do the farm work, and the boat owners have the same operators year after year. Now Edit' tells me Old Man Renard is going to build cabins. Now that he has Charbonneau's store and moved down here, he's started building on his old store property. No, you missed that too. You were fool enough to give him the idea."

"Flory, I don't want to hear de name Renard. I hate dat man. I hate him as much as I hate Fadder Rat who have a face so narrow dat he cannot make de sign of de cross. An' I don't care if Renard build de Roman Empire!"

"Armand, if you knelt down like you asked me to do when you came west and I stayed in Brownsburg, remember? Remember the letters you wrote saying how much you missed and needed me, and at the end of each letter you said, 'Don't forget to say your prayers, my dear wife.' Well I did Armand, and now I'm asking you to kneel and ask God to help you stop drinking. I know he would answer your prayers."

"You say you pray to God every night for me. Why would he answer my prayer and not yours, Flory?"

"Get on with it, Armand. One day you'll be sorry. Mark my words, you'll be sorry."

* * *

That spring Juliette started to rip out the clothes that the aunts had sent and design them to suit her. The straight black satin coat was turned back to front and made into a sleeveless dress. Four flared georgette gussets were appliquéd with black satin flowers and bordered the bottom. They were let in at the back and front, one on each side. When she swung round the gussets stood out in a perfect flare.

"Good gracious! I can't believe it. Why you even made it flare, and look at all the flowers you stitched on. You are going to be a lovely seamstress, dear."

After those words of praise, Maman's sewing machine was never closed. It was one of Juliette's greatest joys, knowing she would never need for clothes. She began to sew pants, mitts, and breeks for the fishermen, and that brought in extra money to help the family.

That spring Cecile and Juliette went to St. Paul. After years of ordering shoes from the catalogue and keeping them whether they pinched or blistered, Flory thought it was time for Cecile to be fitted properly. The girls had never seen so many boxes of

CORSETS AND SHOES

shoes, and having to choose a pair was one big decision to make. Cecile sat trying on pair after pair. When she thought her mind was made up, Juliette came along with another pair.

"Look at these! Aren't they beautiful! I think they're the prettiest shoes I ever saw. Prettier than any in the catalogue, aren't they Cil."

"You can have a pair too. Try them on."

"Can I? Really? Did Maman say I could? You were going to fool me. Maman gave you enough money to buy me a pair? Oh, I'm so happy! I've wanted high heels for so long, and I've been practising how to walk for months."

"Be sure they fit, and make sure you can walk in them."

"It was the first time ever that they bought something away from home and on their own without having to scan through the catalogue, always with Maman's approval. All the pretty dresses they saw weren't nearly as tempting as the coloured high-heeled shoes the tourists wore.

Juliette had been practising how to walk in heels for some time. She would put flashlight batteries in the thumbs of fish mitts. This would provide the heels. Every day after school she practised walking and dancing back and forth the whole length of the dance hall. *When the time comes,* she thought, *I won't be walking clumsy and stiff like some of the girls in their first high heels.*

No matter how much she begged Maman for a pair, the answer she received was always, "No, you're too small, and not even grown yet. I won't allow it. You know very well if we didn't have this dance hall it would be the furthest thing from your mind."

"But Maman, suppose I never grow any taller than I am now. Would I have to wear oxfords all my life?"

"You'll wait another year or two."

Now at last her dream had come true.

Flory looked down at Juliette's shoes. "Why didn't you buy a military heel? These are much too high. Walking on stilts, at your age! What will people think?"

"Look Maman! Look how I can walk, dance, and twirl around and around."

"Yes dear, I see, but I still say you're much too young to be walking on stilts."

Juliette felt grown. She felt the softness of the leather. She breathed in deeply, smelling the newness. In the morning she placed them at the foot of her bed. Her heart filled with joy as she hippity-hopped to school.

Forrest Ross was the teacher. Juliette watched him a lot, because his mouth was

A MATTER OF COMPULSION

always white from eating chalk. He was a dreamer, walking back and forth with chalk-white lips and a far-away look. Besides, there was too much going on at her own house day in and day out to ever be able to concentrate on studying.

When school was out she ran all the way home. Something always happened. Every day, it seemed. Whatever it was today, she felt it would be happy.

Papa's second cousin, Mme. Lafleur, was there. They had sold their hotel in St. Paul. She had bought herself a car and now travelled from town to town selling the Spencer Garment. When Juliette walked in Mme. Lafleur and Maman were having a serious conversation about the miracle of the Spencer Garment.

"When you wear this special corset, it will change your stout body into an hourglass figure. We'll go to your bedroom, then I want you to remove your clothes and lie flat on your back, completely relaxed."

"Good heavens! All my clothes? Whatever for?"

"Non, non. You can keep your underwear on. I must show you the difference. These are not ordinary corsets. They are made to mould the figure. They are not straight up and down. They have a curve like a woman should have."

Flory removed her clothing and lay flat on the bed. "I've never heard of such a thing. Why I only have to measure my hips with a string, send for my corset, and it doesn't fit half bad."

"Half bad? Look at your corsets. They look like a piece of brocade for making curtains. Non, these mail order corsets never fit. A good pair of corsets should make you look like you did fifteen or twenty years ago."

"With every child I had I put on pounds. You had a big family, and you certainly kept your figure, the way you can wear that smart suit and all."

"Oh non, Flory. It is only the Spencer Garment that gives me my figure. I couldn't get this suit on without it. Now roll over so that I can place the open corset on the bed. I'll tell you when to roll back on top of it. Roll over easy! The corset strings are very long. I will start to tighten them from the bottom. Here we go. Up, up to the top! There now. You may feel they're too tight, but wait until you stand. Now I tie them in a long bow, then again in a shorter bow, and now we tuck the whole thing down the top of the garment."

Juliette could see that Maman's face was fuller and rosier. She didn't know if her temperature had risen or if she was overly flushed from happiness.

"How do I get up?"

"Swing your legs to the side of the bed." Mme. Lafleur and Juliette pulled Flory

CORSETS AND SHOES

up and onto her feet.

"I'm stiff."

"Non, non Flory. Stand still. We are not finished. You must have the miracle brassiere. Lean forward. More, more. A little more. That's better. This way the breast drops into place."

"I'll hold you Maman, so you won't fall."

"Now Flory Pilon, look at this brand new woman."

"Maman, I'll get your blue lace dress to slip on and see for yourself how thin you are."

Flory's face looked strained. It seemed like such a chore to raise her arms to get into her dress. Her tongue kept hitting the roof of her mouth with a "Tsk, tsk."

"The petticoat is loose Flory, and look at all the lively folds in the over-lace, eh Juliette?"

"It sure makes you look good, Maman."

"Yes, it's all very lovely, but how can I stand being bound in all day long? I can see Armand having to help me roll over, then pulling me up to my feet. If I know him, he'd leave me there! I'll say this, they are good quality. I just don't want the children having to help mother put on her corsets. Yes, it's all very lovely, but do you mean to tell me I have to go through this every day? No, you aren't nearly as stout as I am. Please, can you loosen them a little? I can't have Armand helping me and pulling me onto my feet!"

"I'll show you how stout I am. You think I have a good figure? Well watch this." She opened her blouse and pulled out the big double bows. Each corset string was plucked a little looser and with each pluck a soft white ball of fat popped out.

Flory stood rigid, in the same position she had been in when she stood up. "Well if you can wear that smart suit and look the way you do, I'll take the corset and brassiere. I won't be able to sit much, but I'll look good standing."

"When you get used to them, you won't have to lie on the bed. We do that to show you what it can do. The idea is that the back of the corset has to tuck under your rear end."

"How do you go to the toilet?"

"You just turn the back up, Flory. There's no problem. Now I want to ask you if you will come with me tomorrow. I'm going out to see the farmers. I want them to see how slim you look in your new Spencer Garment."

"I don't mind going, but I don't think I can get into the car. I can hardly walk now."

"Ah, I was the same with my first set. Now I hate to take them off. My body with no support collapses. No, I feel like a woman in my Spencer Garment. I'll be here at one o'clock to help you with your corsets."

Walking to her room, Juliette thought how exciting it must be to have your very own car and travel around selling the Spencer Garment. One day maybe she would be able to do great things like that. She had the feeling that she could sell even better than Mme. Lefleur. If Mme. Lafleur hadn't tightened Maman's corsets until she looked like a mummy, she would have looked less like a statue.

She closed the door. She was alone to enjoy walking in her new high-heeled shoes. There, just where she left them, was a pair of elf shoes with turned up toes.

I'm dreaming. It can't be true. Dear Jesus don't make it be true. My beautiful shoes are ruined, with only half a heel. She had my heels cut off! I hate her! I hate the shoes! I hate living here. She's cruel. She's mean. She has no heart. Maman doesn't love me one bit. Me being so helpful and kind with her rotten corsets. Oh God, I wish I was brave enough to cut three inches off the bottom of her hateful corsets. Then I'd tell her I did it so she could go to the toilet without having to turn them up. Wherever could I go to live? I wonder what she'd do to me if I did cut three inches off her corset. Whatever would I do? I can't go anywhere, and I know it.

Just last week when she was at the sewing machine I opened one of her drawers. There was a small, fancy box. On the lid in big print was the word "Cigarillos." I opened it because I thought it held Papa's cigars. Then I saw what it was. All fancy and neatly rolled French safes. I knew what they were for and I didn't mean to giggle, but I did. Boy, didn't she jump at me. "Do not go anywhere alone with a man. You'll scream with the pain. He could take you away and sell you to the white slave traffic."

* * *

"Maman, you broke my heart and I'll never forgive you! Cecile wore high heels when she was younger than I am. She looks more grown up and she's taller. I'll never wear the bloody things now!"

"How dare you use that word!"

"You were the one who brought it from England. Remember 'Murder, bloody murder'? Papa would never have done such a thing to me."

CORSETS AND SHOES

Flory looked over her glasses. "Maybe he wouldn't, but there's a lot he would do. I don't want to hear one more word from you."

"No, you waited until I was at school. You didn't even ask me if I'd mind a little taken off. You had to do it right away and have them cut exactly in half with the toe curled up to my instep. I'll never forget what you did! You make my blood curdle!"

"That will be it, young lady. Go to your room. You'll get over it."

"I said I'll never forget what you did and I meant it!"

* * *

"Hector, do you know what Maman did yesterday? They took my new shoes to the shoemaker and had the heels sawn off, all but a little bit, and the toes are curled up higher than the heels and . . . you're laughing? I hate all of you! I hate Papa when he drinks! I hate Cecile for not asking Maman to wait until I got home from school! I hate Maman when she's mean, and I hate you! Hector, I'll never wear them. Never! Never!"

Her eyes were flashing. Then the tears streamed down her cheeks. "I waited for you to come. You were the only one I could tell."

He stroked her hair back, then nestled her head in his arms. He wiped away the tears. She felt the flutter of his long eyelashes on her cheek. All life's hurts melted into nothingness.

* * *

The new set of drums had arrived and Romeo was in his glory. Never a day went by without hours of practise. He was going to show the neighbours what he could do on a real set of drums. They would eat their words. He'd show them that the Pilons did not have a tin pan orchestra.

"Gee cripe, we should be proud, Flory. Romeo, he have his drum an' he sure play good. So he play de piss pot for a while, but he get de beat, de tempo, eh?"

"Yes, he's done all of that. You should see my lovely jardinière, all dented and pounded around the edges. What a pity! And stop calling my jardinière by that terrible name!"

"It did not hurt de bird, and when you put a plant in dat, nobody notice de edge.

A MATTER OF COMPULSION

Speaking of plant, behind at Bedard slough dere are beautiful green bull rush. For de Grain Grower's Pique-nique Dance I have an idea. We will haul dem here. Ray Bedard has de truck an' we can get as many as we need. Ah, dey are beautiful, an' smell fresh. When de time come we will do it."

"For what, Armand? What will you do with them?"

"We will hang dem from de rafter. It will look green an' fresh Flory, an' when de people dance it create a breeze dat will make de bull rush wave back an' fort'."

"Did you say bull rushes? Bull rushes?"

"Yes, I say bull rush. Bullshit! You cannot see ahead, Flory. Non, never! You forget dat dere is two dance hall now. I know it will look beautiful. It look like de palm de priest sell to de good cat'oliques on Palm Sunday, only bigger an' longer. You see how nice dat will look?"

* * *

When Mr. Zigler came for the moving picture season, he brought in a large box and asked Flory if she would be interested in buying some of his daughter's clothes.

"I'll take a look at them. If they fit and are not too expensive, I'll consider it."

Flory held up the first dress. Nothing anywhere, not in any catalogue, or even in her wildest dreams, could have been more beautiful. It was a soft taffeta, the colour of ashes of roses. Row after row of scalloped frills fell from the tiny waist. As Maman examined the dress for quality the colour kept changing to a misty silver.

"Try it on, Cecile. It looks as if it will fit, but I do believe it is shorter in the front."

"Oh my, if it had been ordered for the Royal Palace it could never be more perfect," Juliette said.

Flory stood back, nodding her head, and with a smile of approval she said, "Why it's meant to be that way. It's shorter in the front and gradually falls longer in the back. It's beautiful!"

"It is, Cecile. I've never seen a more beautiful dress in my whole life. You look so pretty in it."

Maman held the second dress up. It had a dusky rose velvet top and a full silk skirt that was two shades lighter. Tucked in at the waist was one large velvet rose and two small buds that hung lazily over the silk skirt. It was the second prettiest dress they

CORSETS AND SHOES

had ever seen.

"Try it on, Juliette. Oh yes, and try these on."

She took out a pair of black satin slippers with high heels. The satin on each side was cut into lacy flowers that were embroidered round the edges. Wide silk bows were tied low on the instep.

Juliette's eyes began to fill, but no, she would not cry. She would say a little prayer asking that they fit. She slipped them on. They cuddled her feet. She could feel Maman's eyes upon her. *She's trying to make me happy. Then why do I have this big lump in my throat? I have to look at her. I can feel her eyes asking.* She looked up with misty eyes and smiled. "Thank you, Maman. I love them more than I hated the broken ones."

"I don't want you wearing these clothes at just any dance. They're just too pretty to make common, do you understand?"

"Yes, Maman. Thank you, Maman."

MORE TROUBLES

Brother Marvin and Sister Martha travelled from town to town preaching the gospel. No sooner had they rented a place in town, when down every road leading to the lake their glorious voices, accompanied by the strumming of a guitar, could be heard. Suddenly there would be a crowd.

Brother Marvin stood to praise the Lord for saving his soul. "I was a sinner," he said. "I frequented bar rooms. Yes, and dens of iniquity. Never once on this God-given instrument did I ever play for our Saviour. Let us sing his praises. Let us sing *What a Friend We Have in Jesus*."

It certainly was different from the Catholic church where the sermons were stern and solemn. There hadn't been a Protestant church in Legal. The school, convent, and church were bundled together on one large property. The few who didn't attend church but attended school were called the Protestant kids.

Brother Marvin, at the end of the religious meeting, asked if anyone could donate food, no matter how little. He said, "It would be appreciated and enjoyed in the name of Jesus."

Flory understood that with such a young group attending there could only be a few nickels and dimes donated, so every time she baked, one of the girls took two loaves of fresh bread, saying, "Maman sent a gift for you."

The girls loved the hymns. It was like praying together in harmony.

After one of Brother Marvin's sermons, and at the end of the prayer meeting, he spoke out loudly and clearly. "Who among you accept the Lord Jesus Christ as your saviour?"

No one stirred. There was not a sound until Juliette stood. "I accept the Lord Jesus as my saviour."

"Praise the Lord, sister. Praise the Lord, Sister Pilon."

It didn't take long for the big news to sweep through the village. "We hear Juliette Pilon has left the Catholic church. She was saved last night."

Ray Bedard said, "Saved from what?"

One devout Catholic said, "The Pilons aren't one thing or the other. They only go to mass when they feel like it. They're not much of anything."

Hector was serious when he saw Juliette. "When they told me you were saved I thought that you had almost drowned. I asked who saved you and Ray Bedard said it was Brother Marvin. I told Ray you only had a brother Leonard and a brother

A MATTER OF COMPULSION

Romeo and how come I had never met your brother Marvin?"

"Oh Hector, all I did was stand up and say I accepted the Lord Jesus as my saviour. What's so wrong about that?"

"You were the only one who stood up. Why?"

"I stood up because I accepted Jesus, that's why. Besides it's the same Jesus that they have in the Catholic religion. Remember when we went to the party at your place and all the older women were grouped together, telling of a fire that swept through and burned everything to the ground except for a statue of St. Joseph? It wasn't even scorched, she said. I heard them and I leaned over and said, 'That is a very sad story, and if you ask me I think St. Joseph was very selfish.' Well you could have heard a pin drop. I'll bet there was a lot of talk about me that night. So I expect a lot of Catholics to make a big story about Brother Marvin holding my head and saying over and over, 'Praise the Lord, sister.' And yes, I'm playing for the Picnic Dance."

* * *

Willis's truck pulled in. Papa was ready and waiting with the ladder set up and two roles of binder twine. Load after load of bull rushes were hauled and stacked on the hall porch.

"It look good, Leonard. You an' Willis bring dem in. Romeo and Ray, you will take turn to string de binder twine on de rafter."

"Do we need nails, Papa? Why not secure the twine around the rafter here and there, eh?"

"Good idea, but you still have to make it tight. Dose bull rush are heavy."

Romeo was up the ladder then down, with Ray handing him a bale of bull rushes at a time. Romeo was draping them over the twine so that it looked like a long Hawaiian skirt.

"Gee cripe! Boy dat is beautiful. Green like emerald and fresh like de outdoor. How you like it, Flory?"

"Yes Armand, it does look fresh. I wonder how long it will last without water. It can't last long, can it?"

"I put it up for de Pique-nique Dance. After dat I don't give a damn, but I tell you one t'ing. I have anodder good idea for dose bull rush."

"Not again! When will you ever stop?"

MORE TROUBLES

"Stop? Stop? When you stop you die, Flory. Non, I will not stop."

* * *

"I want you to see something, Juliette. Come here. You may not be able to see, but the drum player from St. Paul had a picture on his drum. I want something on mine. What can you paint on it?"

"How about a bathing beauty, Romeo?"

"A bathing beauty on a drum?"

"Romeo, this is a summer resort where people come to swim and fish. Do you want a fish on it or a bathing beauty like Clara Bow?"

"Yeah, a bathing beauty could look good. Lenny will want one too, so paint one on his banjo in a red bathing suit, eh?"

* * *

The Grain Growers Picnic Dance was a success. Armand was right. When they danced the bull rushes swayed back and forth. He didn't have a worry in the world. Everything was beautiful and simple when he was "three sheets to the wind."

"You see Flory, everyt'ing go well, an' de bull rush look good, eh? Are you proud of our orchestra dat is our own family, Flory? You always complain about my idea, but you will learn dat Armand make more good idea den he make bad one, non?"

"Oh God Armand, when will you learn? You may have great ideas but what are they worth when you never finish anything you start?"

"Yes Flory, everybody enjoy de dance, but you do not. Don't give me hell tonight. I work hard t'inking how to make interesting and happy t'ings for de people to enjoy. What do you do for de business? Not'ing. If I depend on you to run de dance hall, I feel sorry for you."

"It's lovely, Armand. I never said it wasn't."

"Non, an' you never say it was until you say it just now."

* * *

There were many outstanding bills in the mail. Among them was one thin letter addressed to Mrs. Pilon.

A MATTER OF COMPULSION

"Who could be writing to me Armand, posted from right here in Cold Lake?"
"De way to find out is to open it and read it to me."

Dear Mrs. Pilon,

I am sending you a letter for my dear boy. Please remit it as soon as possible. I am feeling very weak and don't expect to see him anymore. Oh Mrs. Pilon, will you please help him out? He is young and not very strong. I really don't know how he will stand the hard life he will have to go through. If I have to go I feel there is no more hope for me. Mr. and Mrs. Lacky promise me they will take care of my dear boy. I am asking God before I go to touch a heart to receive my dear boy. I can't last very long now. I feel I am expected to pass at any time. Oh, what agony I have to face. It is hard to part with my dear Fiona and Clyde. Now Mrs. Pilon, I come to ask you before I am going, to forgive me for the trouble we have once together. I wish to talk to you. Try to come down and see me. Kiss my boy goodbye for me when you see him again. Do not think of our little trouble and come to see me for I am very weak. I would be glad to see the girls also. With many thanks, Sincerely, a poor dying mother.
The folks told me today they don't want my dear boy in the house when he comes back so please better all of you help him so he won't suffer from cold and hunger. Oh what a tragedy is life sometimes. I am suffering terrible night and day. Cannot sleep anymore from suffering.

With thanks, a poor dying mother.

Annette Pawlic

"I cannot believe de mind of dat woman after what she do to you. So now Madame expect us to take her dear boy? What about her dear girl Fiona dat tell all de lie about Juliette stealing ten pound of sugar from Old Man Renard's store? Clyde is

MORE TROUBLES

a grown man. He should not need looking after. I say dis for Mme. Pawlic, at least she have de heart to apologize. It puzzle me why she do not write to her friend an' accomplice Mme. Charbonneau. Would she be happy for her to watch over her dear kid? Non, I am sure she would not. Also, I feel dat all de terrible t'ings they did to you was de reason why de Charbonneau move away from Cold Lake an' sell de store to Renard."

"Yes, I believe you're right. They were as thick as thieves until many of the Catholic farmers stopped shopping at their store. She may well be sick, but I believe the whole problem is on her conscience. I wonder what Clyde did that would make Old Renard so angry?"

"Somebody tell me dat Clyde rig up a piece of wire, very tricky, dat he can slide inside de cash register an' pull out bills. Yes, if it is true what people say, dat Old Renard is de fadder of Clyde, it could be true dat de kid could do a trick like his fadder."

That night the rain fell gently on the roof. An innocent rain that would wet the earth and freshen the air. All the scents and savouries drifted through the open window.

"Ah Flory, breathe deep. It is food for body and soul."

"Armand, you are a love. I mean if . . ."

"You mean let us go to bed. Take down your braid and we be close."

Suddenly the night took on a different mood. They were awakened by thrashing, whipping curtains, snapping in and out of the window.

"Flory, it is no time to sleep. We can lose de roof an' de floor in de dance hall. Wake de kid! We will need all de pail we can find. It is a wind, believe me. We can lose everything we work for. Gee cripe, if it is not one t'ing it is two of dem. Now de ceiling is leaking along de slats. Flory, we have to work, an' fast!"

Flory lifted the fifty-pound bag of flour out of the flour tin while the boys gathered water pails, Gainor's lard pails, and Maman's grey enamel bread pan. Even the bread tins were scattered everywhere. The main worry was the floor in the dance hall. Without it there would be no flour, no lard, no sugar.

"Leonard, Romeo, come wit' me. We will get de tent an' lay it on de floor in de hall. We will set de pails over de tent for double protection."

It was early morning when Flory looked up and saw the bulging beaverboard.

"Armand, if the beaver board breaks away from the slats, there'll be a foot of water. Oh Lord, my congoleum will be ruined."

A MATTER OF COMPULSION

"Get de butcher knife, Flory. I will puncture holes in de beaverboard. We need somet'ing big to catch de water. If it break away we will be in for a swim. Lenny, Romeo, bring some pail an' get de big push broom to sweep de water out of de door, an' you, Flory, get some rag to soak up. Maybe you can save your congoleum. Yes, congoleum is cheap, compare to de dance hall floor. Congoleum do not feed de kid, Flory."

On the third day the congoleum was shovelled out the back door. Heavy, wet, punctured beaverboard sagged from the ceiling.

"Do not shed a tear, Flory. Be happy dat de dance floor is save. Ah chère Flory, everyt'ing will turn out. Just watch me. Armand Pilon will not be beat. You know dat. Tomorrow we move downstair while de upstair will be fix. You like dat? Don't look at me like dat."

"Armand, I asked you time and time again to repair that first leak by the chimney and always there was an excuse. Once when I asked you, you said I was a troublemaker, that it was a beautiful sunny day that should be enjoyed. Not long ago one of the children ran in and told us that for days the poplar leaves were turned silver side up and that it hadn't rained yet. You knew very well that when it did rain it would pour. That roof could have been tarred. No, there's always excuses. All your life, excuses, excuses! You, Armand, are a lazy man!"

"Flory, we would not be human if we were not good and bad." He quickly turned her around and lowered his hand down her blouse.

"Your breast are pink and soft like velvet. How can you be a hard woman dat complain day by day? Also, I hear dat Napoleon Demarne have marry Mme. Label. I see you are surprise?"

"Not the Label family who lived next door to our farm?"

"A sister to de one next to our farm."

"Well let them get on with it."

"Ah Flory, I know you want to t'ink about dat when you are alone."

BERRY PICKING

Berry picking in jack pine country was a holiday and picnic combined. The tent was pitched and everything made ready for comfort. A full day of picking and bets on who would fill the first pail made it all the more exciting. The cranberries and blueberries lay thick and mellow, while all around them Summer's extravagance rested in Autumn's beauty.

A warm, strong wind blew through the jack pines. It was Autumn's way of cleansing, when everything was swept and made ready for the first blanket of snow. The wind was a blessing, for when all the containers were filled, a canvas was spread on the short stubble growth, and with pail after pail of cranberries held high and slowly poured, every stray leaf was blown away.

Huge blueberries, tender and fragile, were poured onto newspapers, row after row, and held in cardboard boxes. They were the first to be preserved, usually in Papa's Catawba wine jugs. It could be very annoying, for the harder you shook the jug to get the berries out, the more stubborn the berries became, until Papa demonstrated how to plunge a long carving fork down the narrow neck. Only then did the berries plop out in solid blobs of goodness.

Flory, mother of her flock, kept watch in case a bear appeared on the scene. A small fire surrounded by rocks burned and smouldered happily, keeping the mosquitoes away. It was a beautiful time to be undisturbed - a peaceful time to think of what lay ahead.

So . . . Napoleon married Mrs. Label, a sister to the Labels who lived next door to us. I wonder does he love her? Does she mend the sheets? Does she bake golden loaves of bread, and does she sew for Clara? Does he love her hair as he loved mine? How he held it close to breathe in the soapy scent of Castile. Napoleon, I pray that you are happy. I am not happy, but I still love Armand for all that he is. There's always tomorrow. Yes, tomorrow. How many years have I been waiting for tomorrow?

* * *

Indian Summer was a special time of year, a dreamy time to walk the lakeside trails. A golden carpet of leaves lay quite untouched, until the first flurries of snow swept them to their hiding places. The cruel winter snow could lunge down overnight, and there it would stay until spring.

Windows gradually frosted, layer upon layer, turning into exquisite tapestries, and oh, the pleasant mingling of pine and poplar drifted from the kitchen stove. How soothing it was to lie a little longer, searching for new faces on the rain-stained ceiling.

* * *

"I, Armand, have decide dat we are going to have a Mardi Gras Dance. Yes, a Hallowe'en Dance, Flory. I am sure Cold Lake has not had one before. We need it. We have only the Christmas tree for the school kids. Then comes the New Year's Dance and the Fishermen's Ball, and the Grain Growers Dance. A Hallowe'en Dance will help. Also, the café is not making money wit only three boarders. Yes, I will order some comical *masques* to make it happy. You agree to dat?"

"Why order masks? It's money spent for nothing. Why not an ordinary dance?"

"A Mardi Gras dance is not an ordinary dance. Non, we cannot call it a Hallowe'en Dance if we do not have de masque. I know for sure dat Ray Bedard will get de crowd going. He is like dat, a born comedien."

"He may be all of that, but don't you think he carried it a little too far at the last picture show? Lights out, everyone dead silent waiting for the picture to start, then all of a sudden the café door flew open, and with terror in his voice he hollered at the top of his lungs, 'Fire! Fire! Everybody outside!' And they did just that, jumping over the benches, knocking people off their seats. Then he hollered, 'No! No! Come back! Come back! It's a joke!' And dear Mr. Zigler and his son Abe up in the projection room, not knowing whether to save their equipment or run for their lives. It's a wonder they ever came back. I'm very sure not one of them thought it was comical, except for Ray himself."

"Ray is like his mudder. She also laugh all de time. Yes, and she is a cripple. She will never walk again. Mme. Bedard has to lie in her bed every day of her life. I will take you to visit dat lady, and you will be puzzle at why she laugh, believe me, Flory."

"What happened to her?"

"She was butted by a goat and never was she able to walk again. Never do you hear dat lady complain. No matter who walks through her door, she starts to laugh,

BERRY PICKING

and from her bed she calls out, '*Viens, viens!* Let me see who came to visit me!' I say dis, Mme. Bedard is a very strong woman. She had six children. I hear dat dey were de first white people to move here, and can you believe dat Ray Bedard was de first white baby born dis side of St. Paul de Metis? Yes, and I believe dat Ray has not stop laughing since dat day."

* * *

A beam of light shone from the kitchen door and across the hall to the opposite wall. At the end of the hall the furnace lights flickered warm and restful, until all the balmy scent of life came out of the new wood. Playing the piano at the dark end of the hall was a special time for Juliette. It was deep, profound, and hers alone.

Suddenly, from halfway down the hall, came a hair-raising moan. Juliette froze. Behind her she saw the horrifying face of death. She screamed. It was unlike any scream Maman or Papa had ever heard.

"Juliette, what go wrong? Tell Papa!" He held her shoulders hard and shook her. She kept on screaming hysterically until there was only one thing to do. Armand slapped her across the face. There wasn't a sound. Her head fell limp onto her shoulder.

"I'm sorry, Juliette. I'm sorry. Papa had to bring you back to your sense."

"Papa, I saw it. Honest to God, I saw it. It was the devil. I could see him in the dark, exactly like the one pulling people down to hell with long ropes."

"What are you talking about?"

"I'm talking about the devil in the school catechism."

"It was your sister Venice. She put a Hallowe'en *masque* on her face to surprise you!"

"Good God, Armand! She's as white as a ghost and hiding behind the door! In the name of heaven, what happened?"

"She did not know about de *masques* I ordered. Dat was de problem, Flory."

"I never ever saw a Hallowe'en mask. Nobody told me. No, but you told Venice!"

"Venice came in while I was putting dem away. Then she ask me of she can try one to see in de looking glass."

"I hate her! She isn't my friend anymore!"

"Do not say dat, Juliette! You will love one anudder again. Papa knows all about dese t'ings."

The two girls shared the same bedroom. They slept together, sang together, laughed and dreamed of fresh tomorrows. True pals, inseparable.

It was a long, lonely time while they were barely civil to each other. Yet it didn't seem to bother Venice. Every time she glanced at Juliette, she was waiting with a broad, loving smile that showed a perfect set of white teeth.

It couldn't go on much longer. After all, the very first Hallowe'en Dance was going to be held in the Pilon Dance Hall. Juliette would be waving Venice's hair. She always did, from the time Venice was old enough to dance. Juliette knew they had to make up, because never could she refuse to do Venice's hair. Then too, when Venice wasn't on the dance floor, she would play a couple of waltzes to give Juliette a break. Papa was right. He knew all about these things. All about the hurting, the forgiving, and the loving.

* * *

Christopher Gleeson had a team of horses that were big, clumsy-looking, and well fed. When Armand needed logs to fire the hall, Christopher was ready and willing to set out for jack pine country. The logs would be cut with what Armand called the Model T saw. Christopher, if he had the time, was always there to help. He was forever headed somewhere, through snow, rain, or scorching weather.

Christopher had a brother Andrew, and a sister Serena, who very seldom missed a dance. There was another brother, Harvey, as well as two younger brothers. Harvey never did dance, yet he never missed coming. Some of the village people called him Crazy Gleeson. Others called him Funny Gleeson. No one but his family called him Harvey.

"You know what, Juliette?" Harvey asked her. "I work for Bertha Oldfield at the Lakeside Hotel right next to this place here, and you know what I did? Bet you don't! Well, I broke glass, all sizes."

"So why did you break glass?"

"I put it in the cat's food. Didn't feed him much this morning. If it ain't dead tonight it won't be my fault. Yeah, and you know what I did? I pet it 'cause I like that cat. That's a nice looking cat and he looked good on the bench. Halloween is for playing tricks on people. That's why I gave glass to Bertha Oldfield's cat. Yeah, well I couldn't think of anything else to do for Hallowe'en."

BERRY PICKING

"Funny, if Bertha Oldfield finds out, she'll have the policeman after you."

"Yeah, but you won't tell because you don't know if it's true. Ha! I gotcha, didn't I?"

"No, I won't tell. I know you and your stories. The other day you told me that every night a bird flies through your window to spend the night with you. Is that true?"

"Yeah. Why aren't you playing the piano?"

"Because it's Venice's turn. She plays the waltzes."

"Boy, if I could dance I'd ask you to dance with me, but I can't. Ha! I sure gotcha again!"

* * *

"Flory, you have to listen to dis! Ray Bedard take Funny Gleeson down to de lake. He make him lay on his belly an' take in water."

"What has he done now?"

"You, Flory, should be more careful with your rubbing alcohol. You leave it on de table. Funny, he smell it, so what you expect? He drink it. It can kill! You did not use your brain! After you rub your leg return it where it belong, not on de table to welcome visitor. I, Armand, take good care of my own alcohol. Your rubbing alcohol Flory, is poison compared to mine."

"Good gracious, can you tell me what he was doing in our living quarters?"

"It sound to me dat he was looking for some alcohol."

* * *

"Somebody tip de privy. I feel happy. It is a good time to dig a new hole before de big freeze comes."

"Armand, you can't fool me. I can tell how many you've had to drink by the number of times you keep running your hand up your fly!"

"I will do what I wish to do. It is my hand and it is my fly. Yes Flory, and what is inside also belong to me. You have many worry wit your own corselet dat make trouble for you."

Flory didn't make much reply, what with Edith and Willis breaking into little muffled giggles.

A MATTER OF COMPULSION

"It must be hard getting cross with him. He's so comical," Willis said.

"Spending every last cent isn't comical to me, Willis. I used to think he was funny. That's exactly why I married him. Yes, he was oh so witty I thought he would be good for me."

Flory loved her blue dress with the silk petticoat and heavy lace that covered it. The only problem was that the petticoat had a habit of tucking itself into the crease of her derriere, which left the over-lace hanging free. As Flory walked away, Armand eyed the problem.

"Edit', Flory has bend over once more. I feel she needs me." With flaring nostrils he followed her and gently plucked the petticoat free. Her whole nerve centre shot to her bottom, causing a sudden jerk that tightened her muscles.

"Oh God, it's you, Armand! Fool! Why didn't you tell me quietly? I could have done it myself! No, you had to make a spectacle of yourself!"

"Flory, nobody see, only Juliette an' Edit'. Why make so much commotion? It is a lesson for you. You should pass your hand behind to check if all is in order. That is what I do wit my fly. No matter if you look like de queen, always dere are problem. You, Flory, take care of de back door, and I, Armand, will take care of de front door. It is as simple as ABC."

* * *

"Where have you been? Where is Venice? I haven't seen hide nor hair of you since morning," Maman asked Juliette.

"Mrs. Gleeson asked us to stay for supper. She said that everything was ready, but something awful happened. The dinner looked so good, too. She had moose balls, mashed potatoes, and gravy."

"What do you mean, she had moose balls?"

She made round balls out of ground moose meat and onions. They were so good Maman, but I only had two, then I got sick."

"Whatever for?"

"Well, a big bluebottle fly fell from the rafters. It was the biggest one I ever saw. It landed on the table, so Funny picked it up and put it on his young brother's plate. Then the young brother put it on Funny's plate. Funny said, 'I'm not scared of flies,' and oh God Maman, he ate it! He put it in his mouth alone with nothing else. I had to come home. I couldn't swallow all the water that kept filling my mouth!"

BERRY PICKING

"Mrs. Gleeson was in the kitchen. I'm so glad she didn't see what he did, and I hope Funny doesn't tell her. She's such a good mother. Do you know she makes all the boys' white shirts? I mean the ones they wear at the dances. And she made Serena a blue velvet dress with white fur around the neckline."

"It's too bad about that boy. I wonder if he could be helped. He told your father that Bertha Oldfield's cat died on Hallowe'en night. Then he admitted putting glass in the cat's food. Can you believe it? Why, if it's true, Bertha Oldfield would have a carroty fit and phone the police."

"I know. He told me not to tell, but you never know whether to believe him or not. He said he liked Bertha Oldfield but he hated her cat. Then the next time he said he hated Bertha Oldfield but he sure did like her cat. I have a feeling he killed her cat to spite her."

* * *

"Class dismissed" was the happiest sound of the day. Ever since the trial, school was not a happy place. There were too many painful hurts. There was no room left in the cluttered brain for unnecessary things like *King Robert of Sicily, Brother of Pope Urbane*. It was all so meaningless, especially when Juliette's heart knew that out there somewhere there were so many precious, ordinary things that could feed the soul.

"Maman, I hate school and I'm not learning anything!"

"Oh not again, dear. What will you do with your life?"

"Whatever I do, I'll be happy. The kids are cruel, all of them. They wait until I start walking home, then they're all behind me, arm in arm, singing over and over, 'Shit brindle hair. Titty Pilon has shit brindle hair,' and May Johns makes special trips to the pencil sharpener, but not to sharpen her pencil. She pretends to be turning the sharpener a few times, then she grabs my hair and jerks my head. I've never been mean to any of them. I try so hard not to cry. I can't take it anymore. Please, please let me quit school!"

"Don't cry, dear. Can't you see they're all jealous?"

"Jealous of what?"

"Well dear, you can attend anything that goes on in the hall, and you do have pretty things to wear. You can play the piano without taking one lesson. Yes, and do you know Mme. Lafleur told me she has fitted many young girls for brassieres,

A MATTER OF COMPULSION

but she said in all her years as a corsetière, never had she seen a more perfect breast than yours."

"You're saying that because they call me 'Titty Pilon,' aren't you?"

"No dear, your mother would never tell a wicked lie like that! It won't be long before Mme. Lafleur comes again, and if you like we will ask her, and young lady, don't forget that all my daughters have been blessed."

"No wonder Old Man Renard and Mr. Christian often tried to touch my breasts, and Venice's too."

"You never told your mother!"

"Why would I? To get the policeman and have another trial? Pawlic would laugh harder and I would be branded Titty Pilon forever after. Would you like that?"

"No dear. When school holidays come we can talk about your leaving school. And by the way, does Elmer Alexander still bring you candy and gum?"

"Yes he does, and he winks at me too, and guess what. Jack Ruggles is bringing me a surprise gift on Saturday!"

"Juliette, of course the girls are jealous. There's always something going on in the hall. And, young lady, it's all for free! The moving pictures, the baseball dances, the boxing matches, the Christmas Tree Concert, the Grain Growers' Picnic Dance, the Fishermen's Ball, and the New Years Ball. Why everything that comes along is held right here at home, and it's our very own hall!"

"I know we're lucky Maman, but I'm not a snooty or stuck-up girl, and I never say anything mean. Maman, I do have three good friends. They never say anything mean, and they are Fern Vadeboncoeur, Grace Ruggles, and Elinore Nolan. It's Pawlic and her lies about me stealing ten pounds of sugar from Old Man Renard's store. That hurts, Maman, and I can't stop worrying and wondering if the girls believe her."

"Of course you'd worry dear, but you know that everything said at the trial was lies, all lies, and even the policeman was paid off by Old Man Renard. No, you walk proud dear. Hold your head high. That will annoy them more than anything."

"The other day I was at the Vadeboncoeur Café and I spilled a five-pound pail of milk. I cried and Fern's sister Marion put her arms around me and said, 'Juliette my dear, you never cry over spilled milk.' Fern would brush her mother's hair, then M. Vadeboncoeur would walk in with a happy hello and a big smile. They are the dearest people in Cold Lake."

"Yes dear, I do believe they are."

BERRY PICKING

* * *

On Saturday Jack Ruggles delivered the surprise gift to Juliette. It was a wooden box with a chicken wire front. Inside were three baby owls, all in a row, looking like little carvings. The only sign of life was the closing and opening of their wise and solemn eyes.

"Oh Jack, it's the most beautiful gift I've ever had! What should I feed them, and where did you get them?"

"The mother must have been killed. I heard them crying for two days with no sign of the mother. If you go to Martin's fish wharf he has boxes of fish heads, and he'll be happy to cut them into pieces for you."

* * *

That year, in every pound of coffee, there was a bonus. It was a lovely gift of a very small spoon. It was the perfect size to feed the baby owls through the chicken wire. The first and second owls took the fish with proper manners, but the third owl swallowed the fish and spoon in one gulp.

"Please, please don't die." Juliette thought of using the small red enema in the closet, but she would have needed help and only Papa would know how to handle that situation. Papa wasn't around, and she felt there was nothing she could do, so she made up her mind not to tell anyone.

It was a long night of prayer, especially since she went down the long list of her family from the oldest to the youngest, and on to the third owl that had swallowed the spoon.

Early morning found her walking quietly out the door and down to the barn.

All three owls were in a perfect row, exactly the same as the day Jack delivered them, and behind the third owl, in a bit of a mess, lay the bonus spoon. Now she could tell everyone about the miracle of the little owl.

* * *

"Juliette, for two weeks you have done not'ing but worry about de little owls. Maman is right. Dey cannot live in a cage. Take de owls back to Jack. He will free

A MATTER OF COMPULSION

dem and dey will learn to hunt for their own food. Your Maman is right. Listen to Papa. Dey cannot survive living in a cage. Jack gave you a gift, now you give de owls de gift of freedom. Dey must go back where dey were born."

"If the mother didn't die, Papa, would she find her baby owls?"

"Yes, for sure she would. Juliette, you cannot perfect nature."

THE HOSPITAL

"Children, I want you to listen. Your mother has to go to the Bonneville Hospital for an operation."

"Bonneville? That's forty miles away. Why not this hospital?"

"Dr. MacFarland said I would have better care. Cecile will come with me. I don't want you worrying. Mother will have a good doctor. The mail rig will be here to take us in the morning."

* * *

"You know Armand, I was thinking how strange life is. Here I am, not well, and I don't know why. I keep thinking of that Old Man Renard beating me and the miscarriage I had. Now I have asked his daughter Edit' to help me. Strange that she is my best friend. She told me not to worry, that anytime Cecile is with me, she will be happy to help here at home."

"You must not worry. There are only t'ree boarders now, and the fish packers who come for a sandwich and coffee at night. It is no problem. Also, Juliette will be home after school, and Edit' is a good worker."

* * *

As close as the girls were, and as deeply as they loved Maman, each one secretly thought their love was the strongest. If love could have been measured, they bravely would have taken the test. When school was out they never walked home. They ran and never stopped until they saw her lovely face.

One day Maman hadn't been home. They froze and stared at one another, then scattered in all directions, each one taking a different course. One ran down the park road to the cottages. Another ran to Edith Lampson's house. The third ran to Mrs. Ryder's who was not at home. Someone there said that Mrs. Ryder and Mrs. Pilon had gone to visit the minister's sister, Miss Farquhar, who made colourful, hand-hooked rugs. The girls didn't dilly dally. After school it was always that way. They had to see Maman before they could do anything else.

* * *

A MATTER OF COMPULSION

Mrs. Lampson was a fascinating woman, with taffy-coloured hair and very highly coloured cheekbones. No one called her "Edith Lampson." It was either "Mrs. Lampson" or "Edit' Lampson," as the French pronounced it.

One day Flory built up enough courage to ask Mrs. Lampson why she put so much colour on her cheeks.

Edith didn't mince her words.

"Flory, I do not put colour on my cheeks. It is my natural colour."

It must have been the shortest conversation they ever had, and never again was it ever mentioned.

* * *

The day Maman went to the hospital Juliette ran home. Maman wouldn't be there. Nor would Cecile. It was Mrs. Lampson standing at the stove making *pain d'or*, or French toast, which was dipped into sweetened beaten eggs and fried. The fat in the iron skillet bubbled and danced around each slice until each turned a crisp, golden brown. They were topped with Maman's wild berry preserves.

Two men were seated at the table and waiting.

No matter how tempting the aroma, never did the girls linger if there were others to be fed. They swallowed their natural juices and walked on by.

Juliette was reminded of the pigs on the farm, and how she enjoyed watching them at their trough, hearing the slurping, succulent noises they made and knowing they didn't have to share one damned slurp with the next pig. No guilt, no conscience, and no prayers asking forgiveness for something God had no time for. She thought of the pigs left behind when they moved to the village.

She thought of one very special day when she found five cents. How brave she was as she stood at Perra's counter, and how easy it was to say, "I'll have one package of shelled peanuts, please."

She had walked upstairs, closed the bedroom door, taken out the tin box and loaded the lid with peanuts. Holding the box with her left hand, then putting her right hand behind her back, she ate like the pigs, making the same juicy sounds.

Then she thought of Maman and the Saturday treat of one ice cream cone to be divided equally among her girls. How fair Maman was as she crumbled the cone into small bits to top each small mound.

THE HOSPITAL

Night would come and as true as the clock ticked, she would ask Jesus to right all the heartaches in life.

* * *

"Will Papa come home three sheets to the wind?"

"Baby, Papa has never hurt any of us, and you do know that you're his favourite one. Maman has a very good doctor, and Cecile is with her."

When Cecile came home she had a happy surprise. Maman was going to be fine. She would take Baby and Venice to visit Maman. Juliette would stay home and help Mrs. Lampson.

Cecile cut and washed Baby's hair, and truly she looked like a doll with a mass of syrup-coloured curls. Venice had long, blonde hair, two shades lighter than any Swede's.

The mail rig stopped at the front door. They were ready and well bundled for a forty-mile sleigh ride. What a happy day! A sleigh ride in the snow! A sleigh ride to visit Maman! Wildly they waved goodbye until the sleigh was over the hill. It was a never-to-be-forgotten joy that was told of many times over.

* * *

The stove needed kindling and coffee and sandwiches had to be made. *Where are Leonard and Romeo? They love Maman, don't they? Can't they help too? No, I couldn't visit Maman. I wrote a letter instead,* Juliette thought to herself.

The café door opened. It was Mr. Turcott who walked straight to the kitchen. "Now what should we feed these men?" he asked, offering his help.

"Oh Mr. Turcott, how did you know?"

In no time he had the fire rippling and the big enamel coffeepot ready to perk. Papa had roasted pork and deer meat together. He always said that one enhanced the flavour of the other. Mr. Turcott made hot mustard while Juliette buttered slices of bread that had been ordered from Edmonton.

The puzzle was, how did Mr. Turcott know that Papa wasn't home? Or that the boys weren't there to help, and that Cecile had taken Venice and Baby to visit Maman.

He didn't leave until the tables were cleared and the dishes done. Oh how she

A MATTER OF COMPULSION

thanked him, and then she kissed his cheek. He smelled so heavenly that she was tempted to do it again.

Before leaving, Mr. Turcott suggested she save the money for Maman. "When she comes home," he said, "she will appreciate a little gift. Juliette, why are you smiling?"

"Because, Mr. Turcott, I could never give the money to anyone in the whole world but Maman."

* * *

The day Maman was to come home, glancing at the school clock and waiting for the bell to ring, was unbearable. The girls filed out of the school in order, but once out of the gate, never stopped.

The café was cozy and warm, and there sat Papa and Maman, so close and peaceful.

"Do you wish for more tea, Flory?"

"Oh it is lovely to be home, to have all of you around me. Juliette, you were a good girl to write to your mother. I did enjoy your letter, and mother will always keep it."

The one thing on Juliette's mind was the money wrapped in a handkerchief and tucked down the top of her stocking. No one knew. It was to be private for Maman alone.

Leonard and Romeo walked in. Now the whole family was together. It would be a long visit, but Juliette could wait, because she held the prize.

At last the moment came. "Maman, one night the fish packers came for their usual sandwich and coffee, but I was alone. Then Mr. Turcott came in. Oh, I was happy to see him. He got the fire going and the coffee perking. We made sandwiches and guess what? He thought exactly the same thing that I thought."

"Yes dear, and what was that?"

"He said I should save the money and give it to you. So here it is Maman. Aren't you happy?"

"Where was your father?"

"I don't know where he was, but if he had been home, you wouldn't have two dollars and forty cents, would you? And the reason is because Mr. Turcott and I also had a sandwich and he paid for them. And if Papa had been home you wouldn't

THE HOSPITAL

have had anything, would you?

"Did Edit' Lampson come to help?"

"Yes, she always came when Cecile was with you and she was here when I came home from school, but she didn't stay after supper. She told me she was making herself a tailored suit, and guess what? She's collecting pretty stones and pebbles of all colours for making vases and things!"

"Yes, dear. A likely story."

"What did you say, Maman?"

"I said 'Yes dear, I like her stories.'"

NEW BABY, NEW SCHEME

"Flory, I cannot believe what I hear today. It puzzle me, I tell you dat for sure. I hear dat Gilbert has sold his hotel to Johnny Johns and two brothers, Patrick and Clive Pride. Can you understand dat? Yes, and Gilbert is moving to Therien."

"Sold the Beauregarde Hotel? Good heavens! Whatever for? And especially with all the talk of the railroad coming in!"

"Yes, I do not know. They make good money wit the whole family working right there. And de beer parlour, never is it empty. If de railroad comes in dey will make a fortune. Dey have a hell of a good business. Also, dey have five girls dat will not be coming to dance."

* * *

Now that the Beauregarde Hotel had been sold, and Flory having no idea what the new owners looked like, she was very sure they had no idea what Mrs. Pilon looked like either. It was the perfect time to have Armand put on the "black list." No, she would not tell him what she was about to do. If anyone told, it would have to be the new owners of the hotel.

After that Armand made himself scarce, staying in his room and feeling shame and remorse. When he walked from his bedroom and out the kitchen door Maman never looked his way.

"Maman, is Papa all right?"

"I don't know dear, and I don't care. He goes down the lane where he can think of something new to invent."

After a week or more, when Flory and Armand were willing to face one another, they slowly became friends again, only to make more promises. Then Armand would put on his butcher apron to make the best batch of baked beans this side of Honeymoon Harbour. It was always the same for each of them. Fear, hate, pity, and love.

* * *

Maman wore her long flour-bag pinafore and was soaping her hands and up her arms. All the tiny bubbles spiralled round and round her arms. It truly was a joy to

A MATTER OF COMPULSION

watch.

"Maman, why doesn't it work for me? I've tried it many times and the bubbles never go round and round," Juliette asked.

"I don't do it, dear. It's because my arms are round and fat. You were my smallest baby and your arms are small."

"That sounds terrible. Was I healthy?"

"Yes, dear. You were all breast-fed and every one of you is healthy. I pray that my baby will be healthy. You do know your mother is pregnant?"

"Yes I do know, but don't you think you have enough to do without having another baby?"

"That will be enough, young lady! How dare you speak to your mother like that!"

"I'm sorry Maman, but I worry about you. You were so sick when Pawlic and old Renard beat you. Then you had a terrible miscarriage, and oh dear Jesus, didn't we pray for you to live! Then you had to go to the hospital!"

"Don't cry dear, and don't worry. Your mother is strong. Your father said that if it's a boy he'd like to name him Jacquôt. I never heard of such a name. I would like to name him Raymond Armand."

* * *

Raymond was born on March 13th, 1929. Armand called him Jacquôt. He had a playpen, which was kept upstairs in the café. He never cried. When he got older Armand would send one of the children to the store every day for either an apple or an orange for him.

It was Baby who minded and cared for him every day. If she went out the door to play with her friends, the door would quickly open and a loud voice would say, "Take Raymond with you!" It was Leonard, Romeo, or one of the other children.

* * *

"Flory, we have to have a talk about something very important. It has been on my mind for a long time. Yes, and I feel that now is the time to start."

"Is it another invention, Armand?"

"Let me say that the world is there for me to use my brain and experiment. Yes I,

NEW BABY, NEW SCHEME

Armand, will prepare for my new hair tonic."

"Hair tonic? With what? Good heavens, what have you thought of now?"

"Do not excite yourself too soon. Get excited when it is on the market. Yes, this week I will get Christopher Gleeson and his horse."

"What has Christopher Gleeson and his horse got to do with hair tonic, Armand?"

"You would not believe it, Flory. There are enough cattails at Bedard's slough to last a lifetime, and ever since we hung them from the rafters for the Grain Growers' Picnic Dance, I never forget. I have never seen sap so clear. It is pure crystalline and fresh as de air we breathe."

"How are you going to extract it from the stem? Surely you can't use the cream separator?"

"Flory, I see you are beginning to use your brain. Oh it can be done, but now it is fixed for making clothespins only. I have it all figured out, if you go along wit me."

"Don't stare at me like dat. I am not going to use your meat grinder or your rolling pin! When you wash clothes you put dem t'rough de wringer, no? So why cannot I put de bullrushes t'rough de wringer! Easy as ABC, eh? Also, I feel certain de bullrushes will pass t'rough de wringer much easier dan Leonard and Romeo's big fleece-lined underwear. De problem is dat de sap has to be sterilized, and also de bottles dat I will order. It will take some experiment before we can get it on de market. Do not forget de lady in Edmonton who say you have de prize hair, eh?"

Flory stopped what she was doing and became very still. She looked at this man, the husband she knew so well. Her gaze missed nothing. She thought of their life together and of all they had been through. It had been a full life—a difficult life in so many ways. Her body began to shake. Armand stared at her with alarm.

"Flory, what is de matter wit you? Why are you shaking like dat?"

"Oh Armand." Tears sprang to her eyes. Her body shook harder.

Flory was laughing! It was a sound Armand didn't often hear. He looked at her in wonder. She laughed harder.

"But why are you laughing?"

"Oh, Armand. You are not going to change." The bad times were very bad it was true, but the other times . . .

Armand took Flory into his arms and held her close. The sound of their laughter filled the air. Their bodies shook in unison.

THE END

AFTERWORD

Things went from bad to worse for Flory's family. With Armand's increased drinking, life became unbearable.

Flory's mother was now living in Victoria, British Columbia, and her letters helped Flory to imagine a better life. One letter, written in springtime, spoke of the broom being out. Flory thought her mother must mean that when the broom used for sweeping was on the porch, the days were warming up. She later learned the broom her mother spoke of was a lovely yellow shrub, imported from Scotland, and now native to Victoria.

Flory made the decision to move to Victoria with the children. Armand would stay behind to sell the dance hall. This was an important decision for Flory, who realized she might never see Armand again. She wondered if he would send any money, or if he would use what there was for drink.

Flory and the children packed their scant clothing and a few precious belongings. Everything else would be sold. A list of goods was copied and posted around town for the giant sale held October 12, 1936.

They made lives for themselves in British Columbia. Initially they all lived together, the children finding work outside the home and paying board to Flory for their keep. Eventually all the children married and all prospered. None of her immediate family stayed with the Catholic church. At the time of publication Flory had twelve grandchildren, twenty great-grandchildren, and thirteen great-great-grandchildren. Flory died in 1977 at the age of 89.

Armand *did* move to Victoria, but he and Flory eventually separated. He became quite the character in the growing city, living in a shabby apartment on Johnson Street in the downtown area. Occasionally an article would appear in *The Daily Colonist* about one or another of his exploits. One such article shared his dream to build co-operative housing units and homes for the aged.

At one point he decided to lay a trap line north of Victoria on Vancouver Island. Juliette and Babe (Baby) supported this latest venture by offering transportation in Babe's Anglia. Each trip ended in disappointment, until finally he rested his head against his thumb, bowed his head, and said, "Gee Cripe, I have fail again!"

The snowmobile, the clothes peg, the hair tonic, the trap line, co-operative housing, homes for the aged – for Armand these, and many other ideas, never bore fruit. However, years after Armand's death in 1964, one of his ideas did pay off. Remember when he found the pigs wallowing in the black sticky goo?

When Armand sold the farm near Legal, Alberta it was prior to 1949. Therefore, he was able to retain the oil and mineral rights. In 2002 an oil company purchased a lease to drill. This year, 2005, natural gas was found on the property and at the time of publication two wells had been drilled, with a promise of good things to come.

Armand's foresight has become a wonderful and unexpected legacy for his family.

ISBN 1-4120-4469-3